When East European communism collapsed in the revolutions of 1989, the newly liberated countries discarded socialism altogether. For the first time, most of Eastern Europe experienced free elections and a multitude of parties, mostly with liberal, conservative or nationalist connotations, made their entry into political life. A bewildered world is now trying to imagine the future course of events. Has capitalism won or is something different emerging? Has market socialism vanished for good? How can the transitionary period be managed and what effect will it have on the standard of living in Eastern Europe?

In this book, ten distinguished experts explore this transition to a market economy in Eastern Europe. In part I, the authors consider what remains of market socialism. Wlodzimierz Brus discusses the future roles of both planning and the market, Mario Nuti argues that market socialism never existed, whilst Gerhard Fink outlines how a normal market economy can be established. In the following section, Jan Adam, Pekka Sutela and Anders Åslund investigate the development of economic thinking and policy making in Poland, Hungary and the Soviet Union and Stephen Fortescue examines the role of Soviet industrial ministries. The final part is devoted to aspects of the Soviet economy under perestroika. Sheila Marnie analyses labour issues, Henryk Flakierski assesses income distribution and Jan Åke Dellenbrant offers fresh insights on current economic levels in Estonia and Finland.

Market socialism or the restoration of capitalism? presents a collection of thought-provoking articles on a most topical issue that few have yet managed to study. It will therefore be essential reading for all students and specialists of Soviet and East European studies, economics and politics.

Selected papers from the Fourth World Congress
for Soviet and East European Studies
Harrogate, July 1990

Edited for the
INTERNATIONAL COMMITTEE FOR
SOVIET AND EAST EUROPEAN STUDIES

General Editor
Stephen White
University of Glasgow

Market socialism or the restoration of capitalism?

Edited by

Anders Åslund

Stockholm Institute of Soviet and East European Economics

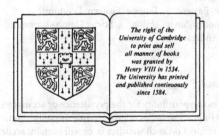

The right of the
University of Cambridge
to print and sell
all manner of books
was granted by
Henry VIII in 1534.
The University has printed
and published continuously
since 1584.

Cambridge University Press

Cambridge
New York   Port Chester
Melbourne   Sydney

CAMBRIDGE
UNIVERSITY PRESS

University Printing House, Cambridge CB2 8BS, United Kingdom

Cambridge University Press is part of the University of Cambridge.

It furthers the University's mission by disseminating knowledge in the pursuit of education, learning and research at the highest international levels of excellence.

www.cambridge.org
Information on this title: www.cambridge.org/9780521411936

© Cambridge University Press 1992

First published 1992

A catalogue record for this publication is available from the British Library

Library of Congress Cataloguing in Publication data

Market socialism or the restoration of capitalism? / edited by Anders Åslund.
  p.   cm.
  Includes index.

  ISBN 0 521 41 193 9 (hardcover)
    1. Mixed economy–Europe. Eastern. 2. Europe. Eastern–Economic conditions–1989–3. Mixed economy–Soviet Union. 4. Soviet Union–Economic conditions–1985– I. Åslund, Anders. 1952–
HC244.M34   1991
330.947––dc20   91–11149 CIP

ISBN 978-0-521-41193-6 Hardback

Market socialism or the restoration of capitalism?

Contents

Part III   Effects of perestroika on Soviet life

Notes on contributors

JAN ADAM is Professor of Economics at the University of Calgary in Alberta, Canada. He has followed the reform process in Eastern Europe for a long time, and recently published *Economic Reforms in the Soviet Union and Eastern Europe since the 1960s* (1989).

ANDERS ÅSLUND is Professor at the Stockholm School of Economics and Director of the Stockholm Institute of Soviet and East European Economics. He is the author of *Gorbachev's Struggle for Economic Reform* (1989, 2nd edn 1991).

WLODZIMIERZ BRUS is Professor of Economics at the University of Oxford. Previously one of the leading reform economists in Poland, he has continued following the reform processes in Eastern Europe and the USSR. His most recent major publication, co-authored with Kazimeirz Laski, is *From Marx to the Market. Socialism in Search of an Economic System* (1989).

JAN ÅKE DELLENBRANT is Associate Professor at the Department of Soviet and East European Studies, University of Uppsala. He has published extensively on regional issues in the Soviet Union.

GERHARD FINK worked at the Vienna Institute for Comparative Economic Studies for many years and was also the Director of the Institute, pursuing research on the economic development of Eastern Europe. Currently he works as a business consultant at IBR Marktforschungsgesellschaft MBH in Vienna.

HENRYK FLAKIERSKI is Professor of Economics at York University, Ontario, Canada. He has specialized in the study of income distribution in Eastern Europe and the USSR. His most recent book was *The Economic System and Income Distribution in Yugoslavia* (1989).

STEPHEN FORTESCUE works at the School of Political Science, University of New South Wales, Kensington, Australia. In his research he has focused on the politics of economic reform in the USSR, a subject on which he has published extensively.

DOMENICO MARIO NUTI was previously the Director of the European University Institute in Florence, and before that Director of the Centre for Soviet and East European Studies at the University of Birmingham. He is now a Director for Soviet and East European Economic Affairs at the Commission of European Communities in Brussels. He has published widely on a wide range of economic issues in Eastern Europe.

SHEILA MARNIE is a researcher at the European University Institute in Florence. She took her degree from the University of Birmingham. Her focus of research is Soviet labour issues.

PEKKA SUTELA has published extensively on the Soviet economic reform process, including most recently, *Economic Thought and Economic Reform in the Soviet Union* (1991). While maintaining a post as Associate Professor at the University of Helsinki, he works as a special adviser on Soviet and East European economic affairs at the Bank of Finland.

Introduction

Anders Åslund

The ten papers in this volume were originally presented at the Fourth
World Congress for Soviet and East European Studies held at Harrogate
Spa in England on 21–6 July, 1990, and this publication occurs under the
auspices of the International Council for Soviet and East European
Studies. The papers have been revised and updated to November 1990.

The autumn of 1989 was the time of the great East European
revolutions, and in 1990 the European stage emerged completely
transformed. Democracy had made a tremendous advance. For the first
time, most of Eastern Europe experienced free and just political elections.
A multitude of new parties, mostly with liberal, conservative or national
connotations, made their entry into political life.

Economically, however, the year of 1990 will go down as one of the
most miserable in terms of economic growth in East Europe, or East
Central Europe as part of it is now called. On the one hand, there is a
tremendous yearning for well-functioning market economies. On the
other, the road to a free economy – to allude to Janos Kornai's recent
book – seems paved with thorns as well as good intentions, and surely will
not lead to heaven.

Currently, there is a broad conviction that only a restoration – or
rather, new emergence – of fully-fledged capitalism can salvage the
formerly socialist countries. This view stands in sharp contrast to
previously prevailing ideas that market socialism was a real alternative
and that the socialist countries would gradually marketize, while
developing more social forms of ownership. Rather than abandoning
these old issues, this is the time to probe more deeply into them. A large
number of questions arise anew. Is central planning really inferior to a
market economy in general? Can market socialism work? How can the
transitionary process be managed? How has economic thinking developed
in the formerly socialist countries? Are these countries intellectually
prepared for a market economy? How are policies actually made? What
are the effects on the standard of living of the first economic changes? And

how might the level of prior economic development – now available for scrutiny, under the new openness – be reassessed?

All these questions are discussed in this volume, which is divided into three parts. The first part considers what remains of market socialism and what this means to the principal direction of events. The second part poses the questions concerning changes in economic thinking and economic policy-making. The third part looks into some particular effects of perestroika in the USSR. Thus, the book starts from the over-reaching principles and moves in the direction of policy formation and examples of the results of application. The first part discusses the formerly socialist countries in general, the second focuses on Soviet affairs – though Jan Adam deals with Poland and Hungary – and the final part is entirely Soviet-orientated.

In a major recent book, Wlodzimierz Brus and Kazimierz Laski have self-critically reconsidered the question of what remains of socialist claims in economics.[1] In the brief first chapter of this volume, Brus draws essential conclusions on the roles planning and the market may play in the future. While Brus does not want to discount planning altogether, the emphasis he gives to the likely predominance of the market is striking, not least in comparison with his previous works.[2]

Mario Nuti, now at the European Commission in Brussels, was until recently Professor at the European University Institute in Florence. He acknowledges that a restoration of capitalism is taking place, but he argues that the recent events in East Central Europe amount to a failure to generate a new 'market socialist' model rather than a failure of market socialism as such, which Nuti argues has never existed. Without claiming that market socialism would have been better, Nuti regrets that it was never properly attempted.

Gerhard Fink, until recently the director of the Vienna Institute of Comparative Economic Studies, provides an overview of the current macroeconomic problems and transition to a market economy of East Central Europe and the USSR. He moves on to suggest how these problems should be solved, providing a brief but impressively comprehensive policy prescription. Fink moves within the mainstream of Western economic thought, effectively advocating a restoration of capitalism.

In the second part of the book, the first two papers by Jan Adam and Pekka Sutela discuss the development of economic thinking in Poland, Hungary and the USSR, respectively. Although the economic debate has been more qualified and manifold in Poland and Hungary than in the USSR, much of the reasoning in these two chapters runs in parallel. Both Adam and Sutela have done substantial work in this field before.[3] They pinpoint previous statements by now leading economists and politicians, demonstrating how much their position has changed recently. Another common point in their analysis is that the level of economic thinking has been very low, although somewhat better in Poland and Hungary. Third, the acceptance of the market came reasonably early, while the breakthrough for large-scale private ownership has occurred just recently.

My own chapter investigates how the institutional framework of Soviet economic policy-making developed in 1989 and 1990. Apart from providing an analysis of how policy is made, my ambition has been to provide a guide to the positions of a large number of Soviet economists, while Sutela offers deeper insights into how the thinking of leading Soviet economists has developed. A picture of continuous and intensive strife at the centre of power emerges.

Stephen Fortescue's chapter pursues the investigation into Soviet economic institutions further by scrutinizing the role and behaviour of Soviet industrial ministries. On the one hand, it is notable how the industrial ministries seem to rebound and recover after various measures have been taken against them under perestroika. On the other, the Soviet industrial ministries are not easily beaten and while their colleagues have gone under in East Central Europe those in the USSR have managed to retain power. Still, if a change of system really takes place, there is little room left for them.

The three chapters in the third part dwell upon particular features of Soviet economic life under perestroika. These discussions have benefited greatly from the large amount of new Soviet data that have been released since 1985. So far, the social effects of perestroika have been less than a cursory look would suggest.

Sheila Marnie has undertaken a detailed study of what has happened to Soviet employment to date. Her assessment points to many problems, but a salient feature is that while unemployment exists in the order of 4–6 million people, it is rather limited and as yet has not grown significantly worse under perestroika. Unemployment remains a relatively small problem under the old system, while the lack of social provisions and economic inefficiency are all the more disturbing.

Henryk Flakierski has studied the correlation between income inequality and economic reform in socialist countries for many years.[4] His general conclusion is that income differentials have increased in the 1980s, but they have not returned to the degree of inequality of the 1950s and 1960s.

There is great confusion over the Western level of economic development relative to other parts of the world. Jan Åke Dellenbrant offers fresh insight by assessing new materials on the current economic level in Estonia and Finland. While Estonia appears to have been slightly more developed than Finland on the eve of the Second World War, today, Dellenbrant concludes, the Estonian level of GNP per capita appears to correspond to approximately 40 per cent of the Finnish level.

The usual dilemma of a conference volume tends to be to find a comprehensive structure. However, the size of the Harrogate Congress has made it possible to select papers of quality which together form a coherent volume. I hope the reader will find that this is the case.

Anders Åslund
Stockholm, November 1990

Notes

1 Wlodzimierz Brus and Kazimierz Laski, *From Marx to the Market. Socialism in Search of an Economic System*, Oxford, Clarendon, 1989.

2 Wlodzimierz Brus, *Ogolne problemy funkcjonowania gospodarki socjalistycznej*, Warsaw, PWN, 1961, translated into English as: *The Market in a Socialist Economy*, London and Boston, Routledge & Kegan Paul, 1972; Wlodzimierz Brus, *Socialist Ownership and Political System*, London and Boston, Routledge & Kegan Paul, 1975.

3 Jan Adam, *Economic Reforms in the Soviet Union and Eastern Europe since the 1960s*, London, Macmillan, 1989; Pekka Sutela, *Socialism, Planning and Optimality*, Helsinki, Finnish Society for Sciences and Letters, 1984.

4 Henryk Flakierski, *Economic Reform and Income Distribution. A Case Study of Hungary and Poland*, Armonk, N.Y., M.E. Sharpe, 1986; Henryk Flakierski, *The Economic System and Income Distribution in Yugoslavia*, Armonk, N.Y., M.E. Sharpe, 1989.

Part I

Market socialism revisited

1   The compatibility of planning and market reconsidered

Wlodzimierz Brus

When this topic for the congress panel was proposed in 1987 I perceived it as a suggestion to reconsider the matter in connection with a new stage of economic reforms in the communist-ruled part of the world: a new stage both in terms of depth and width of the change – the first aspect represented by the clear radicalization of the reform concepts in such countries as Hungary and Poland, the second by the spread of reforms to the former primates of orthodoxy, in the first instance the Soviet Union. Yet, despite the significance of the new stage, it seemed that it was still the *reformist* context within which the problem was to be confronted. Now we find ourselves in a situation when the question is increasingly one not of reforming a socialist planned economy but of *replacing* it with a fully-fledged market system with ownership relations freely adjustable to secure its appropriate functioning (i.e. including predominance of private ownership of means of production should this prove to be the requirement). Some of the supporters of such a replacement refrain from calling the transformed system 'capitalist' ('such as in the developed industrial countries' is one of the preferred designations, sometimes coupled with declarations of the obsolescence of any sharp distinction between capitalism and socialism), and there is still strong adherence to the reform syndrome in the USSR, not to mention China. Nevertheless, we take up here the problem of compatibility between the plan and the market in a situation substantially different from the one in which this panel was conceived; the awareness of this difference must be present throughout our discussion.

The problem of plan–market compatibility is a reformist problem *par excellence*. It does not exist for fundamentalists on either side – whether Marxist comprehensive central planners, or the Hayekian laissez-fairist marketeers. It emerges – rather sooner in practice than in theory – out of disillusionment with results of the more extremist systemic variants. This was the case with the long-lasting impact of the Great Depression of the 1930s on the perception of the economic role of the state in the West. This was also the case with the reformist endeavours in communist countries

7

from the mid-1950s onwards (NEP does not fall, in my opinion, into the same category – because the need to compromise would be and was perceived at the time as temporary, before the socialist system of central planning was complete). It is not my intention to follow the meanders of the market-plan story in the West, or for that matter in the countries of the Third World.[1] My introduction is focused on the evolution of the subject in communist countries.

The first wave of reform proposals in the mid-1950s was based on the diagnosis that the failure of the command ('centralistic') model of planning was due to the lack of any interaction with a market mechanism and the ensuing information and motivational poverty of the system. Neither the informal lubrication of the rigid allocative mechanism by breaking the rules nor the market-like components of retail trade and of some freedom in the field of employment could change the situation. Left to itself, this model of planning seemed to be destined for shedding all 'remnants of capitalism' not only under the weight of the ideology derived from Marxist theory of a marketless socialist/communist economy, but also because of its inner logic. As amply documented in the literature of the time and in the subsequent historical examination[2] the reformists of the 1950s and 1960s wanted to reverse this tendency by restoring the legitimacy of a market mechanism, but within a macroeconomic framework determined by national planning (or – for the smaller East European countries – even some elements of supranational planning, when the Comecon plan coordination structure and the dominant position of the Soviet Union is taken into account). There is no point in describing here the essentials or the different variants of the 'model of central planning with regulated market mechanism' (my own preferred term) which attempted to make the plan and the market compatible by limiting the latter basically to the product market alone (without capital market and labour market in the strict sense), and leaving to the plan the determination of the aggregate savings ratio (and through it, with much less certainty, the rate of growth), of the main changes in the structure of productive capacities (through central allocation of investment flows), of foreign economic relations (through retention, in one form or another, of the state monopoly of foreign trade). Thus, compatibility was to be achieved by making the plan–market relationships analogous to the medieval relationship between theology and philosophy ('philosophia ancilla theologiae'): the market was to become an instrument of the sovereign plan, a better instrument than the primitive tool of direct physical allocation of everything to everybody. This concept of compatibility persisted for a rather long time, to a considerable extent – as I see it now – thanks, paradoxically enough, to the unwillingness of the communist rulers to accept even such a compromise. It was thus scarcely tested, and in the only case which could be regarded as a test (the Hungarian NEM) the weaknesses of the concept itself became not immediately evident because of (1) inconsistency of application, and (2) the mono-archic nature of the political system which was regarded as crucial impediment to rationalization of central economic decisions.[3] Never-theless, despite its limitations, the Hungarian test played an important role both by making clear the need for further change and by some paving of the road to it. The lessons of the Yugoslav experience – despite its specific features which make it untypical for the communist world as a whole – point in the same direction.

Provided that the kind of plan–market compatibility envisaged by the 'naive reformers', to use Kornai's term, is accepted as fallacious, our problem moves into another dimension: is there any role left for the plan in a market coordinated economy, i.e. an economy in which products, capital and natural factors of production as well as labour are allocated as a rule by the market in the process of interaction of independent profit-oriented enterprises? Keeping in mind the assumption that the ownership structure must be such as to create the appropriate conditions for the functioning of the market, I refrain from discussing here the question of relative weights of public versus private enterprises, and hence the legitimacy of using the designation 'market socialism' for a market coordinated economy emerging from the ruins of 'real socialism'.

Needless to say, the answer to the problem in its new dimension can hardly be based now on any evidence derived from practice of the countries concerned. What is obvious is that the old system does not work any more and it finds itself in a state of formal or informal disintegration. But even in the countries which actually moved, or at least showed a clear determination to move, towards a fully-fledged market (Poland, Hungary, Yugoslavia) the situation is strongly affected by the need to reach the 'critical mass' of change indispensable for securing a genuine transition, as well as by the emergency measures aimed at stabilizing the national economies. This, coupled with understandable intellectual backlash against any concepts reminding of the communist past, leaves very few cues as to the detailed pattern (or patterns) these economies are going to follow when the basic tasks of stabilization and systemic transformation are accomplished. Therefore, what remains for us is actually (1) to return to the familiar controversies about compatibility of an economically active government with the principle of market coordination, and (2) to discuss whether the degree and form of such activity found compatible can and should be called 'plan'. Willy-nilly, the experience of capitalist market economies – in particular, the 'newly industrialized countries' of

Asia – must be kept in mind in this kind of discussion. This means, in my opinion, that the former glamour of the question of plan–market compatibility as an element of a battle royal between two diverging principles of economic coordination has gone; the real issue is rather that of painstaking pragmatic tests of validity of government intervention in particular areas of economic activity under particular circumstances. The following survey of the areas concerned refers as much as possible to the problems faced by the former centrally planned economies (CPEs) in their move towards a market system.

The first area of an active role of the state in economic life is that of a *regulator*, establishing and safeguarding the rules of functioning of the market. Apart from the more general ones (like contract enforcement), the widely accepted responsibilities of states (or supranational bodies such as the EC) include promoting competitive conditions, monitoring the operation of market institutions (like stock exchanges), guarding the balance between the right to commercial secrecy and public accountability, helping the supposedly sovereign but practically underinformed consumer to stand up to the pressure of mighty producers and sellers. In this area there seems to be no conflict between state intervention and the operation of the market (although there is a conflict of interests with the monopolists): paradoxically enough, it is not deregulation but appropriate regulation which appears to be instrumental in bringing the real market closer to its textbook descriptions. For the former CPEs the role of the state in this respect is obviously much greater and, in the initial phase of their market-era, qualitatively different. Not only do the monopolistic structures of production and distribution inherited from the past, along with all the consequences of the endemic shortage economy, have to be fought against, but the virtually total absence of the institutional market infrastructure must also be dealt with. Most of these institutions in Western market economies have developed over a long period of time – if not entirely spontaneously everywhere, they have basically been the result of natural evolution. In Eastern Europe, and in China as the case may be, they must be created by conscious (planned?) action of the state in the shortest possible (revolutionary? counter-revolutionary?) way.

Outside this area of providing the 'enabling environment' for the market, the economic activity of the state is more likely to come into conflict with market coordinations. The degree of this conflict varies, and if one should ask for arranging the areas under discussion according to the increasing likelihood of conflict, I would propose to consider them in the following order: the area of human and material infrastructure, the area of macroeconomics, and the area of industrial structure.

The *area of human and material infrastructure* is not easy to define and my rather conventional list (health care, education, environment protection, housing, main transport facilities, energy- and water-supply) does not pretend to make it unambiguously distinguishable from other sectors. In the fields listed the role of the state (central and/or local government) is usually large in all market economies in the provision of goods and services through public sector institutions or in financial assistance through budgetary subsidies. Until the end of the 1970s one could claim some kind of trend towards the 'welfare state', i.e. towards an increase in the share of non-market forms of allocation of resources in this area. Since then, this trend has been arrested or even reversed in some Western countries, and what has become very pronounced is the increase in state–market interaction (for instance, contrasting out the provision of services financed from the public purse). The challenge to the earlier trend and the increase in state–market interaction intensified the debates about empirical criteria of market versus non-market forms of allocation of resources also in the area which I called human and material infrastructure.[4] The gist of the empirical analysis seems to indicate that although the boundaries between the state and the market here are shifting in time, and not necessarily in one direction, the role of the 'visible hand' will remain strong, evidently stronger than in other areas. This is true also of the former CPEs despite the need of pushing back the state in infrastructure as well.

The *area of macroeconomics* – aggregate growth of the economy, utilization of productive capacity, employment etc. – was for a long time regarded by the supporters of national planning as their trump card, even by those who were prepared to admit that sustained growth, elimination of fluctuations in utilization of productive capacities, full employment and other beneficial effects of national planning might imply some price in terms of micro-efficiency. This trump card proved to be spurious, especially in the long run, hence the recourse of the former CPEs to the market also with regard to such aspects as the formation of savings, allocation of investment, and determination of prices and wages. Does this mean a complete withdrawal of the state, passive acceptance of the impact of purely spontaneous processes – including those which are international – on the level and direction of change of economic activity, and their social consequences? Whatever the theoretical laissez-fairist answer, no real-world government in market economies adopts such a stance. Moreover, it would be very difficult, nay impossible, to find governments actually limiting themselves to conventional monetary and fiscal policies in their endeavours to influence developments on the macroscale. Even those as strongly committed to the free market as the Thatcher government in Britain, are usually forced to go further, promoting investment and job-creation through explicit or implicit subsidies, devising special savings schemes, practising various kinds of protectionism and licensing. There are numerous examples of more systematic and comprehensive growth-cum-full-employment strategies applied by the state in predominantly market economies, as well as more or less convincing concepts of possible policy tools which would not undermine the foundations of the market coordination mechanism.[5] The extent to which active macropolicies should be pursued, and whether they are needed because of market failures or because of social objectives overriding the disadvantage of market distortions, cannot be established *a priori*, without empirical examination. It seems however, that in view of the inevitable displacements connected with the transformation of the economic system and in many cases the very painful process of stabilization of the economy, the former CPEs may need, particularly in the nearer future, more comprehensive macropolicies than the developed industrial economies. The interaction of such macropolicies with the operation of the market as the main coordination mechanism cannot be easy and frictionless, but the search for pure solutions is hardly the best guidance here.

The *area of industrial structure* is undoubtedly the one most open to conflicts between the state and the market, or rather the entrepreneurial initiative based on business considerations projected into the future. Central planning showed itself probably at its worst in the attempts to determine the future sectoral structure of the economy, technological developments, shifts in demand for particular categories of goods and services, as well as between the goods and services in general etc. On the other hand it is difficult to see what kind of sufficiently reliable indications of structural changes in the future can be derived from the market whose long-term verdict comes as a rule *ex post* through a chain of short-term adjustments. Hence, the view frequently encountered that neither state policy nor the market are to be relied upon in shaping future economic structures which are the result of entrepreneurial 'creative destruction'; the market's role is to test the entrepreneurial intuition, and to keep in check the risk factor by rewarding the successes and penalizing the failures. The distrust in governments' structural policies, accused also in the West of producing 'white elephants', is reflected in the fact that, at least recently, any coherent industrial policy could hardly be detected in a number of leading market economies, notably in the USA and in Britain. Needless to say, there are famous success stories as well – Japan's in the first place, followed by South Korea and other Asian NICs. What seems most interesting in the Japanese case is the cooperation of the government and business in 'picking the winners' for the future, particularly through joint research and development effort which smooths out the risk, but does not remove it entirely from the corporate sector; joint R&D projects are considered the most important government/firm interaction in the field of industrial policy.[6] Acknowledging the importance of this form, it seems, however, that this is evidently so at a later stage of development, when a country finds itself at the frontiers of technology. At an earlier stage other forms may also prove instrumental, among them some rather unpopular nowadays such as protectionism. There is no reason to forget the 'infant industry' argument, which may be applicable to other situations as well. In particular, it may well be that the legacy of 'conservative modernization' in the former CPEs presents them with such formidable tasks of restructuring that they should consider – also in negotiations with the Bretton Woods institutions and other international bodies – the advisability of combining the opening of their economies with reasonable selective protectionism; blanket liberalization of foreign economic relations may not always be the best option for the badly needed industrial policy.

The brief survey above cannot, obviously, be regarded in itself as a meaningful contribution to the problem of compatibility of an economically active state with the market. In particular, merely pointing to the inadequacy of market allocation (lack of perfect information, externalities, barriers to competition, inability to anticipate etc.) is clearly insufficient because it does not follow from the enumeration of market failures that the government failures will be smaller. As emphasized above, continuous pragmatic testing is probably the only way to find the relatively (i.e. in respect of conditions and accepted social objectives) appropriate scale of state intervention within a general market framework. However, the survey may be useful as a reminder that compatibility is a problem not just for the former CPEs. Nowhere in the world does the economy depend solely on market forces; in this sense one may even say that there is an empirical proof of *some kind* of compatibility of state interventionism with the market.

As for the second part of our query – whether the degree and forms of the state's economic activity which are found compatible with overall market coordination can and should be called 'plan' – the answer depends on the meaning of the term 'plan'. The authors of the French Xth Plan have no doubts on this score when they write 'The Plan and the market are... perfectly complementary'.[7] Statements of this kind supported by the practice of 'indicative planning' in France for over four decades are of course music to the ears of those in the Soviet Union who strive to give substance to the frequently used formula of 'planned market economy'.[8] But it should be clear that the French Plan has little, if anything, in common not only with planning of the classic, command type, but also with the varieties envisaged in the model of 'central planning with regulated market mechanism', under the Hungarian NEM or in the several Yugoslav versions. Moreover, the Xth Plan itself – compared with early French plans – serves as evidence that the active role of the state *vis-à-vis* the market is diminishing over time, probably under the influence of pragmatically assessed experience, and certainly under the influence of progressing internationalization of economic life, of which the integration in the EC is the most important factor. The reading of the cited document prompts one to admit that the Xth Plan is indeed comprehensive in the discussion of the interrelated challenges faced by the French economy in the 1989–92 period, and in the identification of priorities ('one main objective: to progressively achieve a high level of employment' followed by an outline of 'strategy for economic and social growth', education, research and competitiveness etc.), but at the same time it is very general in presentation of the possible ways and means of meeting the challenges and realizing the priorities, except perhaps when straight budgetary commitments for the infrastructural area are involved. This is not perceived by the authors of the Plan as an error, but as a reflection reality ('The instability and growing interdependence of the world economy means that it is no longer possible to set quantified medium-term objectives with any certainty, especially for growth', p. xi). Although the authors could not, nevertheless, resist quoting a growth forecast of 3 per cent annually and formulate 'the 1989–1992 objective for investment to grow twice as rapidly' (p. 22), the reliance is mainly on private investment initiative. It should also be noted that the Plan is quite specific in promising the state's help in making the French economy more competitive before the advent of the integrated European market in 1993 – another interesting case of the state consciously promoting the market.

Would a more structured plan be compatible with the market as the primary coordinating mechanism of the economy? Kalecki, who never ceased to nurture the idea of macroplanning in a capitalist mixed economy under a 'popular front' government, suggested in 1965 at a Polish–Italian seminar[9] the following minimum scope of state economic control for a meaningful plan: (1) over foreign trade and currency operations, (2) over banks and financial institutions, (3) over investment – licensing of private investment and the possibility of direct state investment in cases of too low private investment activity, and (4) over prices of wage-goods (which, in conjunction with the known Kalecki's theory of the relative stability of the share of wages in national income amounted to incomes policy). At the time, the main objection of the Italian participants to Kalecki's idea concerned how condition (1) would square with membership of the EC, but there were other objections as well. The matter was never pursued further, and the unsuccessful later attempts to include more structured planning in the context of 'alternative economic strategy', of the left-of-centre currents in Western socialist parties (the French and Greek experiments in the early 1980s may be regarded as attempts to implement it) would rather discourage its revival. It seems to me, however, that if the problem of compatibility of planning with the market should be seen as worthy of remaining on the agenda of economic debate, the concept of plan must be more akin to the Kalecki version than to the one reflected in the Xth French Plan. Otherwise the issue becomes trivial and the conclusion of compatibility hardly relevant.

Notes

1 One of the most illuminating accounts of a major test of the role of planning in the Third World is Sukhamoy Chakravarty's *Development Planning: The Indian Experience*, Oxford, Clarendon Press, 1987. In a review article of the book, the distinguished Japanese economist Shigeru Ishikawa brings in the experience of other Asian countries and provides interesting generalizations, some of which have been used in this paper (*Structural Change and Economic Dynamics*, Cambridge University Press, forthcoming). See also S. Chakravarty's 'Market Forces and Planning', in O. Bogomolov, ed., *Market Forces in Planned Economies*, Proceedings of a Conference held in Moscow 1989 by the International Economic Association (forthcoming, Macmillan).

2 See, in particular, Janos Kornai's 'The Hungarian Reform Process: Visions, Hopes and Reality', *Journal of Economic Literature*, 24 (December 1986), pp. 1687–1737, which goes beyond the Hungarian experience and literature.

3 The political aspect was presented as crucial in my own book, *Socialist Ownership and Political Systems*, London, Routledge & Kegan Paul, 1975.

4 An excellent analysis of the issues in this area can be found in Julian Le Grand and Ray Robinson, *The Economics of Social Problems. The Market versus the State*, Basingstoke, Macmillan (first edition, 1976).

5 One of such concepts is presented in W. Brus and K. Laski, *From Marx to the Market: Socialism in Search of an Economic System*. Oxford, Clarendon, 1989.

6 The point was convincingly made lately by Yutaka Kosai, President of the Japan Center for Economic Research, in a paper 'Government/Business Relations and Competitiveness: The Japanese Case', presented to the Korea Development Institute's and Economic Development Institute's of the World Bank seminar on 'International Competitiveness: Public Sector/Private Sector Interface', Seoul, April 1990.

7 Ministry for Planning of France. French Planning Office. *France, Europe. Xth Plan 1989–1992*, Paris, 1989, pp. 6–7.

8 This was the formula adopted in February 1990 in the Central Committee of the Communist Party Platform for the XXVIII Congress (section III was entitled, 'For an effective plan-market economy'). The search for support in the experience of French planning could be seen, *inter alia* in an article in

Izvestia no. 119, 28 April 1990, 'Rynok i plan po frantsuski' (Market and Plan in a French manner).

9 The proceedings of the seminar were never published. A brief report can be found on p. 299 of vol. 5 of Kalecki's *Collected Works*, Warsaw, 1985 (in Polish; the English edition of the *Collected Works* is in preparation by Oxford University Press).

2   Market socialism: the model that might have been – but never was

Domenico Mario Nuti

History punishes those who are too late.

(M.S. Gorbachev, 1989)

'It's a poor sort of memory that only works backwards,' the Queen remarked

(Lewis Carroll, Through the Looking Glass)

The moving target of economic reform

The ultimate model for the wave of economic reforms attempted in Central Eastern Europe over the last thirty-five years has been a moving target. At first, reform aimed at improving Soviet-type central planning, replacing central commands with contractual relations, using net value instead of gross physical indicators of enterprise performance, credit instead of budgetary grants, material incentives instead of campaigns, and gearing the system to some market signals, especially to world markets (e.g. Poland, 1956; USSR, 1965; Hungary, 1968; Czechoslovakia 1981).[1]

In a second stage the target was a fuzzy notion of a radically new model, 'market socialism'. Initially, there were talks of a 'socialist market', an expression coined by Gorbachev which was rightly criticized: 'We want sausage', said Gavril Popov, 'not socialist sausage'; 'A market is a market is a market', added Czechoslovak Vice-Premier Valtr Komarek soon after coming to power. Clearly only the institutional environment in which markets operate, and the policies followed by governments, can be socialist or non-socialist, while markets cannot be so labelled; thus, there can be market socialism but not socialist markets. A 'socialist' market may be understood as an egalitarian market where participants have equal income and wealth and 'vote by the ruble' in a genuine economic democracy; however, money, unlike votes, can always be lent and borrowed, and the position of households and enterprises is in any case asymmetric; a market cannot be equalitarian; only policies can be equalitarian. A 'socialist' market may also be understood as a 'regulated' market; however, either the regulation takes the form of price control, in which case we are outside a market system, or it takes the form of state transactions in the open market, in which case there is a perfectly ordinary market. The same objection could be raised against the expression 'social market' familiar from Erhard's Germany, in that government policies implement social concerns; however 'social market' is an established shorthand for a mixed economy with moderate state intervention and social policies. 'Social market' is a label now widely used also with reference to Central Eastern Europe by social-democratic as opposed to liberal reformers.

A notion of market socialism was soon understood as a mixed economy still with prevalent public ownership and a dominant communist party but with generalized market exchange, regulated by public policy, and with a form of political pluralism.[2] The model was not completely developed in its final form, but was rather defined by radical moves in its direction; the lack of a clear and accepted ultimate model did not seem to matter, as the first steps would be the same regardless of the final target (Hewett 1989). Especially in Hungary, Poland and the Soviet Union, substantial and unprecedented changes took place, such as the dismantling of mandatory planning; the gradual remonetization of the economy and establishment of financial discipline of enterprise activity (including procedures for enterprise recovery, liquidation and bankruptcy); the introduction of bonds, shares, and capital markets for their primary and secondary trading; the gradual exposure of enterprises to international competition, through greater access to foreign trade and foreign exchange transactions; the development of non-state economic activities, i.e. by individuals, cooperatives, joint ventures and sometimes even wholly private enterprises, domestic or foreign; the connection of incomes and enterprise performance, and greater mobility of labour; last but not least, some relaxation of the party's grip over political, economic and social life (for an up-to-date account of the progress of economic reform in Eastern Europe see UN-ECE, 1989a, and b, 1990).

Both kinds of reform attempts – at improving the old model and at constructing a new one – failed to cure the inefficiency, inertia and instability of the old system. At present, most of these countries (the GDR through merger with the FRG; Poland, Hungary, Czechoslovakia) are in transition back to multi-party democracy and a full-fledged capitalist economy; the evolution of Bulgaria, Romania and the USSR in theory is still open but in practice no alternative has been developed.[3] No 'Third Way', distinct from a capitalist economy with social democratic policies, has been implemented or even conceived in Western countries either.[4]

It is usually inferred from these developments that the Soviet-type economic system is doomed and that 'market socialism' has failed.[5]

Clearly the rejection of communist monopoly of political power can be regarded as a precondition of any systemic improvement, whether minor or major; otherwise the system's drawbacks are bound to be perpetuated by direct political interference in economic affairs, adverse selection in nomenklatura appointments, lack of political feedbacks, the use of economic weapons in political life, the inability of non-elected government to enforce the austerity needed by economic adjustment processes. However, both minor and major attempts at systemic improvement are likely to have failed not because of the presumed impossibility of the attempted task but because of other factors. These include: the dogmatic unwillingness and political inability to stabilize the economic environment in which reform was to take place and to maintain financial discipline thereafter; the failure to sever the links between the centre and enterprises, to unleash competition, to expose enterprises fully to market rewards (including some appropriation of capital gains) and penalties (without enterprise-specific *ad hoc* and *ex post* compensatory subsidies and taxes, amounting to indirect instead of direct centralization); the failure to undertake reform measures according to an efficient operational sequence instead of meandering, always following the line of least resistance; the lack of a clear cut, coherent and detailed blueprint for the target model; the frequent aimless revisions and sudden reversals under the pressure of interest groups and political currents.[6]

In these conditions, the reform of the old system was and is doomed, and the only viable course is its total rejection. Does this mean that these are the only conditions that the traditional Soviet-type model can generate for its own reform? It may well be that this is the case, i.e. that no socialist economy is capable of following financial discipline (i.e. of sticking to 'hard budget constraints'), of recruiting profit-minded managers to whom devolve economic decisions, of using economy-wide instruments of economic policy, of de-politicizing the economy. It is true that, to date, socialist leaders have proved to be incapable of learning not only from other people's mistakes (which is true wisdom) but also from their own; is this to be regarded as an immutable and permanent state of affairs? Learning being an essential perquisite of the human condition there is something awkward – to say the proof should rest on those who entertain such presumption.[7] If so, it is neither futile nor trivial to consider what a model of 'market socialism' might begin to look like, if it is to differ from a mixed economy under an elected social democratic government: this is the purpose of this chapter.

It should be stressed that speculation about a possible alternative model of 'market socialism' – a 'Third Way' – is a purely intellectual exercise, the exploration of a utopia. It cannot possibly involve claims to superiority over the capitalist system but it might well have been an improvement over the half measures taken in the name of reform. However, market socialism today cannot be regarded as a blueprint for action in Central Eastern Europe: obtuse procrastination on the part of past and present socialist leaders (including also – indeed, especially – Mikhail Gorbachev) has made it impossible for anything but a version of capitalism to be the target model for Central Eastern European countries: when a boat is sinking, it is no time to experiment with the floating properties of alternative rafts.

Nevertheless, it is facile to quip, with the Czechoslovak Finance Minister Vaclav Klaus, that 'The Third Way is the quickest road to the Third World'. The exploration of a model that might have been should be of interest to socialists and non-socialists alike, also in the West.

Market socialism

Economic literature does not provide a comprehensive model of 'market socialism'. Usually Oskar Lange is regarded as the originator of the concept of market socialism, in spite of the fact that he never spoke of market socialism and would not have been the first if he had. In fact, Lange's model involves only a partial market simulation for the trial-and-error iterative construction of a central plan, and belongs to the set of decentralization procedures in central planning. The term appears to have been coined by Heimann (1922, 1934) who first spoke of *Marktsozialismus*; other proponents usually associated with market socialism include Taylor (1928), Landauer (1931), Dickinson (1933), Lange (1938; for a comprehensive survey of pre-War literature, see Landauer, 1959). Even before Heimann, Barone (1908) had discussed the activity of the Minister of Production of his Collectivistic State in terms of actual markets, but only to show the basic equivalence of the two systems. Post-Lange literature on market socialism ranges from Brus (1964), whose work actually influenced Czech and Hungarian reforms and gradually developed more and more decentralized schemes in the light of experience (see Brus 1985), to Nove's 'feasible socialism' (1983) and the statements produced by the more enlightened East European reformers and Commissions for Economic Reform. Nove proposes really an 'efficient' socialism, no more 'feasible' than traditional central planning, undistinguishable from the capitalist mixed economy; while the others seem stronger on criticism than on positive propositions.

A major question is whether 'market socialism' should be understood as a set of specific policies (e.g. full employment, social consumption, social insurance and equalitarian redistribution of income) in a mixed, market economy, or also a set of specific institutions beside those of such an economy. The characterization proposed here includes both policies and institutions.

Kornai (1990: pp. 22–3) contrasts 'market socialism' with what he calls 'the free economy':

A free economy is, of course, a market economy, but the concept is richer and refers not only to the fact that the main coordinator of economic activities is a specific mechanism, namely the market. A free economy is one that allows unhampered entry, exit and fair competition in the market. The notion of a free economy also implies a certain configuration of property rights and a certain institutional and political structure. The system promotes the free establishment and preservation of private property and encourages the private sector to produce the great bulk of output. It is a system that encourages individual initiative and entrepreneurship, liberates this initiative from excessive state intervention, and protects it by the rule of law. A free economy is embedded in a democratic political order, characterized by the free competition of political forces and ideas.

However, we might imagine a model of market socialism that includes all the features of Kornai's free economy but also exhibits additional features strictly related to the socialist project; namely, the privatization of the management of state assets instead of their property; the payment of a national dividend or citizens' income; the transformation of workers – at least on a part-time basis – into entrepreneurs; the use of open-market operations (instead of controls) in all markets on the part of the government as instruments of economic policy, instead of planning, the use of contingent policy commitments, and of state agencies subject to strict budgetary constraints and acting as Employer (or Investor, or Foreign Trader) of last resort.

Markets: competition and balance at single prices

The necessity of markets rests on several strong arguments. First, one can view 'The market as a procedure for discovery and conveyance of inarticulate knowledge' (which is the eloquent title of a paper by Lavoie (1986)). Secondly, and perhaps more importantly, markets are servo-mechanisms, homeostatic automatic devices that adjust price, output and capacity in response to excess demand (respectively, the Walrasian, Marshallian and capital-stock adjustments). Thirdly, markets constrain economic agents to income and wealth budgets.

In order to play these roles, markets have to be competitive on the side of both demand and supply, yield single prices and always clear. Competition requires the splitting of the large enterprises and their associations, currently dominating Eastern Europe in all sectors including agriculture, as well as their total freedom to diversify their output and to move into and out of any sectors. Market clearing is essential to avoid unjustified and inefficient rents otherwise implicit in access to purchase or outlet; the frequent presence of excess demand in socialist countries (see Kornai 1980; Nuti 1986a) is the result of a tragic misunderstanding, a confusion of aspirations and potentials with actual achievements; there can be no market without market clearing at the ruling prices. This means there can be no room for 'price criteria' and 'price formulas' or for intermittent 'price reforms': any price policy should take the form of quantity policies, or income policies; if need be in a passing emergency actual rationing might be considered, instead of the indignity and inefficiency of the kind of queuing where supplies end before all queue members are satisfied. Market clearing should normally happen at single prices, i.e. at uniform conditions for all transactions.[8] Markets as feedback mechanisms ought to be direct and automatic, i.e. not mediated by an intermediate administrative body and depending on its reactions; they are often slow, or unstable, or costly, and in many circumstances they may function worse than plans, but with respect to plans they have the advantages of being automatic where plans may exhibit inertia, and of generating and transmitting information to market transactors. There would have to be market not only for commodities and services but also for productive factors, money[9] and foreign exchange (i.e. currency convertibility). This gives economic agents the opportunity to 'optimize' their behaviour, adjusting it to external parameters and their changes, unimpeded by administrative bodies.

Pluralist ownership

Mises (1951) argued that private ownership of means of production was a precondition of markets, because only ultimate owners have the incentive to control their efficient use. Hence, for Mises there was the dilemma: either socialism or markets, and there could not be such a thing as market socialism.[10] I believe he was both right and wrong. He was right in that the appropriation of all or a sizeable fraction of the capital gains deriving from successful enterprise seems a necessary precondition for the mobilization of entrepreneurial initiatives; but he was wrong in that this is all that is needed. We can imagine an economy where the ownership of all means of production and their further reproduction is in the hand of the state, but these means are leased in competitive leasing markets to private entrepreneurs who retain a residual claim to both income and capital gains and are able to transfer those claims. Capital leasings – present on a small scale under NEP – have reappeared widely in the recent reform, unfortunately also on too small a scale. But there is a model of 'entrepreneurial socialism' by the Hungarian economist Tibor Liska

(1963) based precisely on the competitive leasing of state assets and their compulsory surrender to the highest bidder (however, with the additional bids belonging to bidders, not to the state), all citizens having a capital stake to invest or to use to exercise entrepreneurship (see Barsony 1982; Nuti 1988a, c). Leasings, instead of privatization, are worthy of greater consideration than they have attracted in economic reform to date.

Another form of privatization of management is the maintenance of a large state stake in national capital through state shareholdings in private companies. Thus there can be a large but not exclusive or even necessarily predominant public ownership of productive capacity (state, local and cooperative) coexisting and competing on equal terms with a non-public sector. State and local authorities property is not entrusted to enterprises controlled by administrative agencies, but is sold to independent enterprises in exchange for bonds or equities held by specialized state holdings acting as independent shareholders. There would no longer be any role for so-called 'founding organs' i.e. Ministries (whether branch Ministries, or a single Ministry for Industry, or functional Ministries) or other central agencies: the 'petty tutelage' of central organs over enterprises would have to be abolished.

The expectation that cooperative enterprises might supplant state enterprises within the public sector, through the leasing of state assets to workers' cooperatives, is probably far-fetched; the spectacular hyper-growth of Soviet cooperatives (see Nuti 1989c) is not indicative of this sector's potential because those cooperatives are not subject to traditional limitation of earnings and return on capital. In general, for cooperative members to be fully-fledged entrepreneurs it would be necessary to give them a share of the capital value increments in the assets of their enterprises; this, however, would transform cooperative into private partnerships (see below).

Political and economic participation

There would have to be generalized participation in economic and political decision making at all levels, moving away from bureaucratic power and what Wlodzimierz Brus calls the party's 'mono-archy'. After all, originally this kind of participation was to be exercised through the Soviets' power, and it is an aberration that today 'the Soviets' should be liable to being used – in American and now also in English practice – as a citizenship label, as we might for instance refer to 'the British'. Participation would be necessary, in a phase of transition to the new system at a time of crisis, as a non-resource-intensive good which could be used as a counterpart for austerity in a social pact between the government and society (the other non-resource-intensive goods, i.e. alcohol and drugs, have undesirable side effects).

Supplementary nature of government activity

There would have to be active use of a wide range of policy instruments to implement government policies; however, only government activity would be planned; it would have to be additional, i.e. supplementary to what else happens by itself in the economy and not totalitarian (i.e. not embracing the whole economy); it would be contingent on the economy not following unaided a course judged as desirable by a government subject to frequent electoral verification of popular support. Government activity consists in steering the spontaneously existing economic motion, not in actually providing the engine of the economy's motion.

Socialist policies through the market

In the envisaged model of 'market socialism' commitment to socialist values such as equality, social consumption, social security, and full employment of labour, would be maintained. However, these objectives are not pursued at all costs, or right down to the level of saturation of private or government demand, but only to the extent that their cost at the margin is specifically regarded by the government as commensurate with their achievement. Hence, there are no open-ended (i.e. soft-budget) commitments, but only hard-budgeted allocations to specific targets, directly from the state budget or through independent agencies responsible for their achievement and accountable for their cost-effectiveness. The government policy is asserted primarily through the market, i.e. through budgetary expenditure and the sale of goods and services, physical and financial assets. Provision of social consumption out of the budget would be recognized to be crowding out alternative individual consumption or public targets, and regarded as a good thing not in absolute but in competition with other good things; it would be provided perhaps less generously than previously expected, both in terms of the number of people entitled and of individual entitlement. The commitment to full employment is accompanied by high labour mobility, across firms, regions and occupations; there is no 'job right protection' (a feature of the traditional model theorized by Granick 1987), only a general entitlement to 'a' living job, or rather to a guaranteed income (see below). In a paper on 'Plan and Market' (Nuti 1986b), I envisaged the possibility of a State Agency for Labour hiring at the prevailing wage all unemployed who wish to be employed, and either leasing its labourers at whatever spot price it can get from enterprises, or using their labour for local social needs (especially environmental). This would absolve the government of any duty to look after those unwilling to be so employed; in order to stop enterprises from replacing their labourers with labour from the Labour Agency, usually cheaper, no enterprise reducing its current employment would be eligible for the scheme. A similar principle of government budgeted intervention through the market could be applied to investment policy, or to trade policy (see below). The cutting of social consumption short of saturation, the acceptance of labour mobility and of budgetary limits are partly lessons to be learnt from Thatcherism, especially in view of its popular support; however, market socialism would attach greater weight than Thatcherism to the importance of social consumption and other social values, and would consistently raise tax revenue from capital and capital income (including capital gains) to an extent much greater than Thatcherism.

An open economy

The market socialist economy is open to foreign trade in order to ensure competition in domestic markets and the utilization of efficient opportunities for international division of labour and factor transfers (including technology). This does not prevent the government from undertaking designs of planned economic integration such as those which might arise from the continuation of CMEA, but forces the government to pursue such a design through the market, i.e. assigning tasks to enterprises on a contractual basis for the fulfilment of possible medium and long-term international obligations, and reselling in spot markets the deliveries obtained in return; in such a way the efficiency of planned integration is visible through the transparency of related transactions.

No indirect centralization

Just as prices normally ought to be uniform for all transactions for markets to be efficient, so fiscal and other parameters must be uniform, and there must not be enterprise-specific or even budget-specific subsidies or *ex-post ad hoc* compensatory payments or withdrawals aimed at equalizing the ultimate position of enterprises regardless of their market performance (the large scale of such redistributive cross-subsidization is documented by Kornai 1986, for Hungary). Anything else amounts to indirect or parametric centralization, which perpetuates many familiar disadvantages of central planning (neglect of efficiency, lack of incentives, targets bargaining, etc.).

Minimum guaranteed income

There is some guaranteed income, in lieu of product subsidies which may distort consumption structure; a minimum income is guaranteed also in lieu of some consumption earlier provided as free social consumption, for consumers to be able to exercise some choice even in areas such as medical care or education.

Profit sharing

There is profit sharing by workers of all enterprises, necessarily by statute in cooperatives and optionally by contract in other enterprises (this practice is spreading rapidly in Western Europe, and is the object of further development in spite of British opposition within the implementation of the European Social Charter; see Uvalic 1990). This link gives those workers who wish to take on the risk of entrepreneurship the opportunity – not the obligation – of doing so to the extent that they so desire. The guarantee of a minimum income, and of productive employment, makes this form of risk-taking more approachable by workers. The link ought to have some, sizeable if not dramatic, effect on labour productivity. Possible inequalitarian effects ought to be dealt with through normal taxation; in any case, equality of opportunity should matter more than actual equality of achievement.

Neo-corporatism

The market socialist economy is bound to require neo-corporatist institutions, to move away from what Paul Marer calls the 'atomization of society' towards organized interest groups, and to handle group conflicts which markets are not capable of resolving as well as they handle microeconomic trade-offs, if at all; a social pact seems essential to achieve price stability at full or near-full employment. Neo-corporatist institutions are all the more important if the Party were to retain a special role (as it still might in Romania, Bulgaria and perhaps the USSR).[11]

Conclusion

In brief, economic reform in Central Eastern Europe, which has failed to significantly improve the old system and to generate a new 'market socialist' model, is now leading to the restoration of versions of the capitalist system. This development seems both unavoidable and desirable in view of the dogmatic unwillingness and political inability to stabilize the economic environment and to maintain financial discipline, of the failure to complete essential elements of the reform project and to follow rational sequencing of reform steps. While there is no ready-made alternative at present, it is interesting to explore a course that might have been taken instead, of market socialism understood as a 'free economy' plus a continued commitment to socialist aims and values, if the obstacles to reform had been surmounted.

The implications of such commitments, summarily discussed in this paper, are a combination of policies and institutions, such as the privatization of the management of state assets instead of their property; the payment of a national dividend or citizens' income; the transformation of workers – at least on a part-time basis – into entrepreneurs; the use of open-market operations (instead of controls) in all markets on the part of the government as instruments of economic policy, instead of planning, the use of contingent policy commitments, and of state agencies subject to strict budgetary constraints and acting as Employer (or Investor, or Foreign Trader) of last resort; the promotion of neo-corporative institutions.

The 'market socialist' alternative path is not necessarily 'better' than capitalist restoration, but it would have been 'better' than both the old system and the unfinished reform, preferable from the viewpoint of the old leadership, and interesting for the Western social reformer seeking new solutions for the problems of the capitalist system.

Notes

A previous version of this paper has been published in *Russia and the world*, no. 18, 1990, pp. 12–16, 38–9.

1 On this characterization, see Bauer (1990a, b); he distinguishes among the improvement of the old system, its reform into a new system, and the transition to capitalism. However, Bauer regards the 1968 reform as already an attempt at reforming rather than improving the system. See also Nuti (1988b); on Czechoslovakia, see Drabek (1989).

2 According to Kornai (1990), 'market socialism = state ownership + market coordination' (p. 58); however this seems to be an unduly restrictive definition, in that market socialism is increasingly understood as including even substantial private ownership and enterprise.

3 The closest to a blueprint for the new model is contained in the Abalkin Report (1989), but even that is incomplete, out of sequence, and has been further diluted. 'Even in outline, the Soviet model of socialism for the twenty-first century has not yet emerged' (Davies 1990: p. 27).

4 The recent manifesto by the British Labour Party (1988), for instance, is a vague picture of traditional social democratic policies, listing 'a genuine free society ... real stake in and real democratic influence over the industries and services in which [workers] are employed ... freedom to choose ... redistribution ... extension of democratic control'. 'Democratic socialists believe in

market allocation – but market allocation guided by agreement that the competitive system should pursue the objective of greater freedom, greater equality and greater choice'. The picture of 'market socialism' discussed in the Le Grand and Estrin volume (1989) simply makes a case for markets and mentions egalitarian policies, some planning to obviate coordination and information failure of markets, some profit sharing, cooperatives, and some workers ownership.

5 For a sharp criticism of attempts at market socialism see Keren (1989), Kornai (1990); on the eve of such attempts, Abram Bergson expected market socialism to perform moderately better than central planning though he questioned its ability to improve over the capitalist competitive solution; see Bergson (1967).

6 On sequencing, see Nuti (1990a, b).

7 Indeed, Hewett (1989) finds that 'What is most impressive about Mikhail Gorbachev and those around him is their ability to learn ... mistakes are not important, but learning from them is. Soviet leaders are learning.'

8 There may be exceptions in motivated special cases, such as multi-part tariffs for electricity, which is produced under increasing returns to scale and is not retransferable.

9 See Nuti (1989a, b).

10 He argued that capital markets cannot be simulated; Kornai (1990) concurs: 'We are fed up with simulation' (p. 72).

11 It has been argued (for instance by Marer) that an implicit social pact between the government and workers was always there; this hypothesis is consistent with the observation of official price stability and labour full employment but is not conclusively proven, as there is no positive evidence of this unobservable pact; observations may be the effects of sequential strategies, whereas here we postulate a formal, institutionalized and somewhat guaranteed social pact. Of course, nobody is really bound, individually, by the existence of a social pact, but there is a difference in culture and economic climate and expectations.

References

Abalkin Report [All-Union Conference and Workshop on Problems of Radical Economic Reform, chaired by Vice-Premier Leonid Abalkin] (1989), Radical economic reform: top-priority and long-term measures (material for discussion), Moscow.

Barone, E. (1908), 'Il Ministro della Produzione nello stato colletivistico' (The Minister of production in the collectivistic state), *Giornale degli Economisti*, English translation in Hayek 1935: pp. 247–90.

Barsony, J. (1982), 'Tibor Liska's concept of socialist entrepreneurship', *Acta Oeconomica*, 28, nos. 3–4.

Bauer, Tamas (1990a), 'Hungary on the way towards a market economy', NATO colloquium on 'The Central and East European economies in the 1990s: prospects and constraints', April, Brussels.

(1990b), 'From limits to reform to brakes to transition', Conference paper, London School of Economics, London.

Bergson, Abram (1967), 'Market socialism revisited', 75, *Journal of Political Economy*, 5, October, pp. 655–73.

British Labour Party National Executive (1988), *Democratic Socialist Aims & Values*, London.

Brus, W. (1964), *Ogólne problemy funkcjonowania gospodarki socjalistycznej*, Warsaw, PWE, translated into English under the title: *The Market in a Socialist Economy*, Routledge & Kegan Paul, London, 1972.

(1985), 'Socialism – feasible and viable?', *New Left Review*, no. 153, pp. 43–62.

Brus, W. and Kazimierz Laski (1989), *From Marx to the Market: Socialism in Search of an Economic System*, Oxford, Clarendon Press.

Davies, R.W. (1990), 'Gorbachev's socialism', *New Left Review*, no. 179, pp. 5–27.

Dickinson, H.D. (1933), 'Price formation in a socialist community', *The Economic Journal*, 43, June.

Drabek, Zdenek (1989), 'Czechoslovak economic reform: the search for a minimum market approach', Ms., Washington.

Galbraith, J. Kenneth (1990), 'The great transition: social reality as a guide', conference paper, 5 July, Brussels.

Granick, David (1987). *Job Rights in the Soviet Union: Their Consequences*, Cambridge, Cambridge University Press.

Hayek, F.A. (ed.) (1935), *Collectivistic Economic Planning*, London, Routledge & Kegan Paul.

Heimann, E. (1922), *Mehrwert und Gemeinwirtschaft* (Surplus value and the communal economy), Berlin, H.R. Hengelmann.

(1934), 'Planning and the market system', *Social Research*, 1, November.

Hewett, Ed. A. (1989), 'Is Soviet socialism reformable?', Sturc Memorial Lecture, Johns Hopkins School for Advanced International Studies, 11 November.

(1990), 'Creating a market economy: critical issues', conference paper, IMF Institute, July.

Keren, Michael (1989), 'The New Economic System, the New Economic Mechanism, and Gorbachev's perestroika: bureaucratic limits to reform', conference paper, Jerusalem, November.

Kornai, Janos (1980), *The Economics of Shortage*, 2 vols., Amsterdam, North Holland.

(1982), 'On Tibor Liska's concept of entrepreneurship', *Acta Oeconomica*, 28, nos. 13–14, pp. 455–60.

(1986), 'The Hungarian Reform Process: Visions, Hopes and Reality', *Journal of Economic Literature*, 29, no. 4, pp. 1687–737.

(1990), *The Road to a Free Economy – Shifting from the Socialist System: the Example of Hungary*, New York and London, W.W. Norton & Co.

Landauer, C. (1931), *Planwirtschaft und Verkehrswirtschaft*, (Planned economy and market economy), Munich and Leipzig, Duncker and Humblot.

(1959), (in collaboration with E. Kridl Valkenier and H. Stein Landauer), *European Socialism: a History of Ideas and Movements from the Industrial Revolution to Hitler's Seizure of Power*, Westport, Connecticut, Greenwood Press.

Lange, O. (1938), 'The economic theory of socialism', in Lippincott 1938, originally published in a slightly different version in the *Review of Economic Studies*, 3, 1936–37.

Lavoie, Don (1985). *Rivalry and Central Planning: The Socialist Calculation Debate Reconsidered*, Cambridge, Cambridge University Press.

(1986), 'The market as a procedure for discovery and conveyance of inarticulate knowledge', *Comparative Economic Studies*, 28, no. 1, pp. 1–19.

Le Grand, Julian and Saul Estrin (eds.) (1989), *Market Socialism*, Oxford, Clarendon Press.

Lippincott, B. (ed.) (1938). *On the Economic Theory of Socialism*, Minneapolis, University of Minnesota Press.

Liska T. (1963). 'Kritik es koncepcio. Tezisek a gazdasagi mechanizmus reformiahoz' (Critique and construction. Theses for a reform of the economic mechanism), *Kozgazdasagi Szemle*, no. 9.

Lutter, M. (1981), 'Bankenvertreter im Aufsichtsrat', *Zeitschrift fur Handelsrecht*, 145, pp. 224–51.

Mises, Ludwig von (1951), *Socialism – An Economic and Sociological Analysis*, trans. J. Kahane, Indianapolis, Liberty Classics.

Neurath, O. (1919), *Durch die Kriegswirtschaft zur Naturalwirtschaft* (From the war economy to the natural economy), Munich.

Nolan, P. and S. Paine (eds.) (1986), *Rethinking Socialist Economics*, London, Polity Press.

Nove, A. (1983), *The Economics of Feasible Socialism*, London, Allen and Unwin.

Nuti, D.M. (1986a), 'Hidden and repressed inflation in Soviet-type economies: definitions, measurements and stabilisation', *Contributions to Political Economy*, 5, pp. 37–82.

(1986b), 'Economic planning in market economies: scope, instruments, institutions', in Nolan and Paine (1986), pp. 83–98.

(1988a), 'Competitive valuation and efficiency of capital investment in the socialist economy', *European Economic Review*, 32, pp. 2–6.

(1988b), 'Perestroika: transition between central planning and market socialism', *Economic Policy*, October, pp. 353–89.

(1988c), 'On Tibor Liska's entrepreneurial socialism', *Proceedings of the Second International Polanyi Conference*, Montreal, 10–13 November 1988, on 'Market, State and Society in the Late – 20th Century' (forthcoming, St Martin's Press).

(1989a), 'Remonetisation and capital markets in the form of centrally planned economies', *European Economic Review*, 33, nos. 2/3, March, pp. 427–38.

(1989b), 'Feasible financial innovation under market socialism', in Christine Kessides, Timothy King, Mario Nuti and Kathy Sokil (eds), *Financial Reform in Centrally Planned Economies*, Washington, EDI-World Bank, pp. 6.1–6.31.

(1989c), 'The new Soviet cooperatives: advances and limitations', *Economic and Industrial Democracy*, special issue on Eastern Europe, vol. 10, pp. 311–27.

(1990a), 'Stabilisation and reform sequencing in the Soviet Economy', *Recherches Economiques de Louvain*, 56, no. 2, pp. 1–12.

(1990b), 'Stabilisation and reform sequencing in the reform of Central Eastern Europe', in Simon Commander (ed.), Washington, EDI-World Bank.

(1990c), 'Profit-sharing' in G. Szell (ed.), *Concise Encyclopedia of Participation and Co-management*, Gruyter, Berlin and New York, de Gruyter.

Pareto, V. (1902/3), *Les systemes socialistes*, 2 vols., Paris, Giard and Briere.
Schuller, Alfred (1988), *Does Market Socialism Work?* London, CRCE.
Taylor, F.M. (1928), 'The guidance of production in a socialist state', reprinted in Lippincott (1938).
Thornton, J. (1976), *The Economic Analysis of the Soviet-type System*, Cambridge, Cambridge University Press.
Uvalic, Malica (1990), *The PEPPER Report: Promotion of Employee Participation in Profits and Enterprise Results in the Member States of the European Community*, Florence and Brussels, FUI and CEG.

3   Monetary-fiscal management for macroeconomic equilibrium and growth

Gerhard Fink

Two observations instead of an introduction

1. All too often we hear someone say: 'The problem is that Marxists only told us how to convert a capitalist economy into a planned economy, but now we have to face a completely different problem which never occurred in the past: how to convert a planned economy into a market economy' (Ivan Angelov at a WIIW-seminar on 'The Reforming Eastern Economies and the OECD', 14–16 March, 1990).

2. 'We only have to look up the textbooks by the outstanding macroeconomists to know what we have to do. I would wish the Austrian School of Economics would enjoy the same high appreciation in the West that we give to von Mises, von Hayek, and others' (Vaclav Klaus, Minister of Finance of Czechoslovakia, at a lecture in Vienna, 14 March, 1990).

These two observations characterize the span of opinions about feasibility of reform in a relatively short period of time.

Reudiger Dornbush expressed his view on this problem with his well-known lucidity at a seminar organized by IIASA and the World Bank on 8 March, 1990: 'As long as experts and politicians consider the case of their country to be a very special one there is no way for finding a solution of the major problems of most of the reforming countries in Central and Eastern Europe'. And, indeed, there is practical experience of how to move from an administered system to a market-led economic system, if we only consider the cases of the Federal Republic of Germany and of Austria after World War II. In one specific aspect, the Austrian case is of particular interest: while a large part of Austrian industry which was under Soviet control until 1955 remained nationalized, the whole economy nevertheless basically followed market principles. But beyond that there have been lots of successful and unsuccessful reform attempts in various developing countries.

Sources of inflation and 'shortage'

At the end of 1989, most reforming countries of Central and Eastern Europe suffered from significant imbalances: where prices were controlled, the population had to live with shortages in supply, and where prices were uncontrolled, inflation soared, reaching on average in 1989, 1,250 per cent in Yugoslavia, and 240 per cent in Poland. Therefore, the most important task of the new governments in Central and Eastern Europe is to eliminate the underlying imbalances which lead either to hyperinflation or to hypershortage.

The sources of these imbalances can be found either in the state budget, in the local budgets, in the enterprise sector, or with the population. Since the population has only limited possibilities to finance excess expenditure in an inflationary way, the most important sources of inflation are to be found in the other three sectors.

In 1976 Igor Birman advanced the hypothesis that a part of the revenue of the Soviet state budget is financed by the emission of cash.[1] In addition, he found 'it is quite possible that the budget profits began to be considered a source of credit resources at approximately the time that the practice of granting long-term credits (instead of direct budget financing) to state enterprises began to be sharply increased.'[2] From 1975 to 1978, according to his calculations the deficit of the Soviet state budget covered by non-cash emission increased from 15 billion rubles to 22 billion, i.e. from 6.8 per cent to 8.3 per cent of total budget revenues.[3]

It was not until 1988 that these findings received official Soviet confirmation in the form of a statement by Minister of Finance B.I. Gostev indicating the deficit in the state budget of 1989 to be planned at a level of 35 billion rubles.[4] Further analysis has shown that the deficit might be even substantially larger and amount up to 139 billion rubles.[5] By October 1989 Soviet experts assumed the deficit to amount to 100 billion rubles.[6] Thus, the deficit amounted to about 15 per cent of national income.

Even if one assumes that only part of this deficit was financed by issuing new money, it is obvious that inflationary pressure was high. However, inflation could not fully exert its influence on prices which largely remained under control and went up to 7.5 per cent in 1990 according to newspaper reports.[7] 'In 1988 personal incomes grew by 40 million rubles whereas the output of consumer goods was up 25 billion rubles only. The corresponding figures for 1989 were 60 billion rubles and 35 billion rubles.'[8] Thus, the Soviet population did not suffer from hyperinflation but from hypershortage.

The other major source of inflation can be identified as the large deficits in the enterprise sector, which in one way or another are finally financed by inflationary issue of money; the traditional form is by way of subsidies from the state budget.

Enterprises running at a loss find various excuses and reasons why they do have losses. Prices may have been set at deliberately low levels by the central authorities in order to promote the purchasers of these products, e.g. food prices for social considerations, or prices for high technology products to stimulate the use of high tech in the economy. When the exchange rate is overvalued, a large proportion of exports cannot be sold abroad at prices covering production costs, etc.

The major arguments for subsidizing are to secure employment or to maintain exports at a level which is necessary according to balance of payments considerations. When subsidies were not easily forthcoming any longer enterprises have found other sources of finance. Most of the financing techniques could be observed first in Yugoslavia in the 1970s.[9] The first source to be mentioned are bank credits. Although banks did not (and still do not) have the deposit base they were willing (or obliged) to supply enterprises with credits to cover current losses. When the banks got into trouble the state bank finally restored their liquidity by issuing new money.[10] Similar developments could be observed in Poland in 1988.

As soon as central authorities efficiently impose credit restrictions, enterprises find other sources of finance. Obviously they have to, since a significant reduction of current enterprise expenses basically would mean reducing employment – and in a so-called socialist economy unemployment must not happen. The next step enterprises take is not paying their bills. Purchasers force their suppliers to extend credits simply by not paying. This phenomenon now can be observed in Yugoslavia, Hungary,[11] Poland, and more recently in the Soviet Union, too. Of course, this financing technique to cover enterprise losses cannot be applied over an extended period. And finally either the banks, or the central bank, or the state budget step in and convert the enforced credits into regular credits by issuing new money.

When the last communist government in Poland efficiently imposed a ceiling on credits extended by the banks and when inflation started to soar in early 1989, enterprises found another source of finance by not paying taxes. Government revenues significantly declined in real terms (as they decline in every country with high inflation rates).

Eventually all these deficits are financed in an inflationary way since the population has no reason to save money. The behaviour is virtually the same whether under hyperinflation or hypershortage. The saving ratio is low[12] as is the willingness to maintain money holdings. Inflation rates are usually higher than interest rates for deposits. Under both circumstances (inflation and/or shortage) the population is hunting for goods in order to convert their money into something of value which in turn could be converted into something really needed when the time comes. The best strategy as a hedge against inflation or recurring shortage is converting local money (mostly non-convertible) in real money, i.e. dollars.

Although any other convertible currency also would serve the purpose, dollar bills usually enjoy a preference. The widespread use of dollars has made people more familiar with the face of a dollar bill than, with, for example, a Dutch guilder or Austrian schilling bill. Because of fear of falsification, the value of Austrian schilling or Italian lire bills used to be much less on the Polish black market than officially suggested by the dollar/schilling or dollar/lire exchange rates. Of course, some people made a business out of changing zloty into schilling, going to Austria changing schillings into dollars, and back home converting the dollars into zloties.

Eliminating the 'money overhang'

Over the years the population has accumulated holdings of cash and short-term deposits, usually referred to as the money overhang. In the USSR, the money overhang is estimated to amount to '150 billion currently useless rubles, which, in fact, prevent the country from pulling out of the crisis'.[13] This amount has to be neutralized, eliminated or absorbed, parallel with stabilization measures taken to eliminate the current deficits. Three types of measure can be taken to eliminate the money overhang:

1 to depreciate the real value of cash balances;
2 to offer alternative spending possibilities, and;
3 to pursue policies which increase the savings ratio and the amounts voluntarily held by the population.

Money balances can be depreciated by means of money reforms or by a high rate of inflation. The German monetary union foresees a depreciation of savings deposits beyond a certain amount and of cash holdings, while current incomes and smaller savings deposits will be converted 1:1, because of social considerations.

In Poland money holdings depreciated by the high rate of inflation of 240 per cent in 1989. The effect on wages was less pronounced, since current incomes were increased in nominal terms.

In the USSR it is proposed to offer to the population new spending possibilities – a measure which was used earlier in Hungary and Poland, too. Abel Aganbegian proposes to sell flats to the population, to expand the system of advance payments for purchases of videos, cars etc. and to offer at increased prices sales of scarce goods by catalogues.[14] Beyond these ideas, one might consider offering the sale of equity to the population and other investment opportunities.

Whether these measures or a combination of them would be useful depends also on other measures taken. Introducing the D-Mark as a means of payment and storage of value, offering a positive real rate of interest on deposits, opening the opportunity to place money at productive industrial investment, and having eliminated the underlying deficits of the state budget, may be a sufficient package of measures to convert the involuntary money holdings into voluntary savings in the GDR.

The idea of selling industrial property to the population in order to soak up the money overhang and to promote privatization sounds only initially promising. The so-called money overhang is large with respect to the level of voluntary money balances of the population. However, the financial wealth is small if compared with the value of industrial fixed assets. Only a small fraction of the industrial wealth accumulated could be purchased by the population.

Privatization

Privatization can be achieved reasonably quickly only when a complex set of measures is taken. Before considering this, however, it should be asked why privatization is necessary at all. In some of the reform-communist circles one can still encounter the view that managers' independence is the decisive feature, and not the issue of who is the owner. However, it does matter who is the owner.

In state or socialized industry, workers tend to blame the government, the party or the trade union for failures in enterprise management of state industry if workplaces are endangered or wages and salaries do not grow according to expectations. Since governments need political legitimization, as do political parties and trade unions, they always give in to workers' demands whether justified or not. Therefore, a government representing the workers' interests is not in a position to represent the interests of capital too.

Under such conditions the room for active and profit-oriented management is limited. Managers have to behave as if elected by the workers, since in any dispute between workers and the management the state representatives always go with the workers and will dismiss the managers to pacify the workers. The result is a state industry lacking efficiency, permanently depending on subsidies from the state budget, and finally turning out to be a waste of scarce resources.

Manager independence is not equivalent to the economic system prevailing in the market economies. Only those enterprises turn out efficient where the managers are accountable to the owners for maintaining long-term profitability.[15] If ownership is too much dispersed, the shareholders have little interest to invest time and money into controlling the managers.. In specific cases as, for example, in various forms of consumer cooperatives or in agricultural cooperatives organizing the purchase of agricultural products, the dispersed owners may even become economically dependent on the cooperative and its managers.

In all these cases, managers tend to pursue their own objectives. They tend to appropriate part of the rent on capital through fringe benefits and high salaries. Managers become more interested in their own career than in long-term profitability of the enterprises they have to manage, thus short-term considerations win over long-term perspectives. The managers increasingly gain influence on the nomination of board members who are more and more often invited by the managers themselves. While receiving substantial fringe benefits and over-doing market research on the Bermuda Islands, the board members easily forget about controlling the enterprise.

It is also true that private enterprises are failing in a competitive framework. However, the private sector as a whole is more efficient than the state sector and adds to the wealth of nations. In a market economy, inefficient enterprises are usually taken over by entrepreneurs who believe they can do it better than the present owners. They buy a sufficiently large number of shares to control the enterprise and replace the present managers by people of their own choice. In a management buy-out, the managers take over, because they believe they know how to better control the enterprise than the present owner – and quite often, before that, have run down the enterprise in order to get it at a lower price.

In the transition from planned to market economy, large-scale privatisation is indispensable. Otherwise the desired wealth effects will not emerge. Since only the goods which have been produced can be distributed, production enterprises should be privatized quickly and at the broadest scale possible.

However, privatization takes place in a highly sensitive social and political environment fully of envy, mistrust, and mobilized illusions about the effects of marketization. The process of privatization can be successful only when it finds a broad social consensus, and when workers of the individual enterprises accept the way of privatization. In order to avoid a further decline in efficiency of enterprises, management control has to be maintained during the period of transition to new and hopefully efficient owners.

The industrial wealth accumulated over the last forty years under communist regimes by enforced savings – wages were kept extremely low and inflationary financing of investment brought about a further deterioration in the real incomes of the population – is far larger than the money holdings of the population (cash plus deposits on savings accounts). Therefore, the selling of industrial property to the population would take too long since the population needs time to regain sufficient purchasing power. Beyond that, in Poland the money holdings of the population were almost eliminated by hyperinflation and in the GDR by money reform.

Because of the lack of purchasing power of the population, two methods are proposed to accelerate privatization. The first method is to give shares to the population without any payment involved either directly[16] or through issuing vouchers,[17] the second would be set up credit facilities to be used for purchasing shares of enterprises.

Both methods are the subject of dispute. It is said that anything given freely will not be esteemed by the population. Beyond that, the voucher method is criticized for being inflationary. The assumption of the critics is that people with low income have a high inclination to sell their shares or vouchers immediately and to spend all the revenues from these sales, while people with higher income and a high propensity to save would spend their money for purchasing shares. According to this view the average propensity to spend is expected to increase. However, given the experience in the former GDR where the propensity to save increased significantly after the money reform, one also can expect a similar change in behaviour in the other countries turning from a planned to a market economy. The opportunity to invest or to find alternative means for storage of value very likely will increase the overall savings ratio.

Moreover, the method of providing credits to the population for purchasing shares is highly inflationary from the outset. Since savings are not large enough for purchasing the industrial wealth, the new credit facilities for purchasing shares can be set up only by money creation. Only by imposing the condition that the state freeze all revenue from the selling of shares to the population can the generation of an additional inflationary impulse be avoided. This condition is very unlikely to be met by governments who have to cope with a too large state budget deficit. But even were this condition met, there is no guarantee that later on shares will not be sold by people with a lower propensity to save to others with a higher propensity to save. Therefore, the method of setting up credit facilities is in all likelihood much more inflationary than the voucher method.

There are a lot of additional features which make selling of enterprises to domestic people rather difficult. Uncertainties about future markets and existing price distortions make it impossible to define the 'true value' of an enterprise. Many people would be disinclined to invest even a dime into many of the existing enterprises. A state agency for privatization would have to restore profitability first and assess the value of the enterprise before selling. This would be a lengthy procedure. Beyond that, the state agency for privatization would immediately lose its credibility if one of the sold enterprises turns out to be bankrupt. If purchasers feel cheated, sales are no longer possible.

Since no simple solution can be found for this complex problem, the procedure of privatization will undergo various trials leading to a combination of everything that might be imagined – selling part to foreign corporations, to domestic investors with and without support by cheap credit, preferential sales to workers, and the voucher method, as well. Economically, it does not matter if it is done quickly, finds a social consensus, and finally leads to a property structure where strong and well-defined owners control the management of the newly privatized enterprises. These private enterprises would have to operate in a competitive framework, thus the legal preconditions to secure workable competition have to be generated as well: e.g. anti-trust and other relevant laws have to be implemented.

Eliminating current deficits in the state budget

The current deficits in the state budget theoretically can be eliminated either by increasing revenues or by reducing expenditure. Since the planned economies are not very efficient, an increase in revenue is hardly feasible. Thus expenditure has to be cut. The following cuts are usually proposed:

1 reduce armament expenditure
2 cut state investment outlays
3 eliminate subsidies for maintaining inefficient enterprises
4 reduce state bureaucracy and secret police
5 eliminate subsidies which were granted to keep prices artificially low (basic goods, rent).

Measures 1–4 directly or indirectly make output fall and will cause increasing unemployment. Therefore, a stabilization which is going to eliminate the unsustainable deficits in the state budget and/or of unprofitable enterprises which will be closed down has to be accompanied by a social programme providing support for unemployed people in terms of income support, retraining and offering new employment possibilities.

Elimination of price subsidies would produce enormous increases in the price of basic goods. After World War II the Austrian government successfully operated with three wage–price agreements (actually two more agreements were concluded, but the last two were of little success, because basically they were superfluous).[18]

The logic of the wage–price agreements was as follows: it was obvious that highly subsidized prices of consumer goods had to be increased at least to the level of production cost. In order to make these increases acceptable to the population a commission chaired by government members, but consisting of employers' and workers' representatives, agreed to increase the prices in several steps and, at the same time, to compensate workers for these increases by a lump-sum increase to keep real incomes constant.

Furthermore, in order to avoid getting into an inflation spiral, both sides agreed on a price and wage freeze for a certain period of time. After this period having elapsed prices and production cost were considered again, and prices and wages accordingly adjusted another time.

This procedure worked pretty well since workers did not suffer real income losses and with prices covering the production cost, a positive supply response was achieved which finally also led to productivity gains not immediately passed on to the workers.

During the period of wage–price agreements the wage levels in different industries became more and more similar. The pressure for wage differentiation became stronger and was one of the reasons why the last two wage–price agreements were less successful.

Both changing tasks for social security measures and Western experience make it seem advisable to form new organisations outside the state budget to organize health care, old age pension, labour exchange and other social security tasks. Separate entities can be made independent from influences which otherwise might spill over from other parts of the state budget into the social security system.

Financing the state budget and stimulating investment

When the economy has been stabilized in order to generate a favourable climate for economic growth and privatized in order to achieve the desired supply response in the economy, the state budget cannot be financed any more by withholding practically all the profits generated by the successful enterprises. A market conform tax system has to be set up. Such a system could consist of an income tax, corporate tax, property tax, and value added tax (although other taxes could also be envisaged).

Income taxation has to find a compromise between the desires of successful and dynamic individuals to get a high return on their activities, to be rewarded for their efforts, and the desires of the less dynamic not to become impoverished. The balance has to be drawn between a significant income differentiation in order to stimulate entrepreneurial activity and wage equalization in order to secure social peace.

Recently in many of the highly developed market economies the marginal tax on income was reduced to around 50 per cent, because in the structural crisis of the 1980s the stimulative aspect had greater weight than the equality aspects. In Austria, the highest tax bracket is at a level three times the average wage.

In the reforming economies of Central and Eastern Europe, we might expect extremely wide income differentiation to emerge. Knowing about the low willingness to accept an extreme income differentiation it seems advisable that the reforming countries do not put the highest marginal tax at such a low level of rate and income bracket. Social acceptance of highly differentiated incomes would be strongly enhanced were, for example, incomes of up to 10 times the average income taxed with rates of up to 75 per cent, and incomes at 20 times the average income or higher taxed at a 90 per cent rate.

In order to avoid the counterproductive effects of such a highly progressive income tax and to stimulate investment, only the incomes not reinvested should be subject to the highly progressive income tax. Reinvested profits should be subject to a low corporate tax only.

A low corporate tax is needed to attract foreign investors. The present practice of granting tax exemptions to enterprises with foreign capital participation already has shown unfavourable side effects. Joint ventures are dissolved after the period of tax exemption had elapsed (and refounded with a new name), the tax base is eroded by these exemptions, and, last but not least, the domestic investor is put in disadvantageous conditions which make it difficult for him to compete with the foreign investor. Since the tax exemptions are counterproductive to the aim of developing a competitive domestic economy, it is necessary to apply a corporate tax rate which is low by international standards and to treat all forms of ownership the same way.

Given the proposed combination of a highly progressive income tax on non-reinvested incomes and the low corporate tax, an enterprise owner can avoid high taxation by reinvesting. Thus, the most efficient entrepreneurs will be stimulated to expand their business activities most quickly. It is precisely this which is the desired outcome after the painful stabilization has taken place.

Property tax can also be seen as a measure towards equalization. However, a too high property tax may easily destroy the accumulated productive capital, because it may force people into selling their property. A low property tax of 1–2 per cent may have stimulative effects, because it induces the holders of property to achieve yields of more than 1–2 per cent which are necessary to maintain the property.

Income tax, corporate tax, and property tax will be scarcely sufficient to cover state expenditure. The bulk of the revenue has to come from a value-added tax or a sales tax. A value-added tax can be applied only when high standard enterprise accounting systems are in use. So far this is not the case in many of the reforming countries of Central and Eastern Europe. Therefore, in the coming years mostly a sales tax has to be applied which could be differentiated by food and non-food items. Since it is to be collected on sales at all levels of production and trade, the rates could be kept relatively low (e.g. 5 per cent on non-food and 2 per cent on food sales). It has to be noted that a multistage sales tax favours large enterprises over small ones. This is the reason why a value-added tax should be implemented as soon as possible.

Creating a new banking system

In almost all of the reforming countries, the banking system is being reorganized. As a first step, commercial banks are set up and the central bank should become responsible only for monetary policy.

In the past, the central banks have been kept under government control and often were obliged to perform as a source of cheap unlimited supply of money. This experience delivers strong arguments to guarantee the independence of the central bank from government by the constitution to be adopted in the parliament. Independence does not imply that the central bank would act in isolated measures. While monetary stability has to be the major aim of central bank policy, other aims such as full employment, balance on current account and reasonable economic growth, have to be considered as well. A central bank should not be in a position to apply instruments which would permit selective and discriminatory decisions according to political or social considerations.

With the commercial banks separated from the previous state bank, the last thing these countries need is a deregulated banking sector and liberal banking policies. It is the first and foremost task of the new governments in the reforming countries of Central and Eastern Europe to make their economies perform again, that is, to produce more of the goods needed and wanted by the population. A too liberal banking policy with free capital movement abroad will hardly generate the conditions favourable for expanding the production sector. Free capital movement would only foster capital flight.

Concluding remarks

The package of measures described in this paper is necessary, but not nearly sufficient to get the reforming countries out of their social and economic crises. Only after free elections in a multi-party system will governments be strong enough to put through everything that is needed and to maintain a broad social consensus.

The social system has to cover health care, an old-age pension, support for low-income people, a labour exchange system, and an ecological programme to do away with the damage done by unrestricted pollution in the last forty years. For the poorer countries in the region, part of these measures could be initiated by a Western support programme.

Such a support programme which should not generate unequal conditions for domestic producers could give a new demand impulse to the otherwise stagnating economies. In the short run the other source of growth can be exports only. A trade policy which seeks to generate favourable conditions for domestic economic growth through expanding exports has to be neutral as between domestic and foreign markets. The effective exchange rate for exports has to be equal to the effective exchange rate for imports. Liberal domestic policies should provide easy access to domestic markets and liberal foreign trade policies should provide equal access to foreign markets.

Structural adjustment programmes – at branch or regional level – have to be applied in tandem with the stabilization measures taken in order to avoid the economies entering a downward spiral.

Regional and sectoral analyses and the design of structural adjustment programmes should also be supported by outside funding. However, it is necessary to warn against basing the development of new production capacities on subsidies provided from outside. All too often small and successful firms which started to expand were destroyed by the granting of large subsidies to their competitors. Foreign support should keep away from the previous planners' mistakes: keep away from starting and maintaining inefficient production by massive subsidies. Flourishing economies have a large number of profitable enterprises. It is the task of government policy to generate the necessary stable and liberal environment to allow profitable enterprises to dominate the economy.

Notes

1 Igor Birman, *Secret Incomes of the Soviet State Budget*, The Hague/Boston/London, Martinus Nijhoff Publishers, 1981, *p. ix.*
2 *Ibid.*, p. 185.
3 *Ibid.*, p. 209.
4 *Pravda*, 28 October, 1988, pp. 4–5, and 29 October, 1988, p. 2.
5 Iwao Ohashi, 'How big is the Soviet budget deficit', WIIW-Mitgliederinformation no. 1989/2, p. 20.
6 L. V. Braginsky, 'Monetary policy in the USSR', in G. Fink and A. Wala (eds.), *New Developments in Banking and Finance in East and West*, Oesterreichische Nationalbank, 1990, p. 144.
7 *Izvestiía*, 28 January, 1990.

8 Abel Aganbegian, 'Realities and forecasts', Special supplement for the readers of the *Barometer*, February 1990, Moscow.

9 I wish to thank A. Ribnikar who drew my attention to these techniques in 1975.

10 See Ante Cicin-Sain, 'The inefficiency of monetary policy in a socialist country', and Neven Mates, 'Measurement of government budget deficit, losses of central banks and the impact of aggregate deficit of the public sector on inflation', papers presented at a seminar organized by the Austrian Bankers Association and The Vienna Institute for Comparative Economic Studies, January 1990.

11 Enforced credits are said to amount to 130 billion forint, that is, about 50 per cent of the amount of short-term credits extended by the banks.

12 E.g., 4 per cent in Czechoslovakia, 7 per cent in the GDR, compared with 14 per cent in the FRG, or 15 per cent in Austria.

13 Abanbegian, 'Realities and forecasts'.

14 *Ibid.*

15 For discussion of the 'principal-agent problem', see for example Manuel Hinds, comments on 'Privatization and capital market', by Sergei V. Alexashenko and Leonid M. Grigoriev, IIASA-Conference on Soviet Economic Reform, Sopron, July 1990.

16 Manuel Hinds, 'Issues in the introduction of market forces in Eastern European socialist economies', paper presented at a seminar on 'Managing inflation in socialist economies', IIASA, Laxenburg, Austria, 6–8 March, 1990, pp. 26ff.

17 This proposal was put forward by Duzan Triska and Vaclav Klaus, CSFR.

18 See Günter Chaloupek, 'Preiskontrolle und Preisgestaltung im Übergang zur Marktwirtschaft', Lecture at CSCE expert meeting in Bonn, 4 April, 1990.

Part II

Economic thinking and policy-making

4　The possible new role of market and planning in Poland and Hungary

Jan Adam

Introduction

Poland and Hungary have committed themselves to a full marketization of the economy. The implementation of the commitment is in different stages in the two countries. Poland is trying to achieve this goal in a short period of time, whereas Hungary is following a policy of gradual change.

At the beginning of the 1980s in Poland and Hungary the market played only a subordinate role. Most reformers still believed that planning had to have a very important function in the economy; many believed that planning and market should complement each other in their functions as coordinating mechanisms. By the end of the 1980s, the situation had changed remarkably. Most reformers came to the conclusion that a market economy is the only way out of the economic crisis.

In this chapter I would like first to examine how the views on planning and market developed in the 1980s in Poland and Hungary, then to discuss the official proposals about the new role of planning and, finally, to express my own views about the possible functions of planning in a marketized economy.

Polish and Hungarian views at the beginning of the 1980s

The views of the Polish and Hungarian economists on the economic mechanism went through great changes in the 1980s. At the beginning of the 1980s (in Poland before the declaration of martial law) the vast majority of economists still believed in the reformability of the existing economic mechanism. In Poland in 1980–1, even the group of economists, which nowadays claims to be, or is identified as, neo-liberal, and which would like to see a full marketization of the economy *à la* highly developed capitalist countries, still called for the introduction of the management system which, in substance, meant a combination of planning and market.

In both countries, in Poland in 1980–1 and in Hungary in 1981–2, economists had the chance to express their views on how to reform the economic mechanism. In Poland, the birth of Solidarity in 1980 along with its successful strike, which was ended by an agreement with the Polish government in which the latter committed itself to an economic reform, was such an occasion. It prompted organizations and individuals to come up with reform blueprints.

In Hungary in 1978, under pressure from the worsening economic situation, the Central Committee of the Party took the decision to abandon the old policy of ambitious economic growth for a slower but balanced growth, and in addition, to open the economy more to the world market (Lengyel 1987: p. 131) in order to be able to tackle problems of external equilibrium. Though this decision was not combined with any important changes in the system of management, nevertheless it slowly opened the door to systemic debates, all the more because the authorities started to solicit suggestions for reforms (Lengyel 1988: p. 44). Soon economists responded to the challenge by submitting reform proposals to the authorities, most of which found their way into publications.

The Polish reform blueprints were more comprehensive than the Hungarian, since they were earmarked for a reform which was in the process of preparation. The suggested reforms in Poland differed in many aspects and the same was true about the Hungarian proposals. The Polish reform proposals had many features in common with the Hungarian, but were also marked by differences.

Let me first mention the common and contrasting features of the reform proposals and then dwell on a brief characterization of some of them. Most reform proposals called for the elimination of the administrative system of management (the directive-distributive system, as the Polish economists call it) and the expansion of market forces. The reformers agreed that to this end it was necessary to reduce substantially government interference in the economy and thus increase the autonomy of enterprises. Still, economists attributed great importance to planning in the management of the economy. This is true not only of L. Balcerowicz (1980) who is the leading neo-liberal and, in his function as finance minister, the architect of the Polish drive to full marketization of the economy, but also of the Hungarian economists M. Tardos (1982) and L. Antal (1982). Of course, they had in mind plans which would be binding only on the government and other planning institutions, and which would not be broken down into targets for enterprises.

In the early 1980s, economists did not think of privatization of the state sector; for example, in his reform proposal, J. Beksiak (1981)[1] called for the development of different forms of ownership, but when he enumerated the various forms, no mention was made of private ownership; instead, family ownership was listed. What economists had in mind primarily was how to remove property rights from the control of government administration, more precisely branch ministries. Interestingly enough, to accomplish this purpose, all reform blueprints in Poland called for the introduction of self-management. This is not to say that most Polish economists at that time were convinced adherents of self-management. Some, no doubt, were, mainly those who shared Solidarity's ideology. Some economists saw in self-management only a good shield against the government's interference in enterprise affairs.

In Hungary, the number of economists who supported the idea of self-management was small. Even T. Bauer's (1982) authority was not sufficient to recruit many converts to the idea. M. Tardos's (1982) idea of holding companies found a much greater response.[2] The holding company, as a superstructure above enterprises, should have the right to control the activities of enterprises, establish new enterprises, liquidate existing ones, and redistribute assets. It has not only to prevent the authorities from interfering in enterprise affairs, but even more, to be an instrument for promoting interest in the expansion of enterprise capital (therefore, the holding company should be guided in its decision-making by long-term profitability). Furthermore, Tardos hints that holding companies should also contribute to the establishment of a capital market. However, the fight for a capital market started in earnest only in the second half of the eighties.

The following company idea was subjected to criticism from various directions; critics felt that an executive body of the company appointed by the Presidential Council of the National Assembly, as M. Tardos assumed, would not be able to meet the tasks (Lengyel 1988: p. 29). It has, however, survived in a modified form, whereas the self-management idea was jettisoned as useless baggage by the leading reformers. The practice of self-management, which was introduced in Hungary in 1985, is on the wane. In Poland, the idea still survives in some circles, but the institution introduced in 1982 will probably be decimated by the rapid push to a marketized economy.

In Poland, much more than in Hungary, great stress was put on a radical reorganization of the government administration and the elimination of branch ministries, including the branch departments in the planning Board. This demand had to do with the belief that the branch ministries, as the bearers of group interests, had achieved too much power and had pushed the economy in a direction which was contrary to the national interests.

More concretely about planning

A good insight into the views on planning and indirectly on the market's role in the beginning of the 1980s can be obtained from comparing the reform proposal of a collective, headed by L. Balcerowicz[3] with the Polish Economic Association views, and, in Hungary, from the 1983 debate on Planning.

According to L. Balcerowicz, planning should focus on strategic problems, on the growth pace of the main sectors of the economy and on the main structural branch changes, including investment. It should also focus on the development of consumption, mainly collective consumption, and the main trends in research and development. Of course, the methods used in planning should be in line with the developing market forces. Central investment should be confined to the infrastructure and extractive branches. In other sectors, the central authorities should limit the regulation of investment activity to the extent needed in order to make sure that it is in line with the plan. The authorities should become investors only if indirect methods fail.

In 1980, most economists did not want to go as far as Balcerowicz did, which is clear from the blueprint put together by a large collective representing the Polish Economic Association (PEA). In its detailed blueprint, which was edited by J. Mujżel and J. Pajestka (1980), it is stated: 'Central planning is the basic principle of the socialist system'. To put it in brief, the role of planning should be: to forecast future economic conditions on a world and country scale as well as future societal tendencies and aspirations, to make rational choices in basic strategic matters and to see that they are implemented and, finally, to protect the national interest.

The role of planning is best seen in how investment decisions and financing are carried out. In the PEA's blueprint, the government has to play a greater role than in Balcerowicz's proposal. The PEA blueprint called for central decisions about investment in technical infrastructure, in large industrial enterprises (!) which aim at changes in the structure of the economy and in large programmes intended to satisfy certain societal wants. The first kind of investment should be financed from general revenue, the second and third only partially.

The 1983 Hungarian debate on planning is of importance since it shows how a large number of the leading reformers viewed planning.[4] R. Nyers, who chaired the debate, summarized it by saying that no extreme views came to the fore to challenge the existing system of management, based on the combination of planning and market. some derived the need for planning from the value system of socialism, and others saw planning's task as primarily in promoting efficiency and correcting the market's shortcomings. According to him the latter view dominated existing planning (*Vita*... 1984: p. 32). I. Hetényi, the former minister of finance and deputy chairman of the Planning Board, who introduced the debate, evaluated it in retrospect in the following way: 'In the debate the unanimous view was that there was a need for national economic planning and the planning should be developed in such a way that it supports a decentralised, better working market' (Hetényi 1989: pp. 69–70).

Of course, there were quite important differences in views on the role of planning, the relationship of planning and economic policy, types of plans and democratization. As to the role of planning, it is possible to say that three groups of views crystallized in the debate.

In one group, the role of planning, as designed in the 1968 reform, was seen as correct in substance, and not in need of change. According to A. Balassa (*Vita*... 1984: pp. 76–7), who represented this view, planning's function is, among other things, to detect the possibilities of economic development, and to determine the growth rates, equilibrium conditions and the main proportions. The state should help financing of investment to implement the most important structural changes.

The second group included quite a broad range of views. All agreed that planning should play an important role in the expansion of the infrastructure and in some non-competitive branches such as energy. As to the competitive sphere, some took more or less the position that the government should stay out of production. To M. Tardos, the government role in the development of the competitive sphere should be limited to the setting of priorities and 'the determination of the degree of their support' (*Vita*... 1984: p. 189). In other words, if the government feels that a certain branch or line of production should be developed preferentially, that fact should be publicized, and organizations which are willing to involve themselves in such projects should get government support. In brief, Tardos suggested solutions which A. Lerner proposed in his *Economics of Control* (1944).

T. Bauer (*Vita*... 1984: pp. 111–14) took a middle position as to the planning of investment. He saw an important role for the government in major investments and their financing. On the other hand, the government should not interfere in what he calls natural enterprise investment (what is called induced investment in the West). In addition, he suggested excluding from planning trade contracts with CMEA countries, the rationale being that concern about fulfilling trade contracts was one of the reasons for government interference in enterprise affairs.

Polish and Hungarian views in the second half of the 1980s

The number of economists who lost faith in the reformability of the socialist system grew fast, mainly in the second half of the 1980s. In Poland, this was the result of the failure of the 1982 reform and the worsening economic situation after a period of slow improvement. Even the introduction of the second stage of the reform could not stop the erosion of trust in the existing system. In Hungary, it was the reaction to the 1984 changes in the system of management which were viewed by many as 'too little, too late' and to a worsening economic situation.

The loss of the belief in the reformability of the management system has also resulted from the observation of Western economies and the frustration over the gap in prosperity between the two groups of countries. The increasing contacts of Polish and Hungarian social scientists with their peers in the West have also contributed to the undermining of the belief in the existing real socialism. IMF and World Bank officials can claim credit too for the changes in the views in the two former socialist countries. Last but not least, aspirations to achieve full national sovereignty and to bring about democratization of the system have also had an effect.

More and more economists have started to believe that the introduction of a market economy is the only way out of the economic crisis. Many have adopted M. Friedman's view that the market economy requires minimal government intervention, and some have concluded from this that market and planning are incompatible, even if Friedman himself does not take such a radical view (see Friedman 1983). Others have taken the position that planning can only play a minimal role in a well-functioning market economy. In the past, economists have asked how far reaching market forces can be without impeding the working of the planning system; now the question is: how extensive can planning be without hampering the working of market forces? Of course, there are still some economists who would like to see a planned economy combined with market relations, but their number is rapidly declining. Planning regardless of its form, is associated with the old centralized system in the minds of a growing number of economists and is dismissed out of hand.

Perhaps the changes in the systemic views in the two countries can best be demonstrated by discussing the criticism of planning and the 1988 debate on planning and market, both in Poland, and in Hungary, the 1987 blueprint of reform (*Turning Point and Reform*).

The Polish criticism of planning is of great interest for two reasons. First, it focuses on a shortcoming in planning which has been little aired in the East European literature, and second, it is derived from Polish experience, an experience which has not been so strong in other countries. I have in mind the role of conflicting interests which, according to some Polish authors, is an insurmountable impediment to an effective working of central planning.

C. Jósefiak and A. Lipowski have perhaps best articulated this shortcoming. Józefiak (1984: pp. 128–35) mentions conflicting interests between levels of management concerning the size of output targets and inputs, including labour, and conflicting interests between branches of the economy, within branches and regions. The representatives of interest groups enter into coalitions or competitive relations. To advance their interests, these groups try to push through their representatives to important positions in decision-making. Since in the centralized system no mechanism exists in the economy which would solve the conflicting interests within the framework of rationality, much damage can be inflicted on the economy. One could add that the Party bodies themselves are not immune to the consequences of conflicting interests.

When investment funds are allocated from the centre, the propensity to invest is very high, and central planners are under strong pressure from interest groups. The decision-makers on questions of the allocation of investments must be made up of people of high integrity and authority to be guided only by the interests of the economy. Józefiak maintains that in many cases the decision is made not by 'objective economic criteria but the power relationship between competing interest groups' (Józefiak et al., 1984, p. 134).

A. Lipowski (1988, pp. 219–40) shows that the decision-making about important economic issues is much influenced by political considerations, and what is called national interest is often group interest. Since what is presented as national interest depends on the changing relationships between group interests and other factors, elements of uncertainty are introduced into the economy.

In addition, the author argues that no synthetic criterion of rationality on the macroeconomic level exists. Future needs, in the absence of a market, and the possible manifestation of consumer preferences cannot properly be predicted. On top of this, in a centralized system strong incentives which might encourage enterprise managers to behave rationally, are missing. All this, combined with the considerable influence of group interests, must devalue planning. Lipowski backs up his conclusion with the statement that planning in the 1970s in Poland was of a ceremonial nature, which he regards as quite normal (Lipowski 1988, p. 233).

K. Porwit (Debate 1989), who cannot be regarded as an opponent of planning, criticized planning for becoming too subservient to the bureaucratic hierarchy. Planning was adversely affected by the lack of rational prices and 'money categories'. Only when market relations are introduced can planning – not, of course, centralized planning – be effective.

The 1988 debate on planning and market in *Życie Gospodarcze* was initiated by one of the editors of the above mentioned weekly, M. Mieszczankowski. His paper, titled 'The Final Structure Is Not Known' (1988) was in fact a challenge to a debate about the final shape of the reform. In the paper he tried to prove that the 'transplantation' – as he called it – of market relations into a socialist economy cannot work. Some of the arguments he used were from the old ideological arsenal. His paper touched off a great debate which lasted almost the whole year. Most participants in the debate, which took place at a time when Solidarity's influence was starting to grow, but when it was still not clear what the result of its struggle would be, took a negative position towards his arguments and expressed themselves in favour of a market economy with some limitations.[5] As in some other debates, here too the market was idealized by some and presented as a self-regulating mechanism, able to work with minimal government intervention. As J. Lipiński mentioned in one of his papers (1988), many Polish economists – and this could be applied to many Hungarian economists as well – view the market as a perfect competitive institution.

The Hungarian reform blueprint 'Turning Point and Reform'[6] (Antal et al. 1987) was a watershed in the development of the thinking on systemic problems of a large, and important, group of reformers. In this blueprint, the authors gave a scathing critique of the existing system of management as well as of the economic policy, and called for a comprehensive and radical reform which would apply not only to the economy but also the power structure. They demanded the elimination of all obstacles to the working of the market mechanism. According to them, this also makes it necessary 'to eliminate or restrict political privileges and exclude inequalities of a political nature from the economy' (p. 652).

The change in thinking is best seen in the suggested changes in economic policy; from them it is clear that neo-liberalism and monetarism made significant inroads in the theoretical arsenal of the Hungarian reformers. They suggested, namely, a switch from great stress on fiscal policy to monetary policy. Regulation of the money supply should become the focal point of economic policy. The administrative limitations should be replaced by monetary restrictions which should play a key role in the management of demand.

The blueprint also suggested opening the door to various forms of ownership with great stress on joint-stock companies. Since, in the meantime, the idea of self-management had lost appeal (many of the authors did not favour it from the beginning), the authors were faced with the problem of what to do about self-managed enterprises.[7] In the blueprint, such enterprises were indirectly encouraged to give up voluntarily certain decision-making rights. Some other authors suggested (e.g., Sarkozy 1987) that self-managed enterprises should voluntarily turn into joint stock companies.

As for planning, according to the text published in *Közgazdasági Szemle*, it should undergo great changes. Existing planning, which was much permeated by natural balancing, should be replaced by planning in value terms. The main focus of the new planning should be on the drafting of a macro-financial plan and on its preservation. The departure point should be the working out of preconditions for internal and external equilibrium. In the non-competitive sphere, mainly the infrastructure, the role of planning should be greater and direct.

'Turning Point and Reform' was published with some modifications in *Közgazdasági Szemle*,[8] accompanied by a 'standpoint' written by some members of the Economic work-team, an advisory group of the Central Committee of the Party (Standpoint... 1987).[9] The writers of the 'standpoint' mainly reject the part of the study which deals with planning and which really almost adds up to a rejection of planning. They maintain, and rightly, that the study overestimates the importance of monetary policy, and that it alone cannot solve such current problems as a restructuring of the economy.

Government stand on market and planning

Both countries have decided to introduce a full fledged market economy. The Polish government is determined to achieve it in 1990–91 and, to this end, it introduced in January 1990 a series of provisions – which could be called, because of their extreme austerity, a shock treatment – to stabilize the economy, bring about market equilibrium and lick inflation. In Hungary, the transition is supposed to be achieved at a slower pace. The different pace has to do with several factors. The Polish economy is in a much greater mess than the Hungarian; the Polish ministers in charge of the economy, being ardent believers in marketization, feel that quick marketization is the only solution to the dire economic situation. The consideration that it is prudent to make unpopular changes at a time when the Solidarity movement is very popular and is at the beginning of its rule, played, no doubt, an important role. The Hungarian government leaders, faced with parliamentary elections, were reluctant to engage in policies which would antagonize the population. If the way the two countries have tried to solve the problem of prices in the past is any guide to generalization, then it can be said that historically the Hungarians have solved their problems, gradually, whereas the Poles have had a tendency to solve them in jumps.

Let me make clear right from the beginning that in the short period of time which has elapsed since the two countries declared their determination to marketize their economies, the potential role of planning has declined dramatically. There is still a Central Planning Office in Poland, but no longer in Hungary; it was abolished in 1990 by the present government, which has come into existence from the recently held democratic elections. Some of the planning activities have been transferred to the Ministry of Finance. Most recent documents which deal with systemic problems, in Poland, Premises for the Choice of the Long-Term Strategy of Economic Development (1990) (hereafter Long-Term Strategy), a document of the Planning Board, and in Hungary, the Proposal for the Reform of the Economic System (1989) (hereafter Reform Proposal), do not even contain the word planning.

My further analysis relies on the Polish Outline of Planning (1989) (hereafter outline), worked out under the guidance of the new chairman of the Central Planning Board. I use this material rather than the official Economic Programme[10] (1989), because the former gives a better insight into the intended role of the government and of planning.[11] The Outline is more a theoretical and systemic-oriented document than the Programme, which does not contain any mention of planning. For a general understanding of what is going on in Poland, the Programme is more important.

The main Hungarian documents used here are the Proposal of the Economic Reform Committee for 1990–1992 (1989) (hereafter Proposal), the Summary of the Development of Government Economic Activities (hereafter Summary) and the mentioned Reform Proposal. In December 1988 (*Figyelö*, no. 49) the Consultative Council for Economic Management published a detailed outline for the creation of a socialist market economy. The material was intended as basic background material for the six appointed economic reform committees. The Proposal[12] and the Summary[13] mentioned above are the work of the first and third reform committees, respectively. The Reform Proposal[14] is, in a sense, a summary based on the submissions of the six economic reform committees.

The Polish Outline and the Hungarian Proposal first discuss the intended role of the government in the economy and then derive from it the role of planning, which is the best way to go about this problem. In the Polish Outline it is stated that the departure point for planning is the role of the State and the Agreement at the Roundtable between the Communist Government and Solidarity.

There are great similarities in the formulation of the role of the government. Both documents suggest that it is the government's task to provide the legal framework (the rules of the game) for the working of the market and to create market relations in the transitional period to the market economy. There is also an agreement that the state should be active in areas where the market cannot or should not work, such as social policy, infrastructure, protection of the environment, security and defence. The Polish Outline and the Hungarian Proposal call for government intervention to influence or correct the negative effects of market activities. In this regard, the Polish Outline sees two areas for government functions: (1) 'promotion and strengthening of development tendencies in the economy', and (2) stabilization of the economy. The first function should be achieved by creating a conducive environment, but also by granting incentives to selective productions which may have a significant impact on the growth of the economy. Facilitation of proper economic cooperation with foreign countries is an important component of this effort. The second function consists primarily of remedying the negative effects of the market.

The Hungarian Proposal suggests using government intervention in certain cases to influence the market for the sake of promoting economic efficiency and development, and mitigating fluctuations. The government should also play a role in maintaining equilibrium in the labour market and in preventing socially unacceptable, wide income differentiations (pp. 69–70). In the transitional period the government intervention should be significant, and should include financial help; it should be involved in the transformation of the outdated economic structure, mainly concerning the relationship between production and infrastructure spheres. The latter, particularly communications, education and research, should be expanded by allocating more government investment. The government should also help technological, among other forms of progress, by supporting research. In energy production and distribution, communications, and railways, decisions about the structure should rest in the hands of the government, whereas the competitive sphere should be left to market forces (p. 81).

Disregarding the major role of government in both countries in creating market relations in the transitional period, it is possible to argue that the functions of the government in the documents mentioned are in principle not much different from what liberal or post-Keynesian Western economists maintain. For example, Samuelson (1988: p. 44) believes that the government intervenes in a market economy for the sake of economic efficiency, equity and stability. However, when it comes to the macro-economic policy both countries intend to follow, M. Friedman's monetarist views are quite noticeable. Both countries are committed to giving monetary policy a key role in the macro-regulation of the economy. This is quite clearly articulated in the Hungarian Reform Proposal which reads:

The monetary regulation gets a key role in regulating domestic demand and inflation, and in influencing business fluctuations [*konjunkturalis folyamatok*]. The central bank works out concepts, more precisely concrete goals for the amount of money in circulation, requirements for balance of payments and principles for credit and foreign exchange policies. (p. 34)

The functions of planning are formulated differently in each country, yet, in the final analysis, they are similar. The Polish outline sees the function of planning in the first place in helping to formulate the social economic policy of government and, in the second place, in outlining the ways this policy should be achieved. The first task is to be carried out on the basis of studies and analyses about the goals achieved and by outlining the possible choices and goals on the basis of prognosis.

The Hungarian Proposal deals with planning only very briefly; it devotes little more than a page to it. (The situation is more or less the same with the Summary which discusses economic policies. The Reform Proposal, as already mentioned, does not discuss the role of planning in the marketised economy at all.) It puts strategic planning in first place. Its role should primarily be in restructuring the economy. Little is said about the methods to be applied. Strategic planning has also a role to play in the harmonization of long-term economic and social policy. Again, no elaboration is given (p. 71).

The second function of planning is to provide the government with analyses of the economic situation, prognoses, economic policy concepts, system of goals for the economy and suggestions for short-, medium- and long-term provisions.

The Polish Outline also deals with strategic economic planning when it discusses multiple year plans (national plans). The time horizon of these plans is to be determined from time to time, depending on the economic situation, or adapted to the cyclical life of parliament. In the national plans, the goals of government activities as well as the methods for achieving them are outlined. It is, of course, expected that economic activities in the competitive sphere will be determined predominantly by market forces. Nevertheless, the national plan is to envisage the direction in which development should be promoted as well as the amount of funds available for this purpose. The same refers to the desire to correct the negative effects of the market.

Judging on the basis of materials it seems that the Polish Planning Board would like to have more say in the formulation of economic policy than the authors of the Hungarian Proposals are willing to give their planners. In Hungary, many politicians are against the Planning Board having too great a role in formulating economic policy (see, e.g., Hetényi 1989: p. 86).

Planning has also to have a role in reconciling conflicting interests. The Polish outline gives planning the task of creating a platform for a voluntary reconciliation of conflicting interests, whereas the Hungarian Proposal calls only for the detection of conflicting interests and their possible effect (p. 71).

As already indicated, the analysis given is based primarily on Polish material put together by the Planning Board, an institution headed by a chairman who is on the left within the Solidarity, at a time when the neo-liberals in the ruling party determine policy. Planning is nowadays a dirty word, as a Polish colleague wrote to me. Whether the Polish outline of Planning will remain one of countless documents without any practical use, will, of course, depend on the success of the current efforts to rapidly transform the Polish economy into a market economy. If this experiment succeeds, the neo-liberals' self-confidence will substantially increase and planning will have to play a minimal role, if any at all, in an already marketized economy. Perhaps some strategic planning without any real government involvement will be allowed.

In Hungary, the material used was put together under the auspices of the socialist government, a government which committed itself to a marketization of the economy with some role for planning. Most authors of the documents (many of whom were instrumental in bringing about the present changes) are ardent believers in a market economy. The page on planning, which is included in the Reform Proposal, is perhaps only a tribute to the government they served.

The new Hungarian conservative-populist government, which is the result of the recent elections, has committed itself to a gradual transfer to a market economy. Since it has some anti-capitalist elements in its ideology, it is difficult to predict what its stand on planning will be exactly, probably not much different from what has been said about the Polish position.

Possible role of planning

In discussing the role of planning, it is necessary to distinguish between its function in the transitional period to a market economy and its role in an established market economy. In the transitional period, planning can be helpful in bringing about marketization of the economy. In the first place, it can play an important role in the transformation of the structure of the economy. It can also act in a positive way in opening up the economy to world markets. Planning can even be used for an activity which creates conditions for its own far-reaching elimination, for example, privatization of the state sector.

Planning's role in a marketized economy must necessarily be much smaller. Of course, its role depends greatly on the definition of planning. If we take the position, as some do, that planning means forecasting and *ad hoc* intervention in the economy for the sake of mitigating fluctuations in the economy, then even in a market economy there must be a great deal of planning. However, most economists do not regard forecasting by itself as planning; it is, however, an integral part of planning. *Ad hoc* government interventions have little to do with planning (cf. Hayward 1978: p. 11).

When talking about planning, many economists put stress on the pursuit of some aims with regard to the future, coordination of these aims in order to achieve them and having a plan (see Tinbergen 1964: p. 8; Oules 1966: pp. 28–9). J. Hayward (1978: p. 11) advances a definition of planning (shared also by Chaloupek and Teufelsbauer (1978: p. 316)) which is very broad and, as the author himself states, is intended to cover all kinds of planning systems. Planning 'is attempted through the strategic use of the instruments of economic and social policy by the government, in concert with other economic and social organizations, to attain explicit quantitative and/or qualitative objectives in the short, medium and long term'. Even if the definition does not mention the word 'plan', it is clear from the further text that a plan is assumed.

The planning debates in both countries show that there is a tendency to include in planning activities which may not necessarily be integrated in a plan. Some of the suggestions are also motivated by the desire to give employees of the Planning Office some work. For example, the Polish chairman of the Planning office, J. Osiatyński (1989), suggested in an interview that the activities of the Office should be expanded by taking on the business of providing enterprises with market information.

I would now like to suggest what the role of planning could be in Poland and Hungary. The framework of this chapter allows me to concentrate on only some aspects. I will not discuss here the planning of the infrastructure which is generally accepted. I will use the functions mentioned in the documents of both countries as points of departure and proceed from the less controversial to a more controversial suggestion.

1. In my opinion, the most important planning activity in a market economy should be what can be called 'strategic planning'. There is enough evidence to maintain that planning of the whole economy from one centre cannot be efficient and is necessarily combined with shortages.

There is no proof, however, that planning, limited to important macroeconomic issues combined with market relations, need be inefficient. No such combination has been tested in practice; what existed in Czechoslovakia and Hungary in the 1960s or in Hungary in the mid-80s was not really a genuine combination. Even if we take an opposite position, the reform was too short-lived to allow reliable conclusions.

However, the reality is that the two countries are going to have a market economy, and, therefore, planning must be adjusted to it in the sense that it should not hamper its working but, on the contrary, help in areas where the market may be vulnerable. Planning can also be helpful in remedying potential negative effects of the market.

Strategic planning means letting planning focus on structural changes, more precisely, using planning for the optimization of the economic structure (cf. Karpiński 1989). This does not mean subjecting structural changes to some plan objectives. It means only that *certain* important productions and technologies, which are of importance for the restructuring of the economy from the viewpoint of domestic and foreign demand and for an increase in the competitiveness of the domestic economy in foreign markets, are picked out for special care.

The role of the plan, be it long or medium term, which is binding only on the government, is to identify these productions and technologies and outline ways of handling them. Up to this point there may be agreement among economists; even opponents of planning do not mind if the government supports very significant production and/or technologies. The Polish Outline and the Hungarian proposal also stress the need for strategic planning. However, they do not elaborate on how this support should be given. The question is: should the government become the investor or should it decide who is the investor on the basis of a tender and contribute to the financing of investment by cash and/or guaranteed loans? In brief, should the government have control over investment? Or, should the government simply declare certain productions and technologies to be subsidized, and allow a subsidy to whomever has good credentials and promises to get involved in the field?

Most adherents of full marketization of the economy are against government involvement in investment.[15] On the one hand, they are afraid that such involvement may impede the working of the market and, on the other (this may be more important), they distrust government's ability to get things right. The greatest shortcomings of the centralized system were its inability to ensure smooth changes in the structure of the economy in accordance with the changes in demand at home and abroad and its inability to maintain an acceptable pace in technological development.[16]

In my opinion, government involvement in a limited number of investments may produce better results than a pure system of subsidies which, in the final analysis, does not commit the receiving parties to any concrete results.

It is vital for the two countries to lessen substantially the technological gap which divides them from the West. To rely on market forces alone to do the job, is a gamble. In some countries, such as Japan and South Korea, the government has been instrumental in promoting technological progress, and there is no reason why this could not be done in the two countries under review.

2. Planning may play an important role in the reconciliation of conflicting interests. I have primarily in mind conflicting interests between employers and employees. Many market economies leave the solution of conflicting interests to the market and combat ensuing negative effects with monetary policy, mainly with increase in interest rates which produce unemployment. If the countries are determined now to allow high rates of unemployment, it is not advisable to rely on the market alone; they must have an incomes policy in place. To make such an incomes policy rational it must be based on realistic forecasts and plans for the development of the economy.

Incomes policy need not mean the imposition of certain solutions or the introduction of a mandatory price and wage policy (see Adam 1990). If the employers and employees can agree without upsetting the economy, there is no reason for the government to interfere. In many cases, the awareness that the government can act may be sufficient to encourage the two bargaining parties to come to a viable compromise. However, if the two parties cannot agree, or if the agreement is such that in the long run it will produce inflation, the government should step in.

3. In this point, which is the most controversial, I would like to touch on the possible role of the planning authority, more on the elected body, the Planning Commission (or Council) than the executive body, the Planning office. In my opinion, it can play an important coordinating role in formulating medium- and long-term economic and social policy. Short-term economic policy, mainly as it refers to *ad hoc* interventions in the economy, should be left in the hands of functional ministries, mainly the ministry of finance. Of course, the formulation of medium- and long-term economic and social policy cannot be the realm only of the planning authority; all other ministries must have an important input since they know best the problems on their turf and can best defend their interests.

On the other hand, it should be remembered that the planning authority has two advantages which make it fit for the coordinating role of medium- and long-term economic and social policy.

Due to its planning activities, the planning authority has more than other institutions a comprehensive body of information based on research about the state of the economy and its various components, and forecasts about possible development.[17]

Second, compared to other central economic institutions, the planning authority is the most neutral to group interests. In its coordinating role, it should reconcile the conflicting group interests without really allowing a great injury to national interests. This is, of course, a difficult task, because the members of the Planning Commission themselves are mostly representatives of certain interests. It can be hoped that market forces may keep group interests partly in check. In addition, it is important that significant economic and social policy problems be publicly aired and that the decision-makers be under the scrutiny of the public.

Before the collapse of the socialist system in both countries, the possible coordinating role of the planning authority was often discussed. As might be expected, there was no agreement even among the adherents of planning. For example, B. Csikós-Nagy (1988) believes that the Planning Office is the most important brain centre for the formulation of economic policy. Apparently, he has no objection to this function being continuously retained by the Planning Office, though, as he writes, it often introduces subjective concepts into planning. On the other hand, Hetényi (1989) – as already mentioned – does not like the idea of the Planning Office becoming the centre of economic policy.

It seems that too many adherents of planning the position of the planning authorities in formulating economic policy depended very much on how they viewed the relationship between economic policy and planning. Those who viewed economic policy and planning as two separate activities were not very much in favour of a central role for the planners. On the other hand, those who believed that planning and economic policy were interwoven or even that economic policy was part of planning, had usually no objection to the Planning Office being the centre or coordinator of economic policy.[18]

Notes

I would like to thank the Social Sciences and Humanities Research Council of Canada for the extended research grant which enabled me to work on this study.

1 J. Beksiak, who is a former member of the Wakar school, discussed his proposal with many well-known economists, among them, L. Balcerowicz, R. Bugaj and C. Józefiak.
2 The idea of holding companies was suggested by other economists, mainly by S. Kopátsy (see Sárközy 1982); nevertheless, it is associated with the name of M. Tardos since he popularized it.
3 The collective included, among others. M. Dąbrowski and A. Lipowski.

4 The debate, which was based on submitted papers, was attended by, among others, L. Antal, A. Balassa, T. Bauer, O. Gadó, I. Hetényi, R. Nyers and M. Tardos. The papers presented there as well as the debate were published by the Economic Institute of the Hungarian Academy of Sciences in its Studies (*Vita...* 1984).

5 Many rejected the very idea of contemplating the final goals of the reform; some saw this idea as an attempt to impose on society a model thought out in advance, as was the case with socialism.

6 This is a collective work written by social scientists, primarily economists, from various research institutes, the media and communications, and edited by research fellows of the former research institute of the ministry of finance, apparently under the leadership of Laszlo Antal.

7 In 1985, approximately 60 per cent of enterprises became self-managed (for more see J. Adam (1989, pp. 131–3)).

8 There are several versions of the blueprint, and, in each of the three versions which I have, the part dealing with planning is of a different size and, in two of them, the text is different.

9 The writers of the standpoint are well-known economists. To mention the most important ones: Ivan T. Berend (former president of the Academy of Sciences), B. Csikós-Nagy (former chairman of the Material and Price Board), I. Hetényi (former minister of finance), R. Nyers (former chairman of the Socialist Party).

10 The official Economist Programme was published in October 1989. Since then, the government has published (December 1989) Principles of socio-economic policy for 1990, which is a substitute for the usual annual plan and which is based on the Programme.

11 However, one important observation is in order. The Central Planning Office is chaired by J. Osiatyński, who belongs to the left wing of Solidarity, whereas the Programme is primarily the product of the minister of finance, who is a neo-liberal. Since most economic portfolios are occupied by neo-liberals, it is questionable what kind of influence Osiatyński can and will have.

12 The Proposal was edited by T. Ivan Berend, the former president of the Hungarian Academy of Sciences, and was prepared by, among others, A. Balassa and T. Nagy.

13 The Summary was worked out by a committee presided over by the minister of planning, E. Kemenes.

14 The Reform Proposal was prepared by, among others, L. Antal, A. Balassa and I. Hetényi.

15 In the West, business is also against such a solution because it does not like government control, whereas subsidies do not entail control.

16 In his study prepared for the Hungarian Academy of Sciences, A. Karpiński (1987: p. 53) argues that one of the reasons for the ineffectiveness of planning was its insufficient orientation to technological progress, one reason being that technological progress was handled in a special ministry without jurisdiction really being precisely divided between this ministry and the planning office.

17 Many adherents of planning in both countries would surely not mind if the Planning office became the headquarters of research as L. Abalkin (1987) suggests for the USSR. However, there is also opposition to such a solution, because it would put the Planning Office in a privileged position to influence

the government and public. Some would rather see research scattered throughout many institutes and not give any one a 'monopoly' position.
18 For an insight into the position of economists on the relationship between planning and economic policy the Polish debate (Debate 1989) about planning is of interest. S. Kuzinski complains about the position of economic policy not being clear enough and states: 'We are talking about planning but it is necessary to say that first is economic policy and then follows planning.' Cz. Bobrowski steps in: 'Isn't it possible to say that planning is one of the forms of economic policy?'

References

Abalkin, L. (1987), *The Strategy of Economic Development in the USSR*, trans. from Russian, Moscow, Progress Publishers.
Adam, J. (1989), *Economic Reforms in the Soviet Union and Eastern Europe since the 1960s*, London, Macmillan, and New York, St Martin's Press.
(1990), 'Inflation and unemployment', in Hungarian in *Gazdaság*, no. 1, 1990, and in Czech in *Politická ekonomie*, no. 8, 1990.
Antal, L., (1982), 'Thoughts on the further development of the Hungarian mechanism', *Acta Oeconomica*, 29, nos. 3–4.
Antal, L., L. Bokros, I. Csillag, L. Lengyel and Gy. Matolcsy (1987), 'Fordulat és reform' (Turning Point and Reform), *Közgazdasági Szemle*, no. 6.
Balcerowicz, L. (1980), *Życie Gospodarcze*, nos. 51–2.
Bauer, T. (1982), *Mozgó Világ*, no. 11.
Beksiak, J. (1981), *Biuletyn AS* (Solidarity Agency), no. 4.
Chaloupek, G. and W. Teufelsbauer (1987), *Gesamtwirtschaftliche Planung in Westeuropa*, Frankfurt, Campus Verlag.
Csikós-Nagy, B. (1988), *Tervgazdasági Fórum*, no. 3.
Debate on Planning (1989), *Gospodarka Planowa*, no. 3.
Economic Programme (1989), (Program gospodarczy, główne załozenia i kierunki), Government document, Warsaw.
Friedman, M. (1983), 'Market mechanisms and central economic planning', *Economic Impact*, no. 2.
Hayward, J. (1978), 'Introduction: inertia and improvisation: the planning predicament', in J. Hayward and O.A. Narkiewicz (eds.), *Planning in Europe*, London, Croom Helm.
Hetényi, I. (1989), *Tervgazdasági Közlemények*, no. 2.
Józefiak, C. (1984), in J. Mujżel and Sz. Jakubowicz (eds.), *Funkcjonowanie gospodarki polskiej. Doświadczenia, problemy, tendencje*, Warsaw, Panstwowe Wydawnictwo Ekonomiczne.
Karpiński, A. (1987), *System planowania w PRL i jego rola w tworzeniu strategii społeczno – gospodarczego rozwoju kraju*, monograph written for the Hungarian Academy of Sciences, Warsaw.
(1989), *Nowe Drógi*, no. 8.
Lengyel, L. (1987), *Medvetánc*, no. 2.
(1988), in L. Lengyel (ed.), *Tulajdonreform*, Budapest.
Lipiński, J. (1988), *Ekonomista*, nos. 3–4.

Lipowski, A. (1988), *Mechanizm Rynkowy w gospodarce polskiej*, Warsaw, Panstwowe Wydawnictwo Naukowe.

Long-term Strategy (1990), (*Przeslanki wyboru długookresowej strategii rozwoju kraju*), Material of the Central Board of Planning, February, Warsaw.

Mieszczankowski, M. (1988), *Życie Gospodarcze*, no. 1.

Osiatyński, J. (1989), interview, *Figyelö*, no. 48.

Oules, F. (1966), *Economic Planning Democracy*, Harmondsworth, Penguin.

PEA about Economic Reform (1980), Supplement of *Życie Gospodarcze*, no. 46.

Polish Outline of Planning (1989), (Tezy do nowej ustawy. Planowanie w gospodarce) *Rzeczpospolita*, 12 October.

Principles of the socio-economic policy for 1990 (1989), (Założenia polityki społeczno-gospodarczej na 1990 r.) *Rzeczpospolita*, 15 December.

Proposal (A gazdasági reformbizottság programjavaslata 1990–1992) (1989), Közgazdasági és Jogi Könyvikiadó, Budapest.

Reform proposal (1989), (*Javaslat a gazdasági* rendszer reformjára), Material of the Reform Committee, Budapest.

Samuelson, P.A., W.D. Nordhaus, and J. McCallum (1988), *Economics*, McGraw-Hill, sixth Canadian edition.

Sárközy, T. (1982), 'Problems of social ownership and of the proprietary organization', *Acta Oeconomica*, 29, nos. 3–4.

—— (1987), *Tervgazdasági Fórum*, no. 4.

Standpoint (1987), *Közgazdasági Szemle*, no. 6.

Summary (*A kormányzat gazdasági tevékenységének fejlesztése, Összefoglaló*) (1989), Material of the Reform Committee, Budapest.

Tardos, M. (1982), 'Development program for economic control and organization in Hungary', *Acta Oeconomica*, 29, nos. 3–4.

Tinbergen, J. (1964), *Central Planning*, Yale, Yale University Press.

Vita a gazdaságirányitás és szervezeti rendszer fejlesztéséröl (1984), Economic Institute, report 27, Budapest.

5 Rationalizing the centrally managed economy: the market

Pekka Sutela

Introduction

Assume, following the Polish economist Leszek Balcerowicz (forth-coming), that 'one can – somewhat pointedly – subsume the development of the concept of the reformed system in the countries of real socialism under the rubric "the imitation of capitalism under increasingly relaxed constraints"'. Balcerowicz merely outlines the idea in a few words, but one can well elaborate upon it. Using the vocabulary discussed below, it is possible to (1) start with the Kautsky-Lenin image of socialism as a 'single [hierarchical] factory', (2) proceed through simulated commodity markets in a 'corporation' model, into (3) real commodity markets and simulated capital markets in a 'public sector' model, and (4) finally accept the existence of personal capital owners, that is capitalism in a technical sense. From this perspective, as Balcerowicz points out, the final stage of reforming the centrally managed economy would, in fact, entail a return to capitalism. Practical reform economics would thus confirm the traditional Austrian assertion that exactly such a transition is in fact necessary for an effective 'reform' of the socialist economic system.

It is clear that we are currently witnessing a transformation of economic 'reform' into 'transition' in at least some of the East and Central European countries. In scholarly discourse, too, the Austrian argument has returned with a vengeance (Brus and Laski 1989; Kornai 1990a, b). More widely than ever before, the non-viability of socialism is taken as evident, all the more so after the popular revolutions of the autumn of 1989.

Naturally, revolutions are not decisive arguments in economic theory and the possibility of efficient market socialism will certainly continue to occupy scholarly minds. However, let us for the sake of this discussion assume that the Balcerowicz argument is an apt characterization of the way in which 'the concepts of the reformed system' have evolved in such countries as Hungary and Poland. That assumed, the question to be posed in this chapter is whether the same doctrinal development has taken place

67

within Soviet reform economics. If that proves not to be the case, other questions arise. Have the Soviet economists perhaps demonstrated the Austrian thinking to be faulty? Or have they, on the contrary, even failed to face the relevant questions? Perhaps their own thinking is simply muddled? Does that have an impact on the prospects for Soviet reforms?[1]

This chapter will not attempt a complete analysis of the validity of Balcerowicz's hypothesis in the Soviet case. It will concentrate, instead, on the first conceptual stages of reform economics in the USSR, those involving the transition from the single factory model through 'using commodity–money relations in planning' in genuine commodity markets. Two other facets of doctrinal development, one concerning issues of property rights and the other focusing on the critical issues of transition, will thus be by-passed in this paper.

Furthermore, there will be no attempt to cover all the relevant Soviet literature. Instead, we will focus on those professional economists who seem most interesting because of either their published views or their present positions in Soviet reform efforts.

Finally, one should emphasize that this chapter is about Soviet thinking on economic reform – or reform economics, in short – not about economic reforms themselves. These are interconnected but separate objects of study.

Stages of economic reform

The 'Pre-stage' of economic reform

Before going to the Soviet case, let us make Balcerowicz's implied chain of argument somewhat more transparent. Though the issues involved are exceedingly complex and still remain largely in an embryonic state, the doctrinal development as outlined in a few words by Balcerowicz, and discussed in more detail elsewhere (Sutela 1989c, d), is deceptively simple. The historical and logical starting point of reform economics is the Kautsky-Lenin image of the socialist economy as a single (nineteenth-century) factor, a deterministic mechanism functioning as clockwork – for 'the German army under von Moltke' – to reach the goals predetermined by society or, more realistically, its ruling elite.

It is debatable whether traditional Soviet-type economies are best interpreted as command or bargaining systems. Let us, however, put this issue aside and follow the mainstream of reform economics in assuming that the Kautsky-Lenin image of future society was the model implicitly or explicitly followed in the practical 'construction of socialism'. It was also legitimized in Marxist-Leninist ideology as the proper embodiment of the economic laws of socialism on earth. For several reasons, the normative model could be only very roughly approximated. Not surprisingly, therefore, there is both logically and historically first the 'Pre-stage' of economic reform. By personnel changes and purges, by organization changes, by the implementation of shifts in investment allocation as well as by the reformulation of centralized pricing rules and incentives schemes, the 'Pre-stage' tries to make the existent allocation mechanism conform more closely to the Kautsky-Lenin image of true socialism. The 'Pre-stage' is, in fact, another attempt to implement the Kautsky-Lenin model.

This phase of economic reform, an endeavour to rationalize and make feasible the single factory model, was entered into immediately after the institution of the centrally managed system, in the Soviet case already in the early 1930s. Over the decades, such rationalization measures have proved extremely persistent, bringing into being a peculiar reform cycle of repeated attempts at *sovershenstvovanie* (as 'system perfection' is called in Sovietese) and their failures. To emphasize the relative futility of the 'Pre-stage', many commentators prefer to distinguish it from reforms proper, regarding it as a set of policy measures. The distinction, however, is a fluid one. Because of the immense literature available, there is no need here for further discussion of the 'Pre-stage'.

Phase I of economic reform

Rationalization of the centrally managed system became politically feasible only as the economic arbitrariness of the heroic (or Stalinist) phase of building socialism gave way to a more normalized society. Driven by the goals of efficiency and increased actual (as distinct from imaginary) control over economic processes, many socialist economists had by the early 1960s already by-passed the 'Pre-stage' and argued for *Phase I of economic reform*. The transition from the 'Pre-stage' to Phase I can probably be seen best in the optimal planning tradition founded on the work of Leonid Kantorovich and Viktor Novozhilov. They argued for the idea of indirect centralization, in which the direct commandeering typical of the single factor model is replaced by parametric guidance. In the limiting case of perfect indirect centralization, all such parameters have been formally derived as shadow prices from an optimal plan. Instead of by direct command, enterprises are guided toward the fulfilment of prescribed goals by economic parameters or 'commodity–money relations'. The independence to act against the wishes of the centre or the markets does not exist in perfect indirect centralization. In direct commandeering, the centre tries to tell the enterprises what to do. In indirect centralization, enterprises have the freedom of finding out for themselves which activities are preferred by the centre. The fundamental hierarchy with absolute priority given to the preference of the centre remains. Indeed, the goal is to substitute the 'planned chaos', inefficiencies and arbitrary petty tutelage of direct commandeering by a scientifically substantiated division of labour. Perfect indirect centralization is a model of the operation of a totalitarian model through simulated markets.

As an allocation model to be implemented in practice, indirect centralization is clearly a technocratic illusion. Relative to commandeering, it does not necessarily bring about any administrative cost savings. In general, no algorithms can produce better decisions than the information given by enterprises allows. These problems are by-passed in the simple models of indirect centralization. The underlying assumptions about the motivation are extremely crude, and there is no attempt to face the crucial problems of dynamic competition. As traditional hierarchical subordination is present in indirect as well as in direct centralization, ministries and planners will inevitably continue their paternalistic tutelage, which reform economists of the Phase I generation typically see as the major problem in direct centralization. Budget constraints will accordingly remain soft. In addition, various indirect centralization proposals entail problems of a more technical nature.

The 'Pre-stage' of economic reform is thus best seen as an attempt to get rid of hierarchical petty tutelage by means of streamlining, rationalization and all-encompassing social engineering. It therefore – not at all as paradoxically as seen by generations of Western commentators – claims to promote both real centralization and decentralization. But when the impossibility of all-encompassing central planning is admitted, be it due to uncertainty, the large scale of the planning problem, the existence of enterprise-specific information and other resources, or any other factor, perfect indirect centralization is seen to be as much a chimera as perfect direct centralization. Outside of simple models, there is no way of deriving all the parameters from an optimal plan. One must therefore be willing to legalize the existence of at least some markets. Enterprises have to be allowed other decision criteria in addition to the parameters set by the centre. Though the exact dividing line is not clear, broadly speaking, from this point onwards the normative image of the socialist economy more nearly resembles a simplified picture of a capitalist corporation than that of a single factory. This *Phase I of economic reform* has been discussed for the Soviet case by Ellman (1973) and Sutela (1984), among others.

The classic exposition of Phase I economic reform thinking is the book by Wlodzimierz Brus (1961; in translation, Brus, 1972). Genuine markets for commodities would be created while retaining decisions on net investment in the hands of the centre for reasons of stability, employment, structure and equity. Capital markets would not exist. Within the broad frame set by the state, enterprises would maximize profits. Along side the state sector, small-scale cooperative and private production would be encouraged. This is essentially the model implemented in Hungary since the 1960s, and explicitly argued for the USSR in the 1970s by Raimundas Karagadov and others (see Sutela, forthcoming).

In retrospect (Brus and Laski 1989) the mistakes of Phase I thinking seem obvious. By retaining net investment in central decision-making, the enterprise is still deprived of the right and responsibility of deciding upon its own future. The fundamental hierarchical subordination with the ensuing consequences of paternalism and soft budget constraints therefore remain. Even commodity markets, therefore, cannot function efficiently, though – as within a capitalist corporation – the degree of real commercialization may vary. More often than not, the industrial ministries will still try to manage the enterprises, now using various indirect and unofficial channels of influence when necessary. As seen in the case of Hungary, Phase I economic reforms will deteriorate into a 'no planning, no markets' situation. Because the state has retreated from some of its totalitarian aspirations, the society will have become a more pleasant place to live in, but the expected breakthrough in productivity remains a dream. It is not clear whether there is actually less or more petty tutelage than in the classic command economy.

Phase II of economic reform

Having seen the relative impotence of Phase I reforms, reform economists soon shifted their analysis. Instead of a misuse of hierarchical subordination, petty tutelage was seen as an inevitable consequence of a uni-hierarchical society. The existence of an umbilical cord between enterprises and ministries was diagnosed as the weak point of socialist economies. There seemed to be two possible and largely exclusive options regarding cutting the mutual dependence. These ways define the two possible variants of *Phase II of economic reform*.

The first possibility would be to institute workers' management either as a counterweight to bureaucratic power or as the new holder of property rights. Until very recently, this alternative had the advantage of seeming somehow socialist and it has been discussed in most centrally managed states. On the other hand, it has been seriously handicapped by the Yugoslavian experience as well as by recent political developments in Central and Eastern Europe, which make the alleged socialistic content of labour management a liability. The return of this option does not seem probable in the foreseeable future.

The alternative to labour management is replacing branch ministries by holding companies and other institutional investors as the executors of state property rights. It is assumed that – with asset values as their only target – they would be less interested in petty tutelage and more independent of politicians than branch ministries could be. Capital markets would accordingly exist, but without individual capitalists. This would be a case of simulated capitalism. The allocation mechanism would resemble the way the public sector is managed in some market economies. In addition to the state sector, allowance would probably be made for increased private and partly foreign-owned production, in particular for creating competition, the importance of which would be much better understood than in Phase I.

Phase III of economic reform

All the centrally managed economies have varying degrees of experience of the 'Pre-stage' of economic reform. Hungary stands as a lone example of two decades of Phase I economic reform and Yugoslavia of Phase II, Option I reforms. There are still no consistent examples of Phase II, Option II reforms, though the creation of institutional investors has been widely discussed both in Hungary and Poland, as well as quite recently in the USSR. Many economists of these countries, however, already by-passed theoretically discussions of simulated capital markets and are preparing and partially implementing ways of creating individual capital owners, that is, capitalism in the technical sense of the word.

Though it is generally admitted that, for various reasons, a large state sector will remain for the foreseeable future, several reasons for preferring genuine capitalism to Phase II, Option II, simulated capitalism, have been presented. They range from political and ideological to economic. Thus, capitalism is seen as necessary for creating a politically stabilizing middle-class, for creating the necessary preconditions of external resource inflow and, finally, for abolishing the priority of allegedly socialist goals – by now deeply discredited – in economic decisions. A simple but powerful argument says that capitalism has somehow been proved to be the natural state of society, into which one should return after having been subjected to painful experiments *in vivo*. Among the more narrowly economic arguments for capitalism, it is claimed that though the creation of institutional investors may be the appropriate way of breaking the hold of state administration over existing industries, only the predominance of personal ownership can form the basis for the rapid increase in the small- and medium-scale enterprises needed for competition and technical progress.

This is *Phase III of economic reform*, the transition to capitalism currently under way in Poland, Hungary and – due to somewhat different circumstances – also in the eastern part of Germany. Other (former) centrally managed economies are still somewhere on the road between classical command economy and Phase III, driven by the often conflicting goals of efficiency and political survival. An extreme but perhaps typical example of this is the USSR, which has since 1987 been in all the phases characterized above, at least as far as scholarly and policy debate is concerned. This may help to explain some of the inconsistencies in recent Soviet policies.

Having thus sketched in extremely broad outline the intricate dynamics of reform phases, we can now turn to the application of the framework to the Soviet case. The discussion to follow is not only limited to the first stage of Soviet reform economics, but is also inevitably stylized and documented in only a fragmentary way. The interested reader may want to turn to papers cited below for a more detailed discussion.

The 'Pre-stage' of Soviet reform economics

Optimal Planning

Soviet discussions on rationalizing the centrally managed economy started even before the new economic system had really been constituted (Sutela 1987). They have been, and continue to be, analysed in detail. It is remarkable that such a high degree of continuity has been obtained in reform proposals between the 1930s and the 1960s. Though the later discussions were much wider and more thorough, they were generally dominated by non-economists (on this, see Petrakov 1970), and many of the economists involved – people like Aleksandr Birman, Jakov Kronrod and Shamai Turetskii – have already participated in the pre-war discussions.

The crucial scholarly difference between the 1930s and the 1960s was in the availability of the optimal planning framework from the late 1950s. Though the optimal planners were always a small, even if vocal, minority among Soviet economists, theirs was the only fairly consistent reform economics of the 1960s, and they succeeded in dominating the professional scene far beyond their numerical significance. The traditional Soviet political economy of socialism had proved its practical impotence beyond any reasonable doubt in the law of value discussion of the late 1950s, and the writings of Leonid Kantorovich and Viktor Novozhilov appeared as a revelation to a new generation of young economists. Among them, such people of later prominence as Leonid Abalkin, Abel Aganbegian, Vadim Medvedev, Nikolai Petrakov and Stanislav Shatalin all either contributed to the new school of thinking or formed their own differing conceptions of the new economics of socialism, at least partly as a reaction to the optimal planning approach (Sutela 1990).

Several of the young economists of the 1960s, social scientist members of the 'Children of the 20th Party Congress', are among the foremost theoreticians, politicians and advisers of perestroika. It might therefore be of some interest to recall that the original Kantorovich-Novozhilov formulation of optimal planning was about rationalizing the hierarchical monolith of state ownership, not about market creation or pluralistic ownership. The optimal planning framework helps us appreciate the importance of scarcity, opportunity cost and efficiency prices. In fact, as an exposition of scarcity economics for Soviet readers it remains unsurpassed. Still, the deficiencies of optimal planning as reform economics are extreme. There is no suitable role for money, finance, macropolicy, competition or dynamics in general. Furthermore, the optimal planning framework can at best be interpreted as a partial model of efficient socialism, and it offers no guidance for the problems of transition.

The original Kantorovich formulation (Kantorovich 1965) of optimal planning is a generalization of the plywood trust problem which totally neglects the question of how to determine the product mix to be maximized. Methodically, as a close collaborator of Kantorovich was later to explain, the whole approach was based on 'the possibility, immanent to socialism, of constructing the economic system. Because socialism, in contrast to prior formations, has a blueprint – marxist-Leninist doctrine – the economic system too must be constructed consciously, proceeding from the theoretical conception of this doctrine' (Makarov 1987). In the vocabulary used above, the economist's task, as interpreted by Kantorovich and fellow optimal planners such as Vasilii Nemchinov, was to find the optimal social engineering approach to serving the Soviet state in the rationalization of the Kaustky-Lenin single-factory image.

In this light, more than just ideological camouflage was involved when Kantorovich strongly emphasized that the use of shadow process – or 'commodity–money relations' in the terminology of Soviet political economy – is a totally different thing from capitalist competition (Kantorovich 1965: p. 150). Kantorovich's insistence is well taken. In a similar way, Novozhilov argued in the early sixties that all prices and other parameters relevant to indirect centralization were to be derived from the centrally determined optimal plan. In this sense, *all* economic questions – without a single area remaining outside of state management – would be handled jointly by the centre and the enterprises (Novozhilov 1963: 52). Relative to the 'planned anarchy' of traditional commandeering, indirect centralization was to be a way of enhancing the degree to which the preferences of the centre are implemented in society.

Optimal planning theory soon largely abandoned the totalitarian 'Prestage' of reform economics. There are still a few people, however, who look at mathematical planning methods as a means of increasing the degree of centralization (Vladova and Rabkina 1989). Though he did not publish much on general reform economics, Kantorovich did not remain within the plywood trust framework, but – according to a knowledgeable source – towards the end of his life supported the leasing of enterprises as the proper way of enhancing efficiency. Novozhilov, in particular, seems to have moved rapidly in a more genuinely market-oriented direction. The theoretical optimal planning framework itself was in fact open to two kinds of interpretation (also see Belykh 1989, 1990). It can be seen as an attempt at perfect totalitarian planning, but when the impossibility or undesirability of complete centralization is acknowledged, it then offers a particular, even if narrow, way of looking at the role of prices in a market economy. Shadow prices and market prices can be seen as alternatives.

This kind of shift from technocratic planning centralism to the advocacy of markets is arguably most clearly seen in the writings of Stanislav Shatalin over the last two decades (Sutela 1990). But already in 1967, Viktor Volkonskii pointed out the mathematical equivalence of an optimal plan and the equilibrium of a (market) game (Volkonskii 1967a). He made his preference for the latter type of solution clear, though he was also perfectly conscious of the existence of market failures.[2]

By the late 1960s the USSR had a small but highly qualified group of specialists in general equilibrium economics. They analysed mathematical models of the competitive market economy, knowing exactly what they were doing, but were generally unable to communicate the recommendations implicit in their models to the larger body of economists. Their level of mathematical abstraction was the essence of the discourse, and at the same time, it made such theorizing possible within the increasingly confining ideological atmosphere. But it also tended to isolate them from the larger body of Soviet economists.

During the latter half of the sixties an interesting development took place in the optimal planning views of a research group lead by Aron Katsenelinboigen. This group was central to the development of the optimal planning framework in the mid-sixties (also see Katsenelinboigen 1980). Deeply influenced by contemporary Western thought on systems, the group argued that reality consists of a hierarchy of systems, each supersystem dictating the goal of its subsystem (Katsenelinboigen et al. 1969). The goal of the economy is given by the society, that of an enterprise by the economy. Furthermore, the highest hierarchical echelon of the economy, that of planners and the leaders of the party/state, was taken to be the sole representative of the needs of the 'society as a whole'. In Katsenelinboigen's construction, planners looked only at the long-term horizon, while the lower echelons had only specific short-term interests. The task, therefore, was to secure the priority of the long-term interest. This was to be done by deriving an axiomatic model of optimal socialism, i.e. engaging in system design on a truly grand scale.

This variant of Tinbergian welfare economics had no theory as to why optimality might be imminent to socialism, why existing socialism was less than optimal and why and how the optimal regime might be implemented on earth, in particular on Russian soil (Sutela 1984, forthcoming). The economist's task was explicitly likened to that of an engineer designing a better piece of machinery. Once the blueprints become available, somebody will surely build and begin using the new device – the optimal regime.

The way in which social preferences are handled in Katsenelinboigen's approach gave it – surely against the intentions of the authors – a totalitarian slant. Already in 1967 Janos Kornai criticized Katsenelinboigen's work exactly on this point. In the USSR as well, the group was repeatedly accused of wanting to create a totalitarian superautomaton, a new Leviathan (see Sutela, forthcoming). Such accusations were answered in a 1969 monograph (Katsenelinboigen et al. 1969). It was at the time the most complete discussion of market relations by optimal planners. The socialist economy, as Katsenelinboigen continually argued, has a global objective function. In fact that was to theoreticians like him a central defining feature of socialism. But just as clearly people have genuinely different preferences, and there must be some medium for articulating them.[3] Simple planning theory shows, Katsenelinboigen claimed, that pure quantity guidance is theoretically possible, but due to uncertainty, the size of the planning task, limited computational capabilities, the possibility of planning mistakes and the existence of enterprise-specific resources, even the best of plans can only be derived in aggregates to be further specified in horizontal contracts between enterprises.

This, one should note, is an extremely weak theoretical foundation for reformism. As in Kantorovich's plywood trust, vertical relations and global objective functions – 'planning' – are still primary and everything else secondary, as if mere decorative addition. Katsenelinboigen and others offer reasons why the single factor image can never be implemented in any pure form, but they do not provide an assessment or criticism of the image itself. Their contractual additions to vertical relations are not necessarily more than an explanation for such traditional features of Stalinist planning as *tolkachi* ('pushers': illegal traders) and horizontal delivery contacts. Even in this form, optimal planning theory was unable to deal with markets. It remained in the 'Pre-stage' of economic reform.

Phase I in Soviet reform economics

The 1960s

It is, in fact, extremely difficult to find arguments of any consistency for genuine markets in the Soviet reform economics of the 1960s. (One may want to add, it is exceedingly difficult to find consistent arguments of any kind.) Most of the Soviet debate took place on a level which was enlightened neither by deep knowledge of existing realities nor by theoretical strictness. Among theoretical economists, Volkonskii's general equilibrium models (Volkonskii 1967) are probably the best example of argumentation for a market-like equilibrating mechanism, though his – realistic – admission of market failures leaves his preferred combination of markets and planning unclear, though he does refer to the ideas of Vasilii Nemchinov (to be discussed below). Increasingly tight censorship must have contributed to this relative silence, though the continuity in two of Volkonskii's monographs (see Volkonskii 1967a, 1973) is notable. In the latter, the emphasis on market failures and the theoretical – not normative – role of general equilibrium models is preeminent. Volkonskii was, however, one of the very few Soviet economists of the 1960s to point out publicly the prospects of bankruptcy and unemployment in an efficiency-searching economy (Volkonskii 1967b).

Looking at the better known mainstream of Soviet reformism one should consider Liberman and Nemchinov, probably the best-known Soviet reform economists of the 1960s. The inconsistencies and lack of clarity in Yevsei Liberman's proposals are generally acknowledged. For instance, it is interesting to note that Liberman, whose vagueness has often been commented upon, was actually uncertain about the centrality of the whole issue. On the one hand he emphasized the necessity of rational prices for centralized decisions, on the other he pointed out that the buyer has no difficulty in including any costs in his investment and cost estimates (see Zaleski 1967: p. 166). Therefore, he argued, 'prices are not very important for the economy'. Implicitly, this amounted to pointing out the existence of soft budget constraints. In Liberman's case, however, it was just an incidental insight, not the basis for arguing for hardened budget constraints (with all the ensuing property right consequences).

Vasilii Nemchinov's idea of a *khozraschet* (economic accountancy) economy is easily the most radical reform proposal of any detail to come out of Soviet reform economics of the 1960s. But even this one is silent about ownership forms, sees the task as one of strengthening, not diminishing, the role of planning and argues against 'free markets and market competition (which) contradict the planned and balanced development of the society' (Nemchinov 1968: p. 100; in general, see Nemchinov 1964).

In essence, Nemchinov argued for central planning with limited independence of enterprises. Obligatory plan indicators – the essence of planning to Nemchinov – were not to be abolished, but their number was to be cut drastically. In addition to plan indicators, enterprises would be guided by normatives (or the parameters of indirect centralization) fixed for a period of ten to fifteen years. Within these constraints, enterprises would be free to organize their activities as best they could. The Nemchinovian *khozraschet*-economy would thus presumably have some degree of direct planning, simulation of markets by normatives and possibly genuine markets.

Over two decades later, in 1987, planning by fixed normatives was made the centrepiece of Gorbachev's economic reform, and the Secretary General himself referred to Nemchinov as the scholarly godfather of the reform ('O zadachakh', 1987). The Nemchinovian idea of fixed normatives survived in Soviet practice for perhaps a year. Normatives which were introduced in the middle of a five-year period without price reform could be neither stable nor uniform over sectors or even over enterprises. Management by enterprise-specific normatives collapsed duly into traditional commandeering. Petty tutelage then became the force for changing both normatives and physical plan targets, not only the latter, as in traditional planning.

Seeing this, reformist Soviet economists had to look for a solution in uncharted theoretical waters. The ideas of direct and indirect centralization having been discredited in practice, nothing remained but the market. This process of elimination was the way in which Soviet economists in general came to an understanding of the necessity of the market economy in 1988–9.

Indeed, the idea of planning by normatives cannot be a third way between planning and markets. It may be understood as an attempt at strict guidance of enterprises, in which case normatives cannot possibly be fixed over a longer period of time. The determinants of the economy do not change once in exactly five (or ten or fifteen) years, in concert with Soviet planning periods. Furthermore, if ministries or their equivalents retain their superordinated position *vis-à-vis* enterprises, there is no way of preventing them from attempting to exercise their property rights by petty tutelage. Because enterprises have specific information and other resources useful in bargaining, the plan bargaining of the traditional system is replaced by bargaining over normatives. The ideal of stable normatives becomes even more illusory. In the other case the illusion of strict guidance is abandoned, and normatives become taxlike policy instruments. This alternative, however, presupposes the existence of a basic market-like allocation mechanism. The optimal planning literature of the late 1960s and the 1970s shows the extent to which the optimal planners' arrival at the latter alternative was constrained not only by censorship and political considerations, but also by their basic frame of thought which argued forcefully that planning can be made to perform better than markets ever do (see Sutela, forthcoming).

In addition to stable normatives, another central feature of the Nemchinovian *khozraschet*-economy is 'plan orders'. After receiving the few remaining obligatory plan targets and normatives, enterprises would compete for legally binding orders issued by planners. Such orders would cover the production deemed indispensable by planners. Any production over and above plan orders could be sold freely, but only in accord with the pricing rules set by price authorities.

Nemchinov's *khozraschet*-economy is probably the first Soviet proposal for a dual-track planning system. An unspecified part of production would be, as just seen, strictly planned through plan orders, while the rest would be freely sold. Nemchinov, however, argued in 1964 that this would not imply a duality between planning and markets. The prices of products in excess of plan orders would still be closely regulated. Such transactions would also be guided by various normatives. Though Nemchinov is short on detail, the problems encountered later when dual-tract planning was implemented in countries like the USSR and China may well have been already imbedded in his proposals.

Gennadii Lisichkin is, after Volkonskii, the most obviously market oriented of Soviet economists of the 1960s. His 1966 book was simply entitled 'Plan and market' (Lisichkin 1966). In contrast to the optimal planners, he firmly insisted upon the difference between genuine markets and the use of 'money–commodity relations' as an accounting and controlling device. They are alternatives, and each has an internal logic of its own, he emphasized. Any attempt to fuse elements of one with the other is bound to fail, Lisichkin warned. In case of a fusion, the dominant alternative would absorb and neutralize any 'alien' elements. In Soviet history, Lisichkin argued, the New Economic Policy of the 1920s is the model of the market alternative, and traditional central planning is the model of the money–commodity relations alternative. For Lisichkin, there was no doubt that the principles of the New Economic Policy were 'the uniquely correct system of economic relations, until such time that full communism is built'.

Lisichkin's book can be seen as a far-sighted criticism of the predominant Soviet reformist emphasis on 'using money–commodity relations'. History has proven him right. The book does suffer, however, from three weaknesses. It is not anchored in any consistent theoretical framework. Second, it has an overly optimistic view of the way in which the Soviet economy actually functioned in the 1920s.[4] Third, Lisichkin seems to have understood markets in a very narrow sense, simply as 'a complicated complex of conditions under which the disposal [*realizatsiia*] of social product takes place' (Lisichkin 1966: pp. 13, 56).

It may be pointed out here that Lisichkin's insistence on planning and real markets as alternatives had a counterpart among optimal planners. Stanislav Shatalin has consistently argued for the distinction between real markets and 'using money–commodity relations' (see, for instance, Shatalin 1982; Sutela, 1984, 1990, for earlier references). In a Preobrazhenskian mode he claimed, until the 1980s, that over a longer period of time the range of planning would increase and that of real markets decrease.

The picture seems indeed bleak for the search for a Soviet market socialist of the 1960s. There is, fortunately for us, one more candidate. He is Nikolai Petrakov, whose 1971 books are the best in the Soviet reform economics of the time (Petrakov 1971a, b).[5] Petrakov started his scholarly career as a political economy interpreter of the optimal planning framework. In a 1966 pamphlet, he emphasized the indirectly centralizing character of optimal planning and the primacy of state interests, but also criticised Vadim Medvedev, at the time a rather obscure young Leningrad political economist, for underestimating the role of markets and the 'law of value' in socialism (Petrakov 1966; Sutela 1990). In a 1970 *Novyi mir* article he (Petrakov 1970) was probably the first Soviet economist to explicitly abandon the Kautsky-Lenin image of socialism as a single factory. People have different interests, and planners are no exception, Petrakov pointed out, they also have their particular interests, and plans are too important to be left solely to planners. There is no simple social goal function; there should be a 'mechanism for defining, specifying and correcting' social goals. This should be decoded as an argument for more political representation.

Markets, Petrakov further emphasized, are not only mechanisms for transmitting existing information. Of more importance is the generation of new information. Both this function and the articulation of interests presuppose the existence of social pluralism – a term which, in fact, Petrakov used in print in 1971. Decisions should essentially be informal compromises which take into account the diversity of existing interests. Instead of the social engineering of optimal planning theory, Petrakov – himself a part of this current (Sutela 1984, 1990) – calls for markets as a basis for politics and pluralism.

It is probably not too far-fetched to conclude that Petrakov's way of connecting pluralism, markets and the generation of information may have been influenced by Austrian economics. While such optimal planners as Stanislav Shatalin continued to argue that the choice between planning and markets should be made strictly on efficiency grounds, Petrakov's argument for markets was partly based on their democratic or, perhaps better, anti-totalitarian character (Sutela 1990). This is particularly evident in his discussion of equilibrium prices. Either prices or bureaucratic discretion must always ration scarce supply among competing demands. The former method, Petrakov argued in 1970, is the democratic and the latter the undemocratic way of allocation.

On a more narrowly economic plane, Petrakov proposed a variant of Nemchinovian dual-track planning. Only 'the most important' production would be included in plan orders, and government would primarily regulate economic activities through normatives regarding resource payments, rents, interest rates, tax schedules, etc. But at least some prices would be centrally determined, though Petrakov is unclear on this point. Normatives would be stable for a five-year period.

There should be no doubt, however, that Petrakov had market pricing in mind for most commodities. Following Novozhilov, his mental tutor, Petrakov argued forcefully for equilibrium pricing and against what he called 'the economy of queues' (Petrakov 1970). Rationing by queues leads to efficiency losses and – central to Petrakov – subjects people to planners' discretion. Given his numerous arguments against the possibility of all-encompassing central planning, this can only be seen as another argument for market pricing. At the same time one should point out that in the early 1970s Petrakov mistakenly identified the task of equilibration solely as a price problem. He seems to have become conscious of the need for a stable currency and scarce money only much later, when his concern for monetary stability led to the controversial 1987 proposal for a parallel currency (Sutela 1990).

By 1973, however, after some high-level political criticism, Petrakov had to withdraw his proposal, which seemed to imply market determination of most prices (Sutela 1990). From then on he argued unequivocally for equilibrium prices derived from plans. This, however, is not the crucial point in Petrakov's thinking. While he criticized both the early technocratic Katsenelinboigenian thinking and Volkonskii's general equilibrium models, his real point concerning markets was more profound than the choice between market and administrative pricing. By linking markets, pluralism and democracy he was one of the very few Soviet radicals of the 1960s who, at least to some decree, succeeded in crossing the abyss between economic and cultural and political radicalism, which was so much in evidence in Soviet discussions of the time (Kagarlitsky 1988).

It was to take until 1988 before Petrakov's 1971 argument about the democracy of markets became frequent among Soviet reform economists (Popov 1987; Iasin 1988; Shmelev 1989; Abalkin 1989a, b). In general, this should be construed as an argument against totalitarianism, not as a claim that all market economies are necessarily democratic or that the transition to market allocation is best achieved by making the economy in some sense more democratic. The two latter claims have also been debated in the USSR, as is well known.

To conclude this discussion on markets and money–commodity relations' in optimal planning theory, let me point out two of the wider issues involved. It does not seem that the importance of monetary stability for the institutionalization of markets was understood even by leading Soviet economists until the late 1980s. When financial issues were discussed at all, it was in the context of increasing the share of credit, as opposed to budgetary finance. That was a simple application of the idea of scarcity price – here interest on credit – and does not seem to have led to any understanding of the wider issues concerning the hardness of budget constraints. Neither can one discern any understanding of the role of competition. On the contrary, many of the optimal planners were happy to follow the traditional Marxist-Leninist argument of competition being something that belongs to the nineteenth century (Petrakov 1973). They supported the drive of the early 1970s for the establishment of huge associations of enterprises (see, for example, Volkonskii 1973). Such monopolists were assumed to be big enough to be able to plan, finance and implement investment without having to depend totally on planners. The same chain of thinking was also applied to ministries. The advocacy of putting ministries on *khozraschet* continued for years.

That such monopolies on 'complete *khozraschet*' could not, in fact, be given the right to set prices, due to their possible usage of monopoly power was understood by at least some economists, but in their view the monopolistic structure of the economy was a precondition determined by technical progress and other such 'objective' factors, not a handicap to be overcome (Sukhotin 1970).

As there is no free competition under modern capitalism, Petrakov argued in 1973 (Petrakov 1973), the only people who could even dream of market socialism were the retrograde petty bourgeois professors in Western countries. Optimal planners were, as were Soviet economists, much influenced both by the Marxist-Leninist theories of monopoly capitalism and by the Galbraithian view of an essentially marketless and uncompetitive capitalism. It is against the background of these predominant views that one should examine the perhaps somewhat naive subsequent emphasis placed by such Soviet economists as Pinsker and

Seliunin on capitalism as being, after all, competitive (see Sutela, forthcoming; Seliunin 1990). Controversies over capitalism in actual practice became debates on the future form of the Soviet economy.

The socialist market

Such views should be compared with the thinking of mainstream political economists of the same period. Vadim Medvedev, the young Leningrad economist mentioned above, actually set the tone that prevailed in much of the later political economy when he argued in a 1966 book that the existence of society-wide interests, in addition to personal and group interests, gives the society its socialist character (Medvedev, 1966). Their priority is secured by the use of obligatory plan targets, and abolishing them – the assumed essence of the Hungarian reform of 1968 – would therefore be a mistake.

Yet, money–commodity relations do exist, Medvedev conceded. They serve socialism because they are planned: supply is predetermined, prices are centrally set and even demand is strongly influenced by governmental policies. During the 1970s, this view of 'money–commodity relations' as planned socialist markets became generally accepted among political economists. Leonid Abalkin, in particular, wrote much on the theme (see, for instance, Abalkin 1973).

Abalkin, the most prominent Soviet political economist of socialism since the 1970s, has continued to write about peculiarly socialist markets until the end of the 1980s. Though his vocabulary has made the acceptance of (some kind of) markets easier in Soviet ideology, at the same time it has created some strange illusions. On the one hand, it has been possible to argue, as does the 1987 Law on Socialist Enterprise, both that enterprises are market (commodity) producers and that they remain as subordinated parts of a hierarchy. On the other hand, confusion is created by claiming, as is also done in the law, that hierarchical relations can actually be regulated by law on an equal basis. Third, and perhaps the worst of all, the idea arises that socialist markets could somehow utilize only the assumedly 'positive' features of real markets, leaving the assumedly 'negative' features to capitalism.

Only very recently has the last mentioned approach received its share of criticism from leading Soviet economists (Abalkin 1989b). It has finally been conceded that markets are markets are markets; there are no peculiarly socialist or capitalist markets. The question of socialism can arise only in regard to the environment and policies under which markets operate. Even here, unfortunate obscurities still exist. Abalkin, for instance, still argued in 1989 that among the peculiarities markets have in a socialist environment are the full employment of labour and the exclusion of 'exploitation', defined as wage labour for private gain. The former requirement sets obvious limitations on structural change and the effectiveness of market incentives in general, while the latter tends to make private production ideologically unacceptable. Among other properties of markets not acceptable under socialism, speculation and the advancement of private or group interests are sometimes also mentioned. The former – taken literally as arbitrage – excludes from socialism the law of one price, one of the foremost efficiency properties of neo-classical markets. The latter, on the other hand, proves a complete misunderstanding of the parable of the invisible hand.

One could actually propose a simple test for the degree of seriousness with which the policy-makers of a given national are contemplating the transition from central planning to markets. If arbitrage is still defined as speculation and remains punishable under the criminal code, no transition is forthcoming. Needless to say, this remains the situation in the USSR in the autumn of 1990.

Normal markets

'We have become convinced on the basis of our own experience', says the so-called Abalkin report on economic reform of autumn 1989, 'that there is no worthy alternative to the market mechanism as a method of coordinating the activities and interests of economic subjects. It is also the most democratic form of regulating economic activity' ('Radical', 1989). The report also states that a diversity of property forms is a condition for a normal functioning of the market mechanism, and continues by stating that markets are only effective in the context of free prices and competition. In addition to commodity markets, financial and labour markets are also needed. In principle, there is no longer talk of certain peculiarly socialist markets, but rather of normal (or full-blooded, as Mikhail Gorbachev has put it) markets – so, or at least, it seems.

The wording of the Abalkin report is typical of Soviet reformist thinking of 1988–90. The market mechanism is arrived at on the basis of the method of exclusion. Markets are what is left after direct centralization by traditional central planning and indirect centralization by either optimal planning or planning by normatives are both seen to have failed (see also Evstigneev 1989). Markets are also advocated on the basis of their alleged democratic character. This argument, put forward by Petrakov in 1970, recurred throughout 1988–9.

This means that Soviet reform economics has at long last completed its transition to Phase I of reform economics, and – though this is beyond the scope of the present chapter – that the transition to Phase II is well underway. It was already well understood by 1990 that commodity markets cannot function well without the existence of markets for factors of production, and the implications of this for property rights are fiercely debated. A holding company solution for state-owned industries has been proposed (Vavilov et al. 1990), and is gaining prominence in government reform programmes. The advocacy of the Phase III transition to technically defined capitalism, however, is still viewed as radicalism. But does this really mean that the characteristics of the market system would be clearly understood by Soviet reform economists? One may search for the answer in the recent work of such writers as Leonid Abalkin and Nikolai Petrakov.

There is, naturally, a seemingly small group of orthodox Marxist-Leninist economists who argue that the ills of the Soviet economy are due to having too much, not too little money–commodity relations and markets (for discussions, see Seliunin 1990; Sutela, forthcoming). Furthermore, they argue that functioning commodity markets presuppose the existence of private property, profit motive, competition and market pricing, as well as markets for capital and labour. Radicals agree; but while the former see this as an argument against markets, the latter see it as an argument for Russian capitalism (Seliunin 1990).

Mainstream reformists such as Leonid Abalkin argue, as seen above, for a market economy but at the same time claim that market socialism is possible. Exploitation – which for Abalkin means non-family wage labour – should still be excluded. Furthermore, Abalkin argues in a Galbraithian vein that as more than half of all transactions in modern capitalism are hierarchical, the same should surely be true of market capitalism, as well (see, for instance, Abalkin 1989b). It remains totally unclear, however, how far the positions of modern corporations and Soviet state hierarchies can be legitimately compared. One does not find in the Soviet economic press competent discussion of the new institutional economics of markets and hierarchies. The conceptual dividing lines between market and non-market activities therefore remain confused.

Abalkin emphasizes that monopoly production and markets cannot coexist (Abalkin 1989b: p. 19). Consequently, current Soviet reform programmes contain proposals for demonopolization. Whether such measures are sufficient or not, at least the problem has been recognized. For some reason Abalkin is not equally worried about monopsonies (also see Abalkin 1989a). The simple explanation can probably be found in his continuing advocacy of state ownership of productive enterprises, which in a sense necessarily implies at least a near-monopsony in many segments of labour markets. Or perhaps his neglect of monopsony is a mere echo of thinking habits developed in a society characterized by overwhelming seller's markets.

Abalkin's general definition of a market includes three characteristics: (1) direct contact between producer and consumer, (2) free choice of partners and (3) competition between producers (Abalkin 1989a: p. 5). There is no mention of competition on the demand side (though that may be implied by (2), which, however, would make (3) superfluous), nor of the ways that prices are formed. These three characteristics belong to markets everywhere, Abalkin argues. What makes socialist markets socialist is the fact that they are embedded in socialist relations of production. The characteristics of socialist markets that arise are thus (a) the absence of private wage labour, (b) the existence of social guarantees and (c) the existence of a well-developed system of planned regulation of markets.

Hence, on one hand, Abalkin strongly opposes any attempts to introduce textbook competitive markets in the USSR. On the other hand, he does maintain that one cannot mechanically contrast capitalist and socialist markets. The exact form of socialist markets, he emphasizes, will be the result of a long developmental process, and one should not try to fix all their characteristics in advance. This is either wisdom or a willingness to submit to severely restricted forms of markets fro the foreseeable future.

As is to be expected, bearing in mind the different scholarly backgrounds of the men, the current approach of Nikolai Petrakov continues to be somewhat different from Abalkin's. In the same way as in 1970, he stresses in particular the need for elastic equilibrium – that is market – prices. There cannot be markets without market prices, Petrakov has persistently underlined (also see Iasin 1989). This, Petrakov has argued with great consistency over the last few years, presupposes the creation of a stable currency, monetary restraint and equilibrium as well as competition in the economy (Sutela 1990; Petrakov 1990). These requirements are best met by implementing the transition through the creation of a convertible parallel currency. While most Soviet reformers – following the East European experience also outlined in the first part of this chapter – concentrate on arguing for the necessity of markets for finance, capital and labour as a precondition for functioning commodity markets (as an example see Evstigneev 1989), Petrakov adds the need for currency markets (see, for example, Petrakov 1988). Though this highly controversial proposal lies beyond the scope of this paper, one should note that for Petrakov – contrary to Albalkin, the political economist – the issue at hand is not how to justify markets in socialism but how to devise a way of transition to markets. A concept like socialist markets has never existed for Petrakov.

'But, if we make a transition to market, we have to follow its laws', Evgenii Iasin wrote in late 1989 in opposition to overly regulated price formation and other excessive state regulation (Iasin 1989: p. 56; also see

Borozdin 1990). This truth seems to have been forgotten by the CPSU and the Soviet government, whose programmatic decisions in the first half of 1990 referred to a transition to something called a planned or regulated market system. Only a small share of prices is to be freed during the next few years. 'Progressive economists', complained Academician Oleg Bogomolov among others, were not listened to when the programme was drafted ('Peremena', 1990). Neither Ryzhkov's government nor the engineers of Gosplan understood the economists' language, he continued. Therefore, what was proposed in May 1990 was, in the understanding of radical Soviet reformers, not a transition to markets at all, but at best a generalization of existing 'semi-markets' with almost complete centrally determined entry and exit of producers, fixed disequilibrium prices and the ensuing rationing to most, but not all, sectors of the economy, in particular not to the management of land and natural resources. This impression is strongly reinforced by the words of a leading planner, who asserted in early 1990 – obviously with no sense of irony – that the future well-regulated Soviet markets will know of no anarchy ('Na puti', 1990).

And, indeed, even many economists of tradition-bound and stubbornly conservative views claim to share the general goal of regulated markets. While they naturally condemn any proposals of privatisation (see, for example, Bachurin 1990), they still also reject calls for equilibrium prices as being utopian, anti-marxist-Leninist and impoverishing. Furthermore they also continue to propose adopting only the 'positive' elements of competition and leaving such problems as unemployment to the capitalists. Concerning markets, the views of such economists and planners have not changed since the sixties. Their approach is still that of using money–commodity relations as a tool of planning.

Conclusion

The failure of economic perestroika since 1987 has not been unconnected with the scholarly approaches and reform frameworks which the Soviet economists had to offer. Years later, and contrary to what one may first perceive, it is not only the problems of ownership and transition that continue to divide Soviet opinions. Even attitudes to Phase I of economic reform, market creation, still differ widely. Emphasizing this does not deny the fact that actual true markets do indeed function differently in different environments. Some of this may be explained by the approach to the transition: putting too much of it in the initial framework threatens to kill the whole project.

We may thus be witnessing a particular example of path-dependency. To reach peculiarly Russian markets with whatever their defining features may be, one perhaps has to aim at markets in general. If a particular

Russian version of markets is set as the goal, the actual result may simply be a continuation of old central management under a new name.

Notes

This is a slightly revised version of a paper presented at the fourth World Congress of Soviet and East European Studies, ICSEES, Harrogate, England, 21–6 July, 1990, Panel on Perestroika and Market Socialism. The comments by panel participants, especially V.L. Makarov and V.M. Polterovich, are gratefully acknowledged. The research upon which this paper is based was conducted at the Centre for Russian and East European Studies, University of Birmingham, England, and the Bundesinstitut für ostwissenschaftliche und internationale Studien, Cologne, Federal Republic of Germany. Preliminary versions of the paper have been presented at seminars at the Bundesinstitut as well as at St Antony's College, Oxford. Financial assistance provided by the Volkswagenwerk Stiftung and the Yrjö Jahnsson Foundation is gratefully acknowledged.

 1 The present author has recently analysed the development of Soviet economic thinking in Sutela (1984, 1989a, 1989b, 1990, forthcoming).
 2 Michael Ellman (1971, 1973) has argued that Volkonskii wrote 'the ideology of capitalism adapted to Soviet conditions'. Though Volkonskii was – together with Aleksandr Birman – one of the very few Soviet economists who, in the 1960s, pointed out the necessity of bankruptcy for efficiency, he seems to have been silent about ownership, warned about the cyclical properties of free markets, wanted to leave 'large' investment decisions outside their sphere and also emphasized the insufficiency of revealed preference information for long-term consumption planning.
 3 Quite evidently, Katsenelinboigen had primarily a democratic political mechanism in mind, and the argument is about somehow democratizing planning, not about market choice as a precondition of democracy. Even under perestroika, some descendants of the optimal planning school have continued to argue that the task ahead is about the democratization of central management, not about market creation (see Sutela, forthcoming).
 4 In this aspect consistently, Lisichkin emerged as a defender of Leninism in the late 1980s.
 5 Petrakov (1971a) was later published in a somewhat diluted form as Petrakov (1974).

References

Abalkin, L. (1973), *Khoziaistvennyi mekhanizm razvitogo sotsializma*, Moscow, Mysl'.
    (1989a), 'Rynok v ekonomicheskoi sisteme sotsializma', *Voprosy ekonomiki*, no. 7, pp. 3–12.
    (1989b), 'Strategiia obnovleniia', *Ogonek*, no. 13, pp. 6–7, 18–20.
Bachurin, A. (1990), 'Kakoi rynok nam nuzhen', *Planovoe khoziaistvo*, no. 1, pp. 42–51.
Balcerowicz, Leszek (forthcoming), 'The "socialist controversy" debate and the

discussion of reform in the socialist countries', forthcoming in Marton Tardos and Janos Matyas Kovacs (eds.), *Reform and Transformation*, London, Routledge & Kegan Paul.

Belykh, Andrei (1989), 'Mathematical economics and Soviet planning', *Carleton Economic Papers*, no. 3, February.

(1990), 'O vospriniatii ekonomicheskikh rabot L.V. Kantorovicha na zapade', *Ekonomika i matematicheskie metody*, 26, no. 2, pp. 238–47.

Borozdin, Iu. (1990), 'Ekonomicheskaia reforma i tovarno-denezhnye otno-sheniia', *Voprosy ekonomiki*, no. 1, pp. 13–25.

Brus, Wlodzimierz (1972), *The Market in a Socialist Economy*, Routledge & Kegan Paul, London

Brus, Wlodzimierz and Kazimierz Laski (1989), *From Marx to Market*, Oxford, Clarendon.

Ellman, Michael (1971), *Soviet Planning Today*, Cambridge, Cambridge University Press.

(1973), *Planning Problems in the USSR*, Cambridge, Cambridge University Press.

Evstigneev, R.N. (1989), 'Logika khoziaistvennykh reform', *Ekonomika i matematicheskie metody*, 25, no. 2, pp. 211–18.

Iasin, E.G. (1980), 'Administrativnaia sistema tsen ili ekonomicheskii mek-hanizm', *Ekonomika i matematicheskie metody*, 24, no. 2, pp. 209–20.

(1989), 'Sotsialisticheskii rynok ili iarmarka illiuzii?', *Kommunist*, no. 15, pp. 53–62.

Kagarlitsky, Boris (1988), *The Thinking Reed*, London, Verso.

Kantorovich, L.V. (1965), *The Best Use of Economic Resources*, Cambridge, Mass., Harvard University Press.

Katsenelinboigen, Aron (1980), *Soviet Economic Thought and Political Power in the USSR*, London, Pergamon.

Katsenelinboigen, A., Iu.V. Ovsienko, and E. Iu. Faerman (1963), *Metodo-logicheskie voprosy optimalnogo planirovaniia sotsialisticheskoi ekonomiki*, Moscow, TsEMI AN SSSR.

Katsenelinboigen, A., I. Lakhman, and Iu. Ovsienko (1969), *Optimalnost' i tovarno-denezhnye otnosheniya*, Moscow, Nauka.

Kornai, Janos (1990a), 'The affinity between ownership and allocation mec-hanisms', WIDER Discussion Paper, Helsinki.

(1990b), *The Road to a Free Economy*, New York and London, Norton.

Lisichkin, G.S. (1966), *Plan i rynok*, Moscow Ekonomika.

Makarov, V.L. (1987), 'Glubokii issledovatel'', *EKO*, no. 1, pp. 87–91.

Medvedev, V.A. (1966), *Zakon stoimosti i materialnye stimuly sotsialisticheskogo proizvodstva*, Moscow, Ekonomika.

'Na puti k reguliruemomu rynochnomu khoziaistvu' (1990), *Planovoe khoziaistvo*, no. 6, pp. 34–43.

Nemchinov, V. (1964), 'Sotsialisticheskoe khoziaistvovanie i planirovanie pro-izvodstva', *Kommunist*, no. 5, pp. 74–87. Reprinted, for instance, in *Kom-munist*, no. 11, 1987, pp. 23–32.

(1968), 'Sotsiologicheskii aspekt planirovaniia', *Izbrannye proizvedenie*, vol. 5, Moscow, Nauka.

Novozhilov, V.V. (1963), 'K diskussii o printsipakh planovogo tsenoobrazovaniia', *Primenenie matematiki v ekonomii, Vyp. 1*, Leningrad, Izdatelstvo Leningradskogo Gosudarstvennogo Universiteta, pp. 46–54.

'O zadachakh partii po korennoi perestroiki upravleniia ekonomikoi. Doklad Generalnogo sekretaria M.S. Gorbacheva na Plenume TsK KPSS 25 iiunia 1987 goda' (1987), *Kommunist*, no. 10, pp. 5–47.

'Peremena dekoratsii' (1990), *Ogonek*, no. 23, pp. [0]–2.

Petrakov, Nikolai (1966), *Nekotorye aspekty diskussii ob ekonomicheskikh metodakh khoziaistvovaniia*, Moscow, Ekonomika.

(1970), 'Upravlenie ekonomiki i ekonomicheskie interesy', *Novyi mir*, no. 8, pp. 167–86.

(1971a), *Khoziaistvennaia reforma: plan i ekonomicheskaia samostoiatelnost'*, Moscow, Mysl'.

(1971b), *Nekotorye voprosy upravleniia sotsialisticheskoi ekonomikoi*, Moscow TsEMI.

'Mify "rynochnogo sotsializma" i ekonomicheskaia realnost'', *Problemy mira i sotsializma*, no. 3, pp. 33–7.

(1974), *Kiberneticheskie problemy upravleniia ekonomikoi*, Moscow, Nauka.

(1988), 'Tovar i rynok', *Ogonek*, no. 34, pp. 6–7, 23–24.

(1990), 'Problemy formirovaniia rynka v SSSR', *Ekonomika i matematicheskie metody*, no. 3, pp. 389–97.

Popov, G. (1987), 'S tochki zreniia ekonomista', *Nauka i zhizn'*, no. 4, pp. 54–65.

'Radical Economic Reform: Top-Priority and Long-Term Measures' (1989), Ms, Moscow.

Seliunin, V. (1990), 'Rynok: khimery i realnost', *Znamia*, no. 6, pp. 193–205.

Shatalin, S.S. (1982), *Funktsionirovanie ekonomiki razvitogo sotsializma*, Moscow, Izdatelstvo MGU.

Shmelev, Nikolai (1980), 'Libo sila, libo rubl'', *Znamia*, no. 1, pp. 128–47.

Sukhotin, Iu.V. (1970), 'Ekonomicheskaia reforma i narodnokhoziaistvennyi optimum', *Voprosy effektivnosti obshchestvennogo proizvodstva*, Moscow, Nauka, pp. 11–79.

Sutela, Pekka (1984), *Socialism, Planning and Optimality*, Helsinki, Finnish Society for Sciences and Letters.

(1987), 'Economic incentives in Soviet pre-war economic thought', in Stefan Hedlund (ed.), *Incentives and Economic Systems*, London, Croom Helm, pp. 135–77.

(1989a), 'Ideology as a means of economic debate or: the strange case of objective economic laws of socialism', *Jahrbuch der Wirtschaft Osteuropas*, Band 13/1, pp. 198–220.

(1989b), 'Reformability of the objective economic laws of socialism', in Marton Trados and Janos Matyas Kovacs (eds.), *Reform and Transformation*, London, Routledge & Kegan Paul (forthcoming 1991)

(1989c), 'Marketization in Eastern Europe', in Ronald Hill and Jan Zielonka (eds.), *Restructuring Eastern Europe, Views from Western Europe*, London, Edgar Elgar (forthcoming).

(1989d), 'The Transition of Eastern Europe to the Market Economy', *The Finnish Journal of Economics*, 85, no. 4, pp. 440–52 (in Finnish).

(1990), 'All the President's Men', *Communist Economies*, forthcoming.

(forthcoming), *Soviet Economic Thought and Economic Reform in the USSR*, Cambridge, Cambridge University Press.

Vavilov, A., et al. (1990), 'Bez aktsionerov net rynka', *Izvestiia*, 5 April.
Vladova, N., and N. Rabkina, (1989), 'Vozmozhno li kontseptsiia ekonomicheskogo sinteza', *Neva*, no. 10, pp. 143–56.
Volkonskii, V.A. (1967a), *Model optimalnogo planirovaniia i vzaimosviazi ekonomicheskikh pokazetelei*, Moscow, Nauka.
    (1967b), 'Tovarno-denezhnyi mekhanizm v optimalnom upravlenii khoziaistvom i tsenoobrazovanie', *Ekonomika i matematicheskie metody*, 3, no. 4, pp. 489–99.
    (1973), *Printsipy optimalnogo planirovania*, Moscow, Ekonomika.
Zaleski, Eugene (1967), *Planning Reforms in the Soviet Union, 1962–1967*, Chapel Hill, University of North Carolina Press.

6 Changes in Soviet economic policy making in 1989 and 1990

Anders Åslund

The purpose of this paper is to trace changes in the system of economic policy-making in the Soviet Union from the summer of 1989 until October 1990. The emphasis will rest on the role of institutions and their interaction, but important individuals will also be highlighted. Our interest is in attempts at fundamental economic reform at the central level, elaborated by consecutive reform commissions of the USSR Council of Ministers. Agricultural reform will be by-passed as it has been discussed in other fora. Our current concern is to examine the institutions and people who make policy rather than what they decide. Thus, the substance of economic reform is not covered in this discussion.[1]

First, the paper summarizes the system of economic policy-making established during the second half of 1985. Second, it proceeds to analyse the new economic and political setting that emerged from 1986 to 1989. Third, it presents a review of economic expertise. Finally, the main thrust of this chapter paper is a scrutiny of changes in economic policy-making in the Politburo and the Central Committee (CC) of the CPSU, the Government, the legislature, the Presidential Council, and the economic brain trust, as well as the role of Mikhail Gorbachev in 1989 and 1990.

The legacy of institutional changes since 1985[2]

During the last four months of 1985, important personnel changes took place in the Soviet government, allowing it to expand its policy-making powers at the expense of the CC of the CPSU. Upon becoming prime minister, Nikolai Ryzhkov provided the Chancellery of the Council of Ministers with a policy-making apparatus. Dr Petr Katsura was appointed to head a new department devoted to the 'economic mechanism' and Professor Anatolii Miliukov became his deputy. In the spring of 1987, Professor Vadim Kirichenko became the head of a new department on economic policy.[3] All three were professional economists.

Reform issues were to be sorted out in the Commission for the Improvement of Management, Planning and the Economic Mechanism established as an appendage of the Council of Ministers in December

1985. Although this commission was directly subordinated to the Council of Ministers, it was in fact controlled by the State Planning Committee (Gosplan). Its first chairman was First Deputy Prime Minister Nikolai Talyzin, at the time chairman of Gosplan.[4] Gosplan functioned as the secretariat of the commission. However, its scientific section was controlled by reform economists from the academic world. As a result, the commission and its scientific section were locked in a continuous tug of war. Moreover, after the introduction of the reform in 1988, the staff of USSR Gosplan was reduced by one third to a total of 2,000 people.

The main source of external economic advice was supposed to be the Economic Department of the Academy of Sciences and its main economic institutes, subjected to considerable reorganizations in 1985 and 1986. Academician Abel Aganbegian emerged as the country's chief economist, heading the Economic Department of the Academy of Sciences from the summer of 1986. The second politically influential economist was Leonid Abalkin, then a corresponding member of the Academy. He became the director of the Institute of Economics in Moscow in the spring of 1986. The scientific section that was attached to the Talyzin Commission, was headed by Aganbegian with Abalkin as his deputy, as might have been expected.

Two other politically influential academic economists were Academicians Oleg Bogomolov (Director of the Institute of the Economics of the World Socialist System, IEMSS) and Tatiana Zaslavskaia from Novosibirsk. Next in political importance were Nikolai Petrakov and Stanislav Shatalin, both corresponding members of the Academy of Sciences and deputy directors of economic institutes located in Moscow. The rise of reform-minded professors of economics was notable, and the Academy of Sciences was revitalized.

Little happened in the Politburo or the CC. The CC Economic Department, with some 100 professionals, remained static. In January 1987, Nikolai Sliun'kov assumed the post of CC Secretary for Economic Affairs and head of the CC Economic Department. By June 1987, he was elected a voting member of the Politburo. One of Aganbegian's associates from Novosibirsk, Professor Vladimir Mozhin, was appointed first deputy chief of the CC Economic Department. Before Sliun'kov's and Mozhin's appointments to the department, their posts had remained vacant for one year and half a year, respectively. These protracted vacancies, while the Council of Ministers was strengthening its role, indicated that the power of the CC Economic Department was meant to decline.

During the first half of 1987, intense work on economic reform was pursued. At the time, General Secretary Gorbachev participated actively in the work, especially inviting the leading reform economists (Aganbegian, Abalkin, Bogomolov and Zaslavskaia) for long informal discussions. Traditionally, the General Secretary of the CPSU has had a personal aide for economic affairs. Even Konstantin Chernenko had an economic aide (Arkadii Volskii). But Gorbachev transferred Volskii, without appointing any replacement, relying instead on informal advisers on economic affairs. The more operative work was led by Nikolai Sliun'kov, who presented the reform proposals to a key CC conference in June 1987. The Talyzin Commission seems to have played a secondary role, acting on commands from the party in the traditional manner

In effect, the Talyzin Commission, Gosplan, and the central economic bodies were overruled by the scientific section on strategic issues. Aganbegian writes: 'The country's leading economists were engaged in the elaboration of the basic laws and also in the preparation of the materials for the June 1987 Plenum.' However, the central economic bodies recovered their power when it came to application. At the same time, eleven applied decrees were developed and, according to Aganbegian, 'prepared by the apparatus of Gosplan, the Ministry of Finance and Gosbank, in fact, without the involvement of scholars.'[5]

The first reform wave culminated in the CC Plenum in June 1987 and the subsequent adoption of the Law on State Enterprises by the Supreme Soviet. Two other important reform laws were the Law on Individual Labour Activity of November 1986 and the Law on Cooperatives of May 1988. However, when we speak of reform, we essentially refer to the Law on State Enterprises, which went into effect on 1 January 1988.

The new economic situation

It did not take long before the effects of the Law on State Enterprises turned out to be virtually catastrophic. Initially, the public discussion focused on the so-called state orders that were supposed to regulate public purchases from enterprises. In fact, these state orders turned out to be the same as the old commands, so that in this regard little had changed. The blame was put on Talyzin. He was perceived as an ineffective leader of Gosplan who failed both to comprehend reform and to carry out the orders of the prime minister. Reportedly, a direct clash between him and his protector Ryzhkov forced Talyzin's removal.[6]

In February 1988, Yurii Masliukov replaced Talyzin as the chairman of Gosplan. Presumably, Masliukov took over the chairmanship of the reform commission at the same time. He seems to have managed to recover some of the powers that Gosplan lost under Talyzin's inept leadership, which Masliukov himself criticizes.[7] He was well assisted by his deputies Stepan Sitarian (elected an Academician in economics in December 1987) and Leonard Vid, who were responsible for economic reform issues within Gosplan.

Soon enough it became apparent that the major change the reform had brought to the economy was that wages and monetary incomes of the population had gone out of control. In 1988, the average state wages increased by 8.3 per cent – more than twice as fast as planned.[8] In 1989, this process accelerated in spite of several attempts to impede wage increases both by administrative means and punitive taxes on wage rises. The monetary incomes of the population rose by 12.9 per cent.[9] Wages had been more deregulated than prices by the reform, and major financial imbalances had been created.

In principle, prices remained fixed, but enterprises were allowed to adjust their assortments rather freely. As a result, cheap commodities vanished from production, while expensive products, that were convenient for the producers, became increasingly popular with manufacturers. Frequently, the physical volume of production declined, while value targets were attained. All signs of a severe crisis were apparent.[10]

Because of the massive imbalances, most markets were demonetarized and virtually ceased to function. Barter trade, which is far less efficient than a command economy, proliferated. At the same time, the reform legislation explicitly prohibited the central administration from interfering in the work of enterprises. In addition, the apparatus of the central economic bodies and ministries had been reduced by one third, from 1.6 million people in 1986 to 1.1 million in 1988.[11]

The economy was stalemated. The old command economy no longer functioned, while no preconditions for a market economy had been created. Gross macro-imbalances prevailed; the marketization had failed; the old system was collapsing. In Masliukov's words: 'As a result [of the reform] the state management structures practically lost control over many of the most important aspects of economic development, including the regulation of monetary incomes of the population ...'[12]

The political responses to the alarming situation that was arising were not adequate. The 19th Party Conference in June–July 1988 focused on political reform. The financial crisis was properly noticed in the autumn of 1988, as the minister of finance revealed that the budget for 1989 contained a substantial deficit, soon assessed at 100 billion rubles.[13] Gorbachev turned away from economic issues altogether, with the exception of agricultural reforms discussed with little success at a long-awaited CC Plenum in March 1989. Instead, Gorbachev concentrated on domestic politics, and on reform of both the party and the political system, as evidenced by the 19th Party Conference. He also devoted a great deal of his time to foreign policy. Strangely, Gorbachev did not deal with economic reform at all from the summer of 1987 until the autumn of 1989. The alienation between Gorbachev and the economists came into the open at the 19th party conference. One of its highlights was a sharp attack by the new chief reform economist Leonid Abalkin on Soviet economic policy, which Gorbachev personally refuted.[14]

While Gorbachev turned his back to reform issues, Gosplan and other central organs of the USSR Council of Ministers consolidated their control of the reform commission. On 5 January 1989, the Council of Ministers issued a decree on the 'Commission for the Improvement of the Economic Mechanism at the USSR Council of Ministers', as the reform commission of December 1985 was renamed. Masliukov also chaired the new commission, with Sitarian as his deputy. Out of twenty-eight members of the renewed commission, no less than four were Gosplan functionaries and an additional fourteen worked for the USSR Council of Ministers. Gosplan provided the secretariat for both the Commission and its scientific section (still headed by Aganbegian).[15] An ensuing decree of 31 March 1989 clarified that the Commission was to have very limited rights,[16] leaving most responsibilities to the ordinary line organization. Gosplan and the central organs of the Council of Ministers had reinforced their already strong control over reform endeavours.

By 1989, the reform had turned out to be an extraordinary economic failure. Popular pressure for economic improvements was rising, fomented by ever-worsening shortages and new political liberties. At the same time, the conservative forces of the government apparatus had organised their opposition. A decisive push for radicalized economic reform was badly needed. In the summer of 1989, after the first session of the Congress of People's Deputies, Gorbachev finally signalled his intention to do something about economic reform again.

The development of economic expertise[17]

Surprisingly few institutional changes occurred within the field of economic science after the first year of perestroika. The predominance of the Academy of Sciences and Moscow continued. A few new institutes were established. Academician Tatiana Zaslavskaia became the director of the new Center of the Study of the Public Opinion in Moscow, and Professor Natalia M. Rimashevskaia of the new Institute of Socio-economic Problems of the Population, formed by parts of the Institute of Economics and TsEMI (the Central Economic-Mathematical Institute) of the Academy of Sciences. Towards the end of 1989, the Institute of the Market was being conceived out of parts of TsEMI, under the leadership of the deputy director of TsEMI Nikolai Petrakov. The system of huge, antiquated hierarchical institutes persisted.

All leading economists, as well as senior economic officials, started travelling abroad extensively, widening their horizons. Exchanges with foreign economists developed on a large scale. Gradually, the vestiges of ideology withered, and few inhibitions survived. Domestic pluralism is impressive and economists who advance these days tend to be among the most solid or eloquent. Still, the basic competence remains low and little has been done to change it. There are many economic researchers but little formal economics in the USSR. Few Soviet students or young researchers go abroad to study economics. As Academician Stanislav Shatalin has stated: 'What worries me? First of all the extremely low level of our economic science and the economic education in general.'[18]

Most top economists have become politicians and adjust their statements to what appears to be politically convenient. Many have become too preoccupied with political tactics after at long last having gained their freedom of expression. As time is short and the discussions heated, many top economists indulge more in economic journalism than research. Soviet economics need a reform. Outside Moscow, particularly in the Russian and Ukrainian provinces, Marxist-Leninist exegesis persists under the label of political economy. In many cases, reform-minded Soviet economic journalists seem to understand a market economy better than Soviet professors of economics.

At the top of the professional pyramid, the most significant change is that Abalkin has replaced Aganbegian as the chief economist, and that Shatalin and Petrakov have advanced. Reform economists have become divided politically between those who want to influence the government from within and those who prefer to stand in opposition. Political divisions between liberals and social democrats have emerged as well.[19] All over, new independent economists have emerged.

After the CC had adopted the first reform programme at its Plenum in June 1987, it was presented at a press conference by Academician Abel Aganbegian, although he was not a member of the CC.[20] This event highlighted Aganbegian's standing as Gorbachev's chief economic adviser – an informal position that he was soon to lose. In June 1988, at the 19th Party Conference, it was Academician Leonid Abalkin who spoke as the top economist, and it was not Aganbegian but Abalkin who became chairman of the government's Reform Commission in July 1989. At about the same time, Aganbegian became the rector of the Economic Academy of the Council of Ministers, the foremost management training institution in the USSR. He soon resigned as head of the Economic Department of the Academy of Sciences, and was replaced by Academician Stanislav Shatalin who later joined Gorbachev's Presidential Council. In January 1990, Nikolai Petrakov was appointed Gorbachev's personal economic aide. Aganbegian did not lose all that much, but was no longer the top economist.

There were many reasons for Aganbegian's demotion. For long, he had made a tired impression. He had simply been in the political firing line for a very long time and seemed to prefer a less exposed position. He is widely and correctly blamed for Gorbachev's first and unfortunate economic slogan *uskorenie* (acceleration).[21] In a combative article, Aganbegian does not refute this charge, but he denies many other accusations. He attacks the government for deficient work routines, involving professional economic expertise only at the stage of elaboration of key strategies. Typical decisions made without economic consultations were the campaign against alcohol and the reduction of imports of consumer goods in 1987. Notably, Ryzhkov himself worked through the eleven applied reform decrees of July 1987 without seeking advice from any economist outside his own apparatus. Aganbegian also points out that an article he wrote for *Pravda* in July 1988 was not published until February 1989, so how could he make his voice heard?[22] However, his successor as head of the Economic Department of the Academy of Sciences – Stanislav Shatalin – has stated that he thinks it was a great neglect by the Economic Department not to elaborate its own alternative programme for radical reform, clearly blaming Aganbegian.[23]

Aganbegian seems to have been particularly damaged by a political incident. In December 1987, he spoke incautiously in London and Paris about a commission concerned with a possible change of the status of the disputed province of Nagorny Karabakh. This news item was broadcast back to the USSR. Two months later, the conflict of Nagorny Karabakh flared up and Aganbegian was partly blamed. Unlike most leading economists, he has not even been a candidate in the many recent political elections.

In the autumn of 1990, Aganbegian appeared to make a political comeback as the President's coordinator of economic reform. In fact, he seems to have been catapulted into this position by the default of others. Abalkin was too discredited as representative of the government, Bogomolov and Zaslavskaia had turned in their party cards, Shatalin and Petrakov were committed to the 500-day programme. Gorbachev could throw Aganbegian into the ring because he had stayed rather passive on the sidelines and remained sufficiently obedient.

Aganbegian has written extensively. The views he expresses are strongly restricted by his official positions. Therefore, he does not stand out as very controversial – nor particularly concrete – and it is often unclear if he pronounces his own views. Mostly, he appears a sensible mainstream market-oriented reform economist.[24] However, on behalf of the Economic Department of the Academy of Sciences, he has strangely argued in favour of a reform of retail prices *after* the stabilization of the market.[25] His old institute in Novosibirsk has lost a lot of its previous high profile since Aleksandr G. Granberg took over. In Moscow, Aganbegian's closest collaborator has been Viktor D. Belkin.

Leonid I. Abalkin has risen fast under perestroika as the natural leader he is. There are many positive things to say about Abalkin. He is extremely hard-working, a prolific speaker and writer. Few people have such a sense of duty and destiny, seemingly carrying the fate of the Russian people on his back. A characteristic statement of his is: 'But somebody must work. Somebody must save the country. There is still a chance to pull it out of the crisis.'[26] Abalkin tends to work for consensus, often devoting a long time to convince people. He displays the rare habit of not telling lies, which frequently gets him into tedious elaborations to avoid political embarrassment. Until 1990, Abalkin's behaviour had earned him few enemies and much respect, rendering self-evident his selections for top jobs.

Criticism against Abalkin centred on the fact that he is very much a political economist. On the other hand, this was why he realized the importance of pluralism of ownership early. He has been one of the main advocates of the Swedish model for the USSR, implying that no system more socialist than the Swedish one is likely to work.[27] For Abalkin, the best socialism is clearly social democracy. Thus, Abalkin has favoured far-reaching marketization and denationalization, though he had avoided the term 'private property'.

Abalkin has become increasingly conservative since he joined the government, though he has never sounded radical. At an early stage, he realised how very poor the state of the Soviet economy was and that the crisis had deepened, but he has a strong sense of loyalty. Strangely, Abalkin was long in favour of reform starting in industry and not in agriculture. He has been sceptical of free economic zones and against currency reform or the introduction of a parallel currency. On nationality issues, he has provoked the anger of the Balts for defending the preeminence of Moscow. Few people have had so many speeches, interviews and articles published in the last two years as has Abalkin.[28]

Abalkin has undertaken a curious turnabout as deputy prime minister. During the first five months he stood out as a leading reform economist. In December 1989, he concluded an uneasy compromise with Prime Minister Ryzhkov, moderating his urge for reform. After a new abortive attempt at forming a more radical reform programme in early 1990, Abalkin gradually passed over to the more conservative camp led by Ryzhkov. By September, Abalkin had completed his transition and fully supported Ryzhkov against the main stream of radical reformers.

Abalkin has retained his directorship of the Institute of Economics which serves as his think-tank. His immediate deputy as the institute, Boris Z. Milner, has a major share of responsibility for organizational schemes for the government apparatus.[29] Abalkin's point man on his favourite issue – ownership – is Lev V. Nikiforov, also at that institute.[30]

Still, the formerly conservative Institute of Economics has not recovered fully under Abalkin and it is considered somewhat mediocre. Moreover, it is working more as a secretariat for Abalkin than as a research institute.

Academician Oleg Bogomolov, long acted as an official Soviet spokesman on relations with other socialist countries. He was an Andropov protégé with a background in the CC apparatus. Throughout the Brezhnev period, Bogomolov stood out as a protector of heretic researchers in various social sciences and his institute has been the principal employer of interesting intellectuals during perestroika. Anatolii Butenko, Ievgenii Ambartsumov, Aleksandr Tsipko and others have critically scrutinized the ideology.[31] Professor Gennadii Lisichkin has long been an outstanding proponent of market economy.[32] Professor Viacheslav Dashishev advocated German unification in a paper from April 1989.[33] Otto R. Lacis, first deputy editor of the journal *Kommunist*, was also shielded by Bogomolov. Besides, this institute possessed the best Soviet expertise on other socialist countries and their economic systems, particularly Professor Ruben N. Evstigneev.

After many years of caution, Bogomolov started showing his true colours in public in 1987.[34] He distanced himself from the party apparatus and joined the fast radicalization of his institute, which became possibly the most radical institute and a centre of unofficial movements. Drawing on his knowledge of the experiences of reform in China, Hungary and Poland, Bogomolov advocated a free market economy and massive privatization.[37] He favours initial reform in agriculture, free economic zones, the introduction of a parallel hard currency and general distribution of shares.

On all these points, Bogomolov opposes Abalkin's ideas. In the election to the Congress of People's Deputies in the spring of 1989, Bogomolov won a popular vote against a reformist party secretary in a district of Moscow, thanks to the support of informal organizations and a coalition with Boris Eltsin. Abalkin supported Bogomolov's opponent. Thus, Bogomolov has opted for the political opposition against the government in the Congress, leaving him outside much of the committee work in which he was previously involved.

Academician Tat'iana Zaslavskaia is really a sociologist and she is fully occupied as the head of the most important Soviet center of opinion polls. She has probably never considered herself an economist and her emergence as one of the top economic advisers is evidence of the shortage of professional economists. Since others have come to the fore, she has apparently withdrawn voluntarily from work on the economic reform. In addition, poor health has limited her activities.

Instead, Academician Stanislav Shatalin has surged forward in importance. He is one of the most highly respected Soviet economists and a long-standing proponent of the market. He comes from TsEMI. After several years at the Institute for Systems Analysis (whose significance declined with the political demotion of its director, Dzhermen Gvishiani), he became deputy director of the new Institute of Economic Forecasting and Scientific and Technical Progress, which was formed in 1985 on the basis of one quarter of TsEMI.[36] Shatalin tends to be controversial in his statements. In 1986, he came out in favour of price and wage reforms as well as currency reform, for which he was severely criticized.[37] Battered, he returned two years later to this theme, retracting his previous views and stating that the retail prices should under no circumstances be touched.[38] In the spring of 1990, he emphatically advocated private ownership on a large scale.[39] Shatalin's new arguments did not make economic sense and he appeared to act as a professional giving in to populist pressures.

In December 1987, Shatalin was elected an Academician (together with Abalkin and Sitarian), and in the autumn of 1989, he succeeded Aganbegian as head of the Economic Department of the Academy of Sciences. In the spring of 1990 he gave large number of interviews, urging the need for a market economy and private ownership, but castigating those wanted to move more rapidly or choose a more radical route towards a liberal economy. In particular, Shatalin argued strongly again a Polish type of transition.[40]

Another academic reform economist who has advanced is Nikolai Petrakov, a corresponding member of the Academy of Sciences. For a long time the top Soviet specialist on finance, pricing and money, his advice was badly needed when the financial crisis grew acute. Furthermore, he has a history of ardent struggle for pro-market ideas since the 1960s, and he has concentrated on systemic issues.[41] Like Bogomolov, he has argued for the introduction of a parallel hard currency.[42] As deputy director of TsEMI, he has had a good group of knowledgeable collaborators, such as Professors Evgenii Iasin,[43] Dmitrii L'vov,[44] Boris Rakitskii,[45] Iurii Borozdin,[45] Vilen Perlamutrov and Aleksandr Bim.[47] The director of TsEMI, Valerii M. Makarov, corresponding member of the Academy of Sciences, has kept a low public profile.

In effect, a trio of leading economists – Leonid Abalkin, Stanislav Shatalin and Nikolai Petrakov – emerged at the top of the federal structure. All three profess rather similar views, but their public posture is very different. Abalkin appears as the loyal servant of the government, Petrakov as its assiduous critic, while Shatalin has uneasily criticized both the government and its radical critics, though in August 1990 he joined forces fully with Petrakov. Clearly, Abalkin is more of a politician than the others, while Petrakov and Shatalin have more credibility among radical reform economists. In terms of views, Petrakov and Bogomolov stand close to each other, but in 1990 they opted for different political strategies.

With glasnost and democratic elections, a number of economists have risen to prominence because of their strongly critical views and staunch advocacy of market economy and private ownership. Pavel G. Bunich, corresponding member of the Academy of Sciences, is a splendid orator and a prolific writer.[48] He enjoys great popularity, but for personal reasons is not among the top economists. Bunich seems to be a politician with considerable potential.

Professor Gavriil Kh. Popov of Moscow University attracted a lot of attention for his many imaginative publications on reform at the outset of perestroika.[49] In the spring of 1988, he became editor-in-chief of the main economic journal, *Voprosy ekonomiki*, which he transformed into an interesting reformist publication. In 1990, Popov became one of the country's leading democratic politicians as mayor of Moscow. Two other reformist professors of economics at Moscow University who have surfaced politically are Gevork A. Egiazarian and Aleksei M. Emilianov.

Professor Nicolai P. Shmelev of the USA and Canada Institute has played an outstanding role in the promotion of glasnost. As no one else, he has exposed the economic crisis and the uselessness of the command system.[50] Shmelev's article in June 1987 set the stage for the CC Plenum on economic reform. It aroused such a reaction that Gorbachev felt forced to come out in his support.[51] The USA and Canada Institute as well as the Institute of the World Economy and International Relations (IMEMO) primarily specialize in foreign policy, but recently they have started playing an important role in bringing home economic experiences from the West. The new director of IMEMO, Vladlen A. Martynov, has gained prominence in reform work of late.

Curiously, Gosplan's Economic Research Institute has also turned radical. In the spring of 1987, Professor Vladimir Kostakov was elected its director by the staff, against the wishes of Gosplan's leadership. He has dealt with the spectre of unemployment. His deputy, Gannadii N. Zoteev, is an economist of broad competence, who specializes in long-term forecasting. Professor Tat'iana Koriagina has emerged as the main expert on the underground economy.[52]

Other radical economists who have gained political prominence are Academician Vladimir Tikhonov of the Economic Academy and Professor Ruslan I. Khasbulatov of the Plekhanov Institute of Economics in Moscow.[53]

However, glasnost has also allowed a number of reactionary economists to rise. Mikhail Antonov attacks economic progress as such in Russophile journals. Aleksei A. Sergeev of the Higher School of the trade unions has emerged as a leading dogmatist.[54] Even the extreme anti-semitic organization Pamiat' heralds an economist, Mikhail Lemeshev of TsEMI.

A new occurrence is the appearance of purely liberal economists with no socialist pretensions whatsoever. On 1 March 1990, *Izvestiia* published a letter by Dr Larissa Piiasheva in which she states: 'According to my conviction, I am a consistent liberal by principle in the European sense and a conservative in the American [sense].'[55] Other prominent liberals are the economic journalist Vasilii Seliunin, Dr Grigorii I. Khanin of Novosibirk and Boris Pinsker. In a multitude of articles, Seliunin and Khanin have pioneered investigations into the poor state of the Soviet economy and the effects of the malfunctioning of the system.[56]

A large number of Soviet economists have become well-known political figures, winning one political office after the other. It is as though they need to acquire political power before they can achieve much. Still, for the future the dismal level of competence even of the top economists is worriesome.

Transformation of the economic policy-making institutions

In 1989 and 1990, the institutions responsible for making economic policy were completely revamped. Most changes were derived from the decisions of the 19th Party Conference in June–July 1988. Its resolutions 'On the democratization of Soviet society and reform of the political system' and 'On the struggle with bureaucracy', contained stipulations of considerable importance.[57] First, the role of the party apparatus was to be checked. Large CC Commissions were to be set up, in fact replacing the CC Secretariat and dissipating its powers; the CC apparatus was sharply reduced and demarcation of the functions of party and state organs further reduced the influence of the CPSU. Second, the Soviet legislature was strengthened through the establishment of an elected Congress of People's Deputies, which in turn elected a Supreme Soviet as a standing legislative, administrative and monitoring body. Third, implicitly the government was to lose powers through the monitoring by Soviets at all levels, and its staff was to be trimmed. Fourth, the groundwork was laid for a strong presidency, or initially chairmanship of the Supreme Soviet, a move obviously intended to increase Gorbachev's powers.

The Party Conference in 1988 seemed astoundingly unaware of the approaching economic havoc. Its main resolution read: 'The country's slide toward economic and sociopolitical crisis has been halted.'[58] Apparently, the Soviet leadership thought it had time to concentrate on political reform and could down-grade economic concerns, but economic priorities changed. The main resolution stated: 'The most important task in the socioeconomic sphere is to accelerate the solution of the urgent problems of the people's prosperity.'[59] This was the time when engineering and heavy industry lost their long-standing top priority.

Both in September 1988 and September 1989, Gorbachev managed to undertake considerable personnel changes in the Politburo and the CC Secretariat. Several of the most conservative communists were retired. However, remarkably little happened to appointments that had a bearing on economic reform. Prime Minister Ryzhkov and CC Secretary Sliun'kov retained their posts, and Gosplan Chairman Masliukov was elevated to a voting member of the Politburo in September 1989 – an unprecedented event. Moreover, the reactionary communist Egor Ligachev became CC Secretary for agriculture and chairman of the new CC Commission on Agrarian Policy in September 1988. Thus, moderate or hesitant reformers maintained their grip on economic reform issues in the party.

The power of the CPSU was effectively undermined by the decisions of the 19th Party Conference. A CC Commission on Socioeconomic Policy was established in September 1988, with Nikolai Sliun'kov as its chairman. These commissions have only met about once each quarter and their meetings appear to have been of a rather formal nature. Politburo meetings have become ever more infrequent and limited in scope. The CC Secretariat ceased to function altogether.[60]

In a parallel development, the number of CC Departments was reduced from twenty to nine, and all CC departments responsible for particular industries, apart from the defence industry and agriculture, were abolished. No less than eleven branch departments disappeared.[61] Many were headed by Ligachev protégés, who were transferred to the provinces. Primarily departments in the economic sphere were abolished, and the CC apparatus lost more power on economic matters than in any other field. A number of special Politburo commissions were established, but apparently none for economic matters.

The CC Socioeconomic Department was assigned a new head, Vladimir Shimko, an engineer who had previously headed a ministry in the military-industrial complex. However, he did not stay for many months and was effectively replaced by his first deputy, Professor Vladimir Mozhin. Nikolai Sliun'kov remained at the helm as CC Secretary for economic affairs, and Anatolii Miliukov became deputy head of the CC Socioeconomic Department and the CC troubleshooter on economic reform issues. However, CC jobs no longer looked like a good career track for aspiring professions.

Thus, the powers of the CPSU were weakened. The CC staff was probably slightly more reformist than the staff at the Council of Ministers, but they were put on a backburner. Although the power of the CC apparatus declined in general, it lost most substance in the economic area. One reason was that economic matters comprised the most typical business of the government, but it was equally apparent that the powers of Prime Minister Ryzhkov and Gosplan's Chairman Masliukov grew at the expense of CC Secretary Sliun'kov. An extensive interview with Sliun'kov before the 28th Party Congress clarified that he had not really been involved in the work on reform during the last year.[62] The contrast with agrarian issues is striking. There Egor Ligachev held his own and maintained CC control over policy-making.

Elections to the new Congress of People's Deputies were held in the spring of 1989, and the Congress convened on 25 May 1989. Its first session changed the Soviet political landscape. An exciting fortnight of televized democratic debate on all diverse issues brought about a breakthrough for open discussion. Reform economists were prominent among the deputies and they made frequent public appearances. Among the leading economists who became deputies were Leonid Abalkin, Oleg Bogomolov, Tat'iana Zaslavskaia, Nikolai Petrakov, Pavel Bunich, Gavriil Popov, Vladimir Tikhonov, Gennadii Lisichkin, Nikolai Shmelev, Aleksei Emelianov (all from Moscow), Rein Otsason from Estonia and Edvardas Vilkas from Lithuania. The Congress of People's Deputies and the Supreme Soviet became important popular tribunes. Gradually, their members grew more radical and independent. Characteristically, Prime Minister Ryzhkov had his economic programme approved by the Congress in December 1989, but was told to refine it by the Supreme Soviet in June 1990.

A score of committees of the Supreme Soviet were established. Several dealt with economic issues (for instance, finance and budget as well as regional economics). One committee dealt specifically with economic reform. It was chaired by a reformist, V.M. Vologzhin, who was the director general of enterprise in L'vov which had been the first to set up a joint stock company.[63] However, these committees were not particularly effective. Usually only a few members of a committee possessed professional knowledge of their issues, and the staff was minimal. Because alternative proposals were rarely at hand, the committees would do little but amend or block government proposals.[64]

On the government side, the central economic organs held their own. Gosplan had marked its strong position through the reconstitution of the reform commission in early 1989 and the promotion of Masliukov to voting membership of the still all-powerful Politburo in September 1989. At the confirmations of ministers in the summer of 1989, the USSR Supreme Soviet blocked several of Ryzhkov's nominations. The new appointees were probably more qualified. Academic merits were highly rated. Notably, Stepan Sitarian became deputy prime minister and chairman of the State Foreign Economic Commission, Viacheslav Senchagov (deputy minister of finance) became chairman of the State Price Committee, Valentin Pavlov (chairman of the State Price Committee) minister of finance, and Vadim Kirichenko was appointed chairman of Goskomstat (the State Committee on Statistics). All these men were highly qualified economists but they had advanced within Gosplan or the Ministry of Finance. On the one hand, they possessed the economic competence to understand reform and kept pace with the radicalization in society. On the other, by interest they were closely attached to the central economic organs and therefore tended to impede reform. Their promotions show how the economists advanced at the expense of engineers in the central economic bodies in the wake of economic reform.[65]

In spite of the aggravated economic crisis, Prime Minister Ryzhkov emerged with more strength as the leading politician beside Gorbachev. His memorable visit to earthquake–ridden Armenia in December 1988 earned him substantial popularity. Remarkably, at a CC meeting on 18 July 1989, Ryzhkov criticized Gorbachev all but by name, complaining that the General Secretary did not devote enough of his time to the party.[66] Never before had such a clear rift between Gorbachev and Ryzhkov surfaced in public. One reason for Ryzhkov's manifestation of dissatisfaction might have been a major political decision made just before the event.

On 5 July 1989, a new State Commission of the USSR Council of Ministers on Economic Reform was formed by a decree from the Council of Ministers,[67] replacing the Masliukov Commission. It differed from its predecessor in several important regards. First, its chairman was not Masliukov but the foremost reform economist, Academician Leonid Abalkin, who was appointed deputy prime minister for this purpose. Second, its status was much higher, because it was a permanent body of the Council of Ministers. Third, it was to have an independent apparatus. Fourth, its tasks were broad, and it was given substantial powers. For instance, it was to report directly to the Council of Ministers, and it could give orders to other central economic organs.

Finally, the composition of this Commission was completely different from the previous reform commission. It was highly professional. Of twenty-seven members, only one represented Gosplan (Sitarian). As many as nine were academic economists, and all of these were outspoken reformers.[68] Of the others, fourteen represented bodies belonging to the Council of Ministers, but not all headed their bodies. It was plain that a selection had been made of officials who were also competent economists.[69] Two progressive enterprise directors were included, but also a reactionary secretary of the Central Council of Trade Unions, K. Turysov, who had also been a member of the previous reform commission.

Still, an ominous feature was that its nascent apparatus was based on the department on the Economic Mechanism at the Council of Ministers, headed by Petr Katsura, who became first deputy chairman of the Reform Commission, and his immediate subordinates S.V. Assekritov and A.V. Orlov became deputy chairmen of the Abalkin commission together with Sitarian.[70] Katsura and his group had increasingly shown evidence of conservative leanings. Abalkin had little opportunity to choose his own staff and his subordinates, who had worked for long for Rhyzhkov, were conditioned by the prime minister's poor understanding of economic reform. Lastly, officials of the Council of Ministers formed the majority also of the new Reform Commission.[71]

The CC had been represented on the Masliukov Commission (by Anatolii Miliukov), but now the party was excluded, as it was supposed to be separated from the government. Similarly, leading economists who had become deputies of the Congress of People's Deputies were not included in the Reform Commission.[72] In any case, the establishment of the new Reform Commission was a great step forward for the academic reform economists. The main loser was Gosplan, but also Ryzhkov and the CC.

Despite the open dispute between Gorbachev and Abalkin at the 19th Party Conference a year earlier, the new initiative obviously came from Gorbachev. At the same time, it was rumoured Gorbachev had offered Oleg Bogomolov the chairmanship of Gosplan and Nikolai Petrakov the chairmanship of the State Price Committee, but both reportedly turned down his offer.[73] In September 1989 (after his holidays), Gorbachev gathered leading reform economists and told them to work out a comprehensive reform proposal as rapidly as possible. The result, promptly published in early October, was the first comprehensive proposal to switch to a market economy, marking a radical departure from all former documents. This new proposal clearly expressed the ideas cherished by Abalkin, including an unambiguous denunciation of central planning in favour of the market, an advocacy of pluralism in ownership, and a radical shift in economic system. It envisaged a stepwise introduction of a market economy from 1991.[74]

Gorbachev underlined his involvement in this reform programme by chairing no less than three publicly reported meetings: 23 October, 1 November, and 13–15 November.[75] At the big economic conference with 1,400 participants from 13 to 15 November, CC Secretary Sliun'kov delivered both the opening and the concluding speech, although Ryzhkov was also present.[76] However, this conference backfired. To his surprise, Abalkin found a strong pressure from the conservative forces.[77] Ed Hewett reported: 'it was shocking to sit through speeches on the need for better planning, and strictly controlled markets, without any obvious sign of understanding by the majority in the auditorium that this neo-conservative approach to the economy has no more hope of working now than it did under Brezhnev.'[78] This conference marked the political rise of substandard dogmatic communist economists. One outstanding example was Professor Aleksei A. Sergeev, who was backed by the reactionary official trade unions.

As a follow-up, the second session of the Congress of People's Deputies in December 1989 was expected to receive a more specific reform programme. Instead, Prime Minister Ryzhkov unveiled a completely different proposal. The transition to a market economy was postponed until 1993. In the meantime (1990–92), a stabilization was to be undertaken through recentralization.[79]

This amounted to a total rebuttal of Abalkin's programme. It is worth noting that it had been promoted by Abalkin, with support from Gorbachev and Sliun'kov, while Ryzhkov had not been visibly involved in the process. At the time when Abalkin's programme was published, Ryzhkov delivered a major speech on the same topic to the Supreme Soviet. He did not contradict Abalkin directly, but rather ignored the Abalkin Commission and its programme, Ryzhkov's speech was centred on five draft laws dealing with property, land, the socialist enterprise, taxation and leasehold.[80] Gorbachev kept an uncharacteristically low profile during the December 1989 session of the Congress of People's Deputies. Abalkin's statements were somewhat ambiguous[81] and at a press conference Abalkin evaded the question of whether he supported the Ryzhkov programme.

The evidence suggests that Ryzhkov was neither involved with nor supportive of the Abalkin Commission. Ryzhkov's own programme had been worked out by Gosplan, though certain rather cosmetic compromises had been made with the Abalkin programme. The discussion at the Congress left no doubt that First Deputy Prime Ministers Iurii Masliukov and Lev Voronin, who were not members of the Abalkin Commission, stood on Ryzhkov's side.[82] Later on, Masliukov emphatically assumed the responsibility for the Ryzhkov programme, leaving little doubt that he was a prime mover behind it.[83]

The Abalkin Commission had suffered a serious setback and was effectively defeated by the alliance of Ryzhkov and Gosplan, backed by other central economic bodies of the government. Abalkin did not come out in open opposition, thus becoming widely identified with the Ryzhkov-

Masliukov programme. Liberal members of his Commission became increasingly dissatisfied because of the lack of radicalism, influence and action. Initially, its most radical member, Tat'iana Koriagina, stated that Abalkin had made clear that 'there can be no limitations on the expression of individual viewpoints, no matter how disturbing they may be. There also can be no limitations as far as our contacts with the mass media are concerned.'[84] But at the beginning of 1990, Koriagina was no longer called to the meetings of the Commission after she had criticized Ryzhkov in the press.

In early January 1990, Gorbachev appointed Nikolai Petrakov, one of the most prominent Soviet advocates of a market economy, as his personal aide for economic affairs. By selecting Petrakov, Gorbachev distanced himself from Ryzhkov's programme. At the beginning of 1990, Gorbachev spent considerable time with Petrakov and other reform economists discussing how to radicalize the economic reform.[85]

On 15 March 1989, Gorbachev was elected president. In his first programmatic speech to the Presidential Council on 27 March, he concentrated on 'the elaboration of concrete measures to radicalize economic reform'. He advocated 'the formation of a normal full-blooded market'.[86] It looked as if at long last Gorbachev could disregard the predominantly conservative Politburo and carry out his own programme.[87]

The new Presidential Council was created to replace the Politburo as the major policy-making body. However, its composition, presumably reflecting Gorbachev's own choice, attracted considerable criticism. Academician Stanislav Shatalin was the Council's single reform economist, while it included Ryzhkov and Masliukov as well as reactionary enemies of economic reform such as the Russophile writer Valentin Rasputin and one of the co-chairmen of United Workers' Front of Russia, Veniamin Iarin.[88] It did not display a reformist majority, but rather suggested that Eltsin was right in criticizing Gorbachev for preferring half-measures and compromises.[89] Did Gorbachev fail to grasp the essence of economic reform? His close adviser Shatalin saw it as follows:

I understand that even [Gorbachev and Ryzhkov], who started perestroika, are not able to, if you want, do not have the biological facilities to change their philosophy instantly, to move from the existing way of thinking of the new realities. As with everyone, they have been fed for decades with the ideas of a strict plan and a technocratic approach to the solution of economic question.[90]

At the first session of the Presidential Council, numerous reform economists, such as Academicians Aganbegian and Bogomolov, were invited to speak, and they all criticized the government programme of December 1989. At the second session of the Presidential Council in April

1990, none of these critical outsiders had been invited, although the topic was economic reform. Moreover, Abalkin had been sent away to Cuba on an ordinary bilateral mission, which could have been handled by any one of the other deputy prime ministers. The only attendee who criticized the government's policy at the time was Petrakov, while Shatalin sat quiet.[91] The president and the Presidential Council had missed their chances to radicalize economic reform. The Presidential Council appeared barely more reformist than the Politburo. The new institutional setting had failed to achieve the aim Gorbachev had set for it, and a new reform plan had fallen flat even before it reached the public eye.

In a parallel effort, a new government commission on 'the acceleration of the transition of a planned market economy' was formed through a decree issued by the Council of Ministers on 11 March 1990.[92] Both its tasks and its composition clarify that this commission superseded the Abalkin Commission, though without replacing it. Reminiscent of the former Masliukov Commission in composition, it was chaired by Ryzhkov himself, with Masliukov and Abalkin as his deputies. Of its twenty members, as many as ten simultaneously belonged to the Presidium of the Council of Ministers. Among the top economists, only Shatalin and Aganbegian were included. Abalkin's subordination was further emphasized by the appointment of Abalkin as head of the new Commission's working group. This Commission was assigned the unrealistic task of completing a full proposal on the transition to 'a planned market economy' as well as twenty-seven draft laws and decrees by 1 May 1990.

Needless to say, this deadline could not be met though several draft laws emerged in the spring, and the main programme was presented by Ryzhkov to the USSR Supreme Soviet on 24 May. From the very outset, Masliukov seems to have taken on the actual chairmanship of the commission and Abalkin reported to him.[93] Masliukov defined his task as follows: 'Being deeply convinced that the state can in no way rely on the automatic functioning of the spontaneous market, I was the initiator and direct leader of the work on and assembling of the documents presented to the third session of the USSR Supreme Soviet' [in May and June 1990].[94]

On 13 June 1990, the Supreme Soviet adopted a decree 'On the concept of transition to a regulated market economy in the USSR',[95] ordering the USSR Council of Ministers to prepare a new programme by 1 September 1990. For this purpose, the Council of Ministers established a new special commission headed by Masliukov,[96] but in fact Ryzhkov himself took charge of this work.

Still, after one year of intense squabbles, Masliukov had formally taken over the supreme reform commission. Again, the reform economists had been outwitted by Gosplan and the apparatus of the central economic bodies of the Council of Ministers. But, Abalkin had constructed an apparatus with the sole task of promoting reform, and his Commission was not disbanded. During the past year, Abalkin has lost a lot of his public esteem, since he has seemed responsible for government policies. However, both in December 1989 and May 1990, it was Ryzhkov who was perceived by the public as the main culprit.

Surrealistically, Ryzhkov, Masliukov and Voronin – three hard-working engineers of the old communist school – seemed to have come out on top, regardless of a rapidly worsening economic crisis and conspicuous popular contempt for the government. However, in the summer of 1990 the whole political stage changed.

The 28th Party Congress of the CPSU, 2–12 July 1990, marked the end of most of the CPSU's powers. In effect, the powers of the Politburo were transferred to the Presidential Council. Old stalwarts of the party, such as Ligachev, Zaikov and Sliun'kov were simply pensioned off. Gorbachev brought some of his favourites from the CC apparatus to the new presidential apparatus. Thus, Nikolai Petrakov became the personal economic aide of the president rather than of the General Secretary of the CPSU, even though Gorbachev held both positions. A new socioeconomic department of thirty-five posts was formed within the presidential apparatus. It was headed by Anatolii Miliukov, who took along about ten of his collaborators from the CC apparatus.

However, the role of the presidency and its apparatus remained spurious. By design, it was a consultative body, but its members could be subdivided into three categories – full-time aides of the present, leading representatives of the government and outsiders. Clearly, this body must be transformed in either direction, but for long it was kept in suspense. Typically, Stanislav Shatalin stated in august 1990: 'Even I, myself a member of the Presidential Council, don't know: what am I? What am I responsible for? What share of responsibility do I take upon myself? There is clarity only for one person – the President... May I ask, for instance, the Minister of Finance to do something or do I have a right to tell him that he must do it? Mistrust and petty offences arise.'[97] The prime minister tried to exploit this ambiguity to his own advantage, stating: 'The Presidential Council must remain a council, [and] not [become] an administrative body.'[98]

In effect, the CPSU was no longer a policy-maker at a central level. The Council of Ministers was the dominant policy-maker, but it had lost its responsibility for final coordination to the Presidential Council. The president, in turn, exploited the ambiguity he had created to lend new legal authority to presidential decrees. However, most of the decrees were prepared by the Council of Ministers, while only Shatalin, Petrakov and possibly Miliukov could argue with prominent members of the Council of Ministers. Incredible as it may sound, Gorbachev had annihilated the central policy-making system without constructing any viable alternative, at the same time as the economic crisis was moving towards its peak. The major policy instrument left was presidential decrees that were supposed to be speedily produced and issued.

A broad popular opinion had long realized that the government was not capable of forming a viable economic policy. The final confidence in Ryzhkov was broken in May 1990. A parallel development was the questioning of the policy-making powers of the centre as such. These tendencies acquired new political weight as Boris El'tsin was elected chairman of the Supreme Soviet of the RSFSR at the end of May 1990. In the middle of June, Mikhail Bocharov presented a 500-day programme for transition to a market economy in the RSFSR Supreme soviet as a candidate for the premiership of the RSFSR.[99] Bocharov lost. But even so the 500-day programme became the programme of El'tsin's administration.

In fact, the 500-day programme had been written in February 1990 as a 400-day programme of a 'Conception of an accelerated transition of the economy of the USSR to a market economy' by the three young economists Grigorii Iavlinskii, Aleksei Mikhailov (Goskomtsen's research institute) and Mikhail Zadornov (Institute of Economics).[100] Iavlinskii had led the work, while employed at Abalkin's Reform Commission, and this programme contained ideas that had been considered but refuted by the Soviet leadership in April. In the summer of 1990, it made its breakthrough as a basis of various reform plans.

At the end of July, Gorbachev seemed to make peace with Eltsin and the radical marketeers. Gorbachev and Eltsin agreed to set up a common 'working group for the preparation of a conception of a union programme of transition to a market economy as a basis of a union treaty'.[101] This working group chaired by Stanislav Shatalin was composed of four different groups of economists. Shatalin and Petrakov were to represent the President; Abalkin, Iasin and Sergei Aleksashenko the Prime Minister. Iavlinskii, Mikhailov, Zadornov and Boris Fedorov (RSFSR Minister of finance) were Russian representatives, while the rest came from the Academy of Sciences (L.M. Grigor'ev, V.A. Martynov, V.M. Mashchits, A.P. Vavilov). Nikolai Shmelev was appointed to the group but did not attend because of travelling abroad, and Abalkin refused to participate for political reasons.[102] The group worked intensely for the whole of August and presented a program of 239 printed pages plus 21 draft laws.[103] This is called the Shatalin Group Programme.

About half the members of the Shatalin group were younger than forty. They represented a new generation that had been brought to the fore by Eltsin. Grigorii Iavlinskii (thirty-eight) and Boris Fedorov (thirty-two) were their leaders. All of them came from Moscow, but they did not originate from any particular organization. Iavlinskii had worked for long at a research institute attached to the State Committee for Labour and Social Affairs before he joined Abalkin's reform commission and later became deputy prime minister of the RSFSR for economic reform. Fedorov had worked within Gosbank (the state bank) and briefly at the CC socioeconomic department. Others worked at various economic institutes of the Academy of Sciences. Significantly, it was necessary to mobilize young economists in order to break barriers of dogma and socialist habits.[104]

While the Shatalin group sat at the Arkhangelskoe dacha outside Moscow, the top economic experts of the government sat at the Sosnye dacha on another side of Moscow and produced their own programme. No cooperation took place between the two groups, and economists made their choice which group to serve – if any. The government group was led by Prime Minister Ryzhkov himself who together with his colleagues refrained from holidays. Now, Abalkin had effectively become the second man in the government, overtaking the two first deputy prime ministers, Masliukov and Voronin. Other particularly influential members were Valentin Pavlov and Viacheslav Senchagov. When the economic issues were becoming more complex, the economists came to dominate the work. The government presented its programme in September.[105]

Thus, in early September the economists were polarized around two different programmes. The government had moved far in the direction of the Shatalin group, but important differences persisted. The Shatalin group wanted free pricing, fast privatization, a swift elimination of the budget deficit, and an extensive devolution of powers to the republics. On neither of these points was the government prepared to go equally far. It still spoke of 'a regulated market economy' and avoided the very word privatization. Amidst a general expectation that Gorbachev would sack the government and adopt the Shatalin programme, Gorbachev instead asked Aganbegian, who had spent the summer with a third commission revising alternative programmes, to try to work out a compromise between the two contenders. Obediently Aganbegian did so, but the programme he produced almost entirely coincided with the Shatalin programme.[106]

Aganbegian's 'compromise' was not acceptable to the government, but rather than sacking it, Gorbachev requested, and received, extraordinary powers to work out a new programme in three weeks time. Allegedly,

Gorbachev participated in this work, but again it was presented by Aganbegian. The new programme was humbly called 'Basic guidelines for economic stabilization and transition to a market economy'.[107] In effect, it maintained most of the slogans of the Shatalin Group Programme, while its contents recalled the government programme, though it was very vague and left most decisions to be made by presidential decrees. Surprisingly, these guidelines were swiftly adopted by the USSR Supreme soviet with a minimum of opposition. The president had exploited the polarization between two camps to block the programmes of both, and gathered even more of the formal powers of economic policy-making in his own hands, while the various republics were declaring that no decisions at the centre were valid without their ratification.

Conclusions

The years 1989 and 1990 have seen a very conscious transformation of the economic policy-making apparatus. It is all too clear that the hand behind this transformation has been Mikhail Gorbachev's, in particular as most changes initially were directed against Prime Minister Nikolai Ryzhkov, CC Secretary Nikolai Sliun'kov and Gosplan Chairman Iurii Masliukov – the three Politburo members in charge of economic affairs.

Until the summer of 1990, Gorbachev's obvious intention was to strengthen the reformers. Institutionally, this course has been pursued through the weakening of the Politburo and the Central Committee apparatus. Meanwhile a number of other bodies gained political power, namely the Reform Commission of the Council Ministers, the Congress of People's Deputies, the Supreme Soviet, the Presidency, and the Presidential Council. Most of these institutional changes enhanced the political prominence of academic economists. In the end, an even more complex balance of powers had developed whereby the new institutions (the Congress of People's Deputies with its many committees and the Presidency) and political activism at the grass roots level undermined the once mighty leadership of the CPSU apparatus, sapped the strength of the central economic organs and Gosplan, and tipped the scales in favour of the Presidency. In parallel, the republics claimed more power, and the large state enterprises quietly extended their powers in the vacuum left by the weakened states.

On the personal level, Gorbachev solicited support from three leading reform economists, Leonid Abalkin, Nikolai Petrakov and Stanislav Shatalin, while keeping the former chief economist Abel Aganbegian as a reserve. Gorbachev tried to sidestep Nikolai Sliun'kov and Iurii Masliukov, while containing Nikolai Ryzhkov in a somewhat ambiguous manner. He succeeded in reducing the influence of Sliun'kov and the CC

Economic Department early on, while Iurii Masliukov and Gosplan fought back vigorously until the summer of 1990. Finally, all traditional centres of power were severely restricted, but no new structures could provide for the necessary coordination of economic policy.

So far, progress towards economic reform has been tardy and marked with failures. The Abalkin Commission, with its previous balance of forces prompting inconsistent compromises ran out of steam not least because of too conservative an apparatus inherited from Ryzhkov and continuous pressures from the rest of the government. When Gorbachev was elected president, he declared his aim to move fast towards radical reform, but he failed to take adequate action. Furthermore, his Presidential Council is characterized by a rather conservative balance and it blocked endeavours for more radical reform in April 1990.

While the USSR Congress of People's Deputies and the USSR Supreme Soviet tend to be reform-minded, though somewhat populistic in their outlook, they have not been fully consulted and tend to act as brakes rather than promoters of radical reform. Their actions seem easily manipulated and pretty arbitrary. Thus, surprisingly little came out of all these institutional changes in the first round. Ironically, even more formal power has been concentrated in the hands of the president, but this power can hardly materialize with less than a declaration of martial law.

The picture that arises from this scrutiny of the institutional and personal framework for the work on economic reform is that an intense struggle has been going on but the dividing lines have moved. The top of the Council of Ministers (Ryzhkov, Masliukov, Voronin, Sitarian, Pavlov and Senchagov) comprises a tightly-knit comparatively conservative camp. Abalkin used to lead the reform economists but during 1990 he switched allegiance to the government. Gorbachev has played an impassive and hesitant role, although the initiative was his. As time passes by, his endeavours to concentrate a maximum of power in his own hands grow ever more ominous.

So far, Shatalin and Petrakov may be perceived as leaders of the reformers, but young economists such as Iavlinskii and Boris Fedorov seem likely to dominate the stage rather soon.

In 1990, the limits of Gorbachev's reformist ambitions might have been displayed. Until he was elected President, it was obvious that Gorbachev fought against severe resistance. His hesitation in the spring of 1990 may be explained by concerns for the Party Congress in July. After the Congress, Gorbachev seemed to heed reformist advice, focusing on both economic reform and the transformation of the union. However, by the end of October Gorbachev's gestures no longer looked credible. He had not only failed to develop but also seemed disinterested in developing well-functioning democratic and confederative structures. Single-mindedly, he

116   *Anders Åslund*

concentrated on reinforcing the presidency, while confusing everyone and avoiding any of the vital decisions. His previous restructuring of policy-making institutions seemed to have become mere destruction. As a result, new policy-making bodies will be needed when the transition to a market economy finally is launched.

Notes

I would like to thank thirty-four of the Soviet econimists and officials mentioned in this paper for useful talks on this topic in 1989 or 1990. Ed Hewett has generously shared his considerable knowledge in this field; Sten Luthman and Marion Cutting have assisted me in various ways. A previous version of this paper has been published in *Soviet Economy*, 6, no. 1, 1990, pp. 65–94.

1 This paper constitutes a sequal to Åslund, 'Gorbachev's economic advisors', *Soviet Economy*, 3, no. 3, 1987, pp. 246–69.
2 This section is based on Åslund, 'Gorbachev's economic advisors'.
3 Previously Petr Katsura served as the economic director of the Avtovaz car works in Togliatti; Anatolii Miliukov accompanied Ryzhkov from the Economic Department of the CC; Vadim Kirichenko had been the director of Gosplan's Economics Research Institute. Katsura's department employed some ten professionals, and Kirichenko's about twenty.
4 This commission will be referred to as the Talyzin Commission. However, Stepan Sitarian, first deputy chairman of Gosplan, seems to have led its work.
5 Abel Aganbegian, 'Prakticheskie dela ekonomicheskoi nauki', *EKO*, 20, no. 9, 1989, p. 21.
6 Anders Åslund, *Gorbachev's Struggle for Economic Reform*, London, Pinters, 1989, pp. 124–6.
7 *Pravda*, 5 July 1990.
8 Goskomstat SSSR, *Narodnoe khoziaistvo SSSR v 1988 g.*, Moscow, Finansy i statistika, 1989, p. 77; *Pravda*, 20 October 1987.
9 *Pravda*, 28 January 1990.
10 For a broad picture, see *PlanEcon Report*, 21 February 1990.
11 *Narodnoe khoziaistvo SSSR v 1988 g.*, p. 36.
12 *Pravda*, 5 July 1990.
13 *Izvestiia*, 28 October 1988.
14 *Pravda*, 30 June and 1 July, 1988.
15 *Sobranie Postanovlenii Pravitelstva SSSR*, no. 7, 1989, Article 19.
16 *Sobranie Postanovlenii Pravitelstva SSSR*, no. 18, 1989, Article 59.
17 A great deal of the evidence in this section has been obtained in conversations with the thirty-four economists and officials mentioned. I have also benefited from information from colleagues with good contacts among Soviet economists, primarily Ed Hewett and Igor Birman.
18 *Ogonek*, no. 20, 1990, p. 24.
19 E.g. *Izvestiia*, 1 March 1990.
20 For biographical details, see Itzchok Adirim, 'A.G. Aganbegjan. Pragmatiker der Wissenschaft und Theoretiker der neuen wirtschaftspolitik', *Osteuropa*, 39, no. 1, 1989, pp. 23–35.
21 Presumably, the first public criticism was expressed by Vasilii Seliunin,

'Istoki', *Novyi mir*, 64, no. 5, 1988, pp. 162–89. The reactionary Mikhail Antonov has been another sharp critic. Now such criticism is commonplace.
22 Abel G. Aganbegian, 'Prakticheskie dela ekonomicheskoi nauki', *EKO*, 20, no. 9, 1989, pp. 17–29.
23 *Argumenty i fakty*, no. 13, 1990.
24 Aganbegian has recently published two books in English: *The Economic Challenge of Perestroika*, Bloomington and Indianpolis, Indiana University Press, 1988; *Inside Perestroika. The Future of the Soviet Economy*, New York, Harper & Row, 1989.
25 Abel G. Agenbegian, 'Ekonomicheskaia nauka – praktike zakonodatel'noi deiatel'nosti', *Voprosy ekonomiki*, 62, no. 2, 1990, p. 4. Unfortunately, this is a frequent, probably even predominent, view among Soviet economists.
26 *Ekonomicheskaia gazeta*, no. 27, 1989.
27 Abalkin visited Sweden extensively both in 1987 and 1988 to investigate the Swedish model.
28 A few of these: *Pravda*, 4 August, 11 and 14 November, 16 December 1989, 30 march, 4 June, 7 July 1990; *Izvestiia*, 22 September and 18 December 1989; *Rabochaia tribuna*, 26 May 1990; *Ekonomicheskaia gazeta*, no. 27, 1990, no. 21, 1990; *Newsweek*, 29 January 1990. See Boris Rumer, 'The "Abalkanization" of Soviet economic reform', *Problems of Communism*, 39, no. 1, 1990, pp. 74–82, for further illumination of Abalkin's programme and additional references.
29 For Milner's ideas on this topic, see Milner, 'Problemy perekhoda k novym formam organizatsii upravleniia', *Voprosy ekonomiki*, 61, no. 10, 1989, pp. 3–14.
30 On leasehold: Nikiforov, 'Arendnye otnosheniia: problemy stanovleniia', *Voprosy ekonomiki*, 61, no. 11, 1989, pp. 3–16. On ownership in general: 'O variantnosti i al'ternativnosti sotsial'no-ekonomicheskogo razvitiia', *Voprosy ekonomiki*, 62, no. 3, 1990, pp. 3–17.
31 The outstanding piece is: Aleksandr Tsipko, 'Istoki Stalinizma', *Nauka i zhizn*, nos. 11 and 12, 1988, and nos. 1 and 2, 1989.
32 Recent good articles by Gennadii S. Lisichkin are: 'Mifi i realnost'', in *Osmyslit' kul't Stalina*, Moscow, Progress, 1989, pp. 247–83; 'Kak zarabatyvaem – tak i zhivem', *Delovye liudi*, February 1990.
33 *Der Spiegel*, no. 6, 1990.
34 Notably, Oleg T. Bogomolov, 'Mir sotsializma na puti perestroiki', *Kommunist*, 64, no. 16. 16, 1987, pp. 92–102.
35 For a recent representative presentation of Bogomolov's current views, see *Ogonek*, no. 23, 1990.
36 This institute has not really taken off. It was created for Academician Aleksandr Anchishkin, who died prematurely in June 1987. Its new director, Iu. V. Iaremenko, corresponding member of the Academy of Sciences, is neither particularly prominent nor clear-sighted on reform issues (see *Izvestiia*, 19 June 1990).
37 *Ogonek*, no. 20, 1990; *Delovye liudi*, May 1990.
38 Stanislav S. Shatalin, 'Sotsial'noe razvitie i ekonomicheskii rost', *Kommunist*, 63, no. 14, 1986, pp. 60–70.
39 *Sotsialisticheskaia industriia*, 30 October 1988.
40 *Liternaturnaia gazeta*, 2 May 1990; *Izvestiia*, 21 April 1990.

41 For a recent review of his views, see *Rabochaia tribuna*, 24 April 1990.
42 Nikolai Ia. Petrakov, 'Zolotoi chervonets vchera i zavtra', *Novyi mir*, 63, no. 8, 1987, pp. 205–21.
43 Evgenii G. Iasin, *Khoziaistvennye sistemyi i radikal'naia reforma*, Moscow, Ekonomika, 1989.
44 On how to move to a market economy: Dmitrii L'vov, 'Obnovlenie fabrik i rynok', *Pravda* 5 April 1990.
45 On bureaucracy: Boris V. Rakitskii, 'Puti k konsolidatsii: uchast' nomenklatury i lichnye sud'by "byurokratov"', *Voprosy ekonomiki*, 61, no. 12, 1989, pp. 56–68.
46 Primarily a specialist on pricing: Iurii Borozdin, 'Ekonomicheskaía reforma i tovarnodenezhnye otnosheniía', *Voprosy ekonomiki*, 61, no. 9, 1989, pp. 13–25.
47 Aleksandr S. Bim, *Reforma khoziaistvennogo upravleniia: zadachi, opyt, problemy*, Moscow, Nauka, 1989.
48 His latest book on reform is: Pavel G. Bunich, *Novye tsennosti*, Moscow, Nauka, 1989.
49 Notably, Gavriil Kh. Popov, *Effektivnoe upravlenie*, Moscow, Ekonomika, 1985, and Popov, 'S tochki zreniia ekonomista', *Nauka i zhizn'*, no. 4, 1987, pp. 54–65.
50 Nikolai P. Shmelev, 'Avansy i dolgi', *Novyi mir*, 63, no. 6, 1987, pp. 142–58; Smelev, 'Novye trevogi', *Novyi mir*, 64, no. 4, 1988, pp. 160–75; Shmelev and Vladimir M. Popov, *The Turning Point*, New York and London, Doubleday, 1989.
51 *Pravda*, 22 June 1987.
52 T.I. Koriagina, 'Uslugi tenevye i legalnye', *EKO*, 20, no. 2, 1989, pp. 60–65; T.I. Koriagina, 'Tenevaia ekonomika v SSSR', *Voprosy ekonomiki*, 62, 1990, pp. 110–20.
53 Khasbulatov was elected first deputy chairman of the RSFSR Supreme Soviet as El'tsin's candidate in June 1990.
54 *Pravda*, 8 July 1990.
55 Larissa Piiasheva wrote a letter under pseudonym that was published as early as May 1987, in which she argued against social democracy from a liberal point of view with the argument that you cannot be 'half-pregnant', L. Popkova, 'Gde pyshnee pirogi', *Novyi mir*, 63, no. 5, 1987, pp. 239–41.
56 Their pioneering article was: Vasilii Seliunin and Grigorii Khanin, 'Lukavaia tsifra', *Novyi mir*, 61, no. 2, 1987, pp. 181–201.
57 *Pravda*, 5 July 1988.
58 *Ibid.*
59 *Ibid.*
60 According to Egor Ligachev in *Pravda*, 5 July 1990.
61 *Izvestiia TsK KPSS*, 1, no. 1, 1989, pp. 81–8.
62 *Pravda*, 25 June 1990.
63 It was chaired by a reformist, V.M. Vologzhin, who was the director general of an enterprise in L'vov which had been the first to set up a joint stock company (*Izvestiia*, 1 April 1990; V.M. Vologzhin, 'Utro sovetskikh aktsii', *EKO*, 20, no. 1, 1989, pp. 41–50).
64 *Izvestiia*, 12 June 1990. For a description of the work of one committee of the

Supreme Soviet, see Mikhail Tsypkin, 'The Committee for Defense and State Security of the USSR Supreme Soviet', *Report on the USSR*, 11 May 1990, pp. 8–11.
65 I have discussed this phenomenon in A. Åslund, *Gorbachev's Struggle for Economic Reform*, pp. 145–6.
66 *Pravda*, 21 July 1990.
67 *Ekonomicheskaia gazeta*, no. 31, July 1989, pp. 16–17. *Sobranie Postanovlenii Pravitelstva SSSR*, no. 28, 1989, Articles 103 and 108.
68 In addition to Abalkin the reformers included, Aganbegian, Shatalin, Ruben Evstigneev, Vladlen Martynov, Boris Milner, Tatíiana Koriagina, Gevork Egizarian and A.P. Vladislavlev.
69 Notably, these included Sitarian of Gosplan (who is not among the fourteen), Minister of Finance Valentin S. Pavlov, Viacheslav K. Senchagov of the State Price Committee, Vadim N. Kirichenko of Goskomstat, and Ivan D. Ivanov of the State Foreign Economic Commission.
70 Orlov has frequently appeared in the press with substantive and reasonably reformist statements (*Izvestiia*, 2 and 3 April and 8 June 1990). Katsura has maintained a rather low profile. In September 1989, the apparatus consisted of some thirty professionals, and its size seems to have stayed at that level, but the Abalkin Commission also set up a considerable number of working groups, involving a few hundreds of officials and academics.
71 One of the few early Abalkin appointment was Evgenii Iasin, who became head of a department, another was Grigorii A. Iavlinskii.
72 Economists who otherwise presumably would have been chosen include Oleg Bogomolov, Tat'iana Zaslavskaia, Nikolai Petrakov, Gavriil Popov and Pavel Bunich. Abalkin was a deputy (elected on the CC list) but resigned after his appointment as deputy prime minister.
73 This came from reliable sources in Moscow in June 1989. The offer to Petrakov is almost beyond doubt.
74 *Ekonomicheskaia gazeta*, no. 43, 1989, pp. 4–7.
75 *Pravda*, 24 october, 2, 6, 11 and 14 November 1989; *Ekonomicheskaia gazeta*, no. 47, November 1989; Ed A. Hewett, 'Perestroika – "Plus": The Abalkin Reforms', *PlanEcon Report*, 1 December 1989, p. 11. Most materials have been published in L.I. Abalkin and A.I. Miliukov (eds.), *Ekonomicheskaia reforma: poisk reshenii*, Moscow, Politizdat, 1990.
76 *Ekonomicheskaia gazeta*, no. 47, November 1989.
77 *International Herald Tribune*, 16 November 1989.
78 Hewett, 'Perestroika – "Plus": The Abalkin Reforms', p. 13.
79 *Pravda*, 14 December 1989.
80 *Pravda*, 3 October 1989.
81 *Izvestiia*, 18 December 1989.
82 *Izvestiia*, 16 and 18 December 1989. Lev Voronin was long-time first deputy chairman of Gosplan, where he worked with both Ryzhkov and Masliukov. All three are engineers by education and former enterprise directors. They have all worked in the military-industrial complex.
83 *Pravda*, 30 June 1990.
84 *Moscow News*, no. 37, 1989.
85 Personal communication from Ed Hewett.

120   *Anders Åslund*

86 *Pravda*, 28 March 1990.
87 Dawn Mann, 'Gorbachev sworn in as President', *Report on the USSR*, 23 March 1990, pp. 1–4, and Elizabeth Teague, 'The Powers of the Soviet Presidency', *Report on the USSR*, 23 March 1990, pp. 4–7.
88 Alexander Rahr, 'From Politburo to Presidential Council', *Report on the USSR*, 1 June 1990, pp. 1–5.
89 Boriṣ Jeltsin, *Bekännelsen*, Stockholm, Forum, 1990.
90 *Izvestiia*, 21 April 1990.
91 Personal communication from two senior Soviet reform economists.
92 'O podgotovke materialov, neobkhodymykh dlia osuschestvleniia perekhoda k planovo-rynochnoi ekonomike', Decree no. 257, I owe this unpublished decree to Peter Rutland; Peter Rutland, 'Abalkin's strategy for Soviet economic reform', *Report on the USSR*, 25 May 1990, pp. 3–6.
93 Personal communication from senior Soviet officials.
94 *Pravda*, 5 July 1990.
95 *Pravda*, 16 June 1990.
96 *Izvestiia*, 22 June 1990.
97 *Moscow News*, no. 33, 1990.
98 *Ibid.*
99 *Sovetskaia Rossiia*, 16 June 1990.
100 *Delovoi mir*, 31 July 1990; *Interfax*, 27 July 1990.
101 *Sovetskaia Rossiia*, 5 August 1990.
102 *Soiuz*, no. 37, 1990.
103 *Izvestiia*, 4 September 1990; *Perekhod k rynku. Kontseptsiia i Programma*, Moscow, 1990; *Perekhod k rynku Chast' 2 – Proekty zakonodatel'nykh aktov*, Moscow, 1990.
104 An early presentation in English of the new ideas are to be found in: P.O. Aven, S.S. Shatalin and F. Schmidt-Bleek, 'Economic reform and integration. Proceedings of 1–3 March 1990 meeting', IIASA Collaborative paper, CP-90-004, July 1990.
105 *Pravda*, 12 September 1990; *Pravitel'stvennaia programma formirovaniia struktury i mekhanizma reguliruemoi rynochnoi ekonomiki*, Moscow, 1990.
106 *Izvestiia*, 15 September 1990.
107 *Pravda*, 18 October 1990.

7 The restructuring of Soviet industrial ministries since 1985

Stephen Fortescue

An examination of the restructuring of the industrial ministries since 1985 is an important aspect of any evaluation of current Soviet economic reform. The traditional 'command-administrative' functions and style of the ministries, which function as the 'transmission belts' for economic and administrative control between the centre and industrial enterprises, are clearly incompatible with the operation of the 'socialist market', the ostensible goal of economic reform. If the ministries are still operating in the same way as they have since the 1930s – whether because they are forced to by 'objective circumstances' or because they choose to for their own selfish bureaucratic reasons – we can safely assume that the reform has a long way to go.

There should be no need here to describe the long-standing 'sins of the ministries'. They have been exhaustively described in the Soviet press in endless stories of bureaucratic misdeeds. Although they have been subjected to less detailed analysis in either the Western or Soviet literature than one might have expected, there are good and clear accounts of the phenomena of *vedomstvennost'* (usually translated as either sectionalism or departmentalism) and *melochnaia opeka* (petty tutelage). The first refers to the ministries' habit of protecting their own narrow interests at the cost of all others, including an obsession with autarchy and non-cooperation with other ministries. The second refers to their determination to closely control every detail of the activities of their subordinate enterprises.[1]

These problems were certainly not suddenly uncovered for the first time by Gorbachev. Nor is he the first to express the desire to do something about them. Indeed, one of the difficulties involved in analyzing proposals for the restructuring of the ministries is that virtually no one is prepared to defend them. Greater independence and initiative for enterprise managers and the breaking down of departmental barriers were no less the catch-cries of Stalin and Brezhnev than of Khrushchev and Gorbachev. There is also a very strong anti-bureaucratic tradition in Bolshevism, based on the Marxist goal of the withering away of the state and Lenin's hopes in *State and Revolution*, mistrust of holdovers from the old Tsarist bureaucracy, and the eternal need to find scapegoats for economic failures. Thus, the conservatives are as likely as, perhaps even more likely than, the reformers to utter harsh words about the ministries and their bureaucrats.

This likelihood is increased by the general rule that in the Soviet Union, even today in conditions of glasnost, everyone feels obliged to adopt the slogans and language of those in power. At the moment those slogans and language are of decentralization and marketization.

Thus, it is not easy to determine how radical or genuine particular proposals or actions might be. However, the radical approach can perhaps be identified.[2] It demands an almost complete destatization of the economy and the consequent destruction of the traditional structure and functions of the industrial ministries. The goal would appear to be the effective abolition of the existing ministries and their replacement at the state administration level by a few or only one ministry, similar to a Ministry of Economy or Department of Trade and Industry as found in the West.[3] It would have no powers of direct administrative control over enterprises, but would have general 'strategic' functions of information collection and analysis, long-term forecasting and participation in the economic policy making of the state. Direct administrative functions, to the extent that they remain under the socialist market, would be assumed by the managerial apparatuses of independent enterprises or associations of enterprises. Such apparatuses might consist of the single owner-operator of a small private enterprise, but for our present purposes are more likely to be large bureaucratic structures managing major industrial conglomerates, like the head offices of major Western corporations.[4]

At the other end of the spectrum are the conservatives, including those in the ministries, who continue to place their trust, to a greater or lesser degree, in the maintenance of central control of industrial activity, through the setting of production plans and central allocation of inputs and outputs. Clearly such an approach requires the maintenance of ministry-type structures.[5]

This is not the place to describe all the ups and downs, advances and retreats of Soviet economic reform – some greater sense of that can be gained from the other chapters in this volume. However, the general trend in both public debate and practice over the last five years has been towards the radical end of the spectrum. Thus, as far as the ministries are concerned, the last five years have seen a steady process of legislative and spontaneous reductions in their functions and powers; savage staff cuts, amalgamations and reorganizations of their internal structures to reflect their reduced role; and the establishment of alternative 'economic' units to replace, complement or compete with them. Over the last twelve months or so the situation has been vastly complicated by the demands of republican and regional structures for economic independence from the centre. Such independence would have a major effect on the control of the central ministries over their enterprises. We will now look in more detail at each of these developments, providing a running evaluation of actual outcomes.

Reductions in functions and powers

We are at a disadvantage in trying to describe the formal powers of the industrial ministries for a number of reasons. The first most general one is the increasingly chaotic complexity of Soviet economic legislation. More specifically, there is the lack of up-to-date legislation dealing directly with the ministries. Indeed one increasingly notes the disappearance of specific reference to them in major economic legislation.

The ministries long-awaited new General Statute (*Obshchee polozhenie*) has still not appeared, and one suspects that it is as far away as ever. This means that legally the old 1967 General Statute is still in force.[6] That Statute, while hardly declaiming the virtues of *melochnaia opeka* and *vedomstvennost'*, leaves the ministries considerable room to operate as the instruments of the command economy.[7]

In recent times the only official document specifically dealing with the ministries is the July 1987 Central Committee and Council of Ministers decree. The decree devotes considerable attention to the nature of the relationship between a ministry and its subordinate enterprises under new economic conditions. The emphasis is very much on the ministries' obligation to

use primarily economic methods rather than primarily administrative methods, to establish conditions for the display of initiative and enterprise by labour collectives, the development of the economic independence of enterprises, the comprehensive use of the principles of full *khozraschet* and self-financing.[8]

The intention is that 'command-administrative' control should be replaced by 'economic' levers such as tax and credit regimes.

For our determination of the legal status of the ministries' relationships with enterprises we rely to a considerable extent on recent legislation on the enterprise, essentially the 1987 Law on the State Enterprise (Association) and its 1989 amendments and the Law on Enterprises which replaced the original legislation in June 1990.[9] The general impression that the original piece of legislation, in particular its amendments, strive to give is of reduced powers of the ministries over producer units:

The relations of an enterprise and a higher organ (ministry, state committee, agency or other higher organ) are built on the basis of management by plan, the observance of the principles of full *khozraschet*, self-financing and self-management of the enterprise.

The original Law on the State Enterprise has been replaced by the new Law on Enterprises. It is noteworthy, among many other things, for the fact that the ministries are not once referred to specifically. However, the Law, basing itself on the Law on Property which preceded it in March 1990, makes regular reference to the considerable economic rights of the *sobstvennik* (owner) of the means of production. The Law legalizes a number of different forms of ownership. However it, and subsequent commentary, suggest that state ownership is intended to remain as the dominant form, certainly in the major industrial sectors where the ministries we are concerned with are concentrated. The Law then goes on to refer to the right of the *sobstvennik* to delegate its powers and functions of ownership to other bodies (Article 14.1). Those other bodies have been identified in subsequent legislation and practice as being more often than not the industrial ministries. As the representatives of the state, the ministries originally claimed the right to dispose of the assets of enterprises and of the enterprises themselves.[10] The establishment of the Fund of State Property of the USSR as the states sole agent for the disposal of its property, put a dampener on those claims.[11] However, the Fund remains a shadowy body, which also possesses the right to delegate its powers to an agent, with again the industrial ministries being the most likely agents.[12]

The state as *sobstvennik* has delegated its power as *arendovatel'* (lessor) to the ministries in cases of enterprises going into *arenda* (lease). That is, it is the ministries which supervise and set the conditions for the transfer of enterprises on to what is seen by many as the most decentralizing of the new forms of economic organization. Not surprisingly, they have used this power all too often to set onerous conditions or to simply liquidate enterprises seeking to transfer.[13]

In a recent decree of the Council of Ministers the state has also delegated to the ministries its right as *sobstvennik* to appoint enterprise directors.[14] This decree, bringing to a formal end the short-lived experiment in election of enterprise managers, increases the ministries' powers of hire and fire by introducing a contract system[15]

Finally, practice seems to have established the ministries as the agents holding the state's shares in joint-stock companies (*aktsionernye obshchestva*, A/Os) (usually a minimum 51 per cent), although the situation is complicated by the fact that the legislation is trying to accommodate both the concept of enterprise self-management and state ownership. Thus, Article 18.1 of the Law on Enterprises states that the Council of Board of an enterprise is made up equally of representatives of the *sobstvennik* and elected representatives of the labour force. That Council has wide powers as set out in Article 18.4, but in the same article is forbidden from 'interfering in the operational-directive activity of the administration'. At the same time the Law contains a number of sternly worded clauses guaranteeing enterprises freedom from administrative control by organs of state power, the latter having to use 'economic levers' in their economic management functions. On top of all that in the first major transformation of a state enterprise into an A/O, that of KamAZ the truck manufacturer, half the voting rights derived from the state's 51 per cent shareholding have been delegated to the labour force.[16]

It is not yet clear what all this means. However, most commentators are confident that the ministries will have control of the state's majority shareholding, and will use it together with strong links with other shareholders and the right of appointment of top management, to dominate the new A/Os as much as if not more than the old enterprises. Certainly the ministries have adopted the share approach with suspicious enthusiasm.[17]

In summary, legislation, while speaking boldly of the rights of independent enterprises, leaves very considerable powers and functions of the ministries. But how do things work in day-to-day practice? Are those powers actually exercised, and if so are they used in a way which continues or rejects the traditional model of ministerial control?

Many reports suggest that *melochnaia opeka* has indeed been drastically reduced. That is, ministerial staff are less demanding in terms of the number of reports and information (*otchetnost'*) they demand from enterprises, and they are less persistent in their checking on day-to-day plan fulfilment.[18]

However, it is too early to declare that the decline in petty tutelage has been matched by what could be called 'grand tutelage'. The ministries will have a major role in drawing up the five-year and yearly plans that still ultimately determine the activities of enterprises. It is true that the long-standing programme to reduce the number of planning indicators continues, and the planning system is based on *normativy* and the *goszakaz* rather than the traditional indicators. A *normativ* is a supposedly objective determination of an enterprise's capabilities rather than a simple extrapolation from the previous year's performance or arbitrary allocation of whatever output target is required for balancing higher level plans. The *goszakaz* is an obligatory order for the production of key items which is either, as in practice, allocated to an enterprise or, as in theory, taken on by an enterprise after competitive tendering. What distinguishes the *goszakaz* from the traditional plan task is that it should not take up the full production capacity of the enterprise. The enterprise should be left with some free capacity which it can use in whichever way it chooses. In the amendments to the Law on the State Enterprise the right to fix *goszakazy* was taken away from the ministries, at the same time as *goszakazy* which took up 100 per cent of the capacity of enterprises were banned. Ministries in the original legislation were expressly forbidden to unilaterally increase plan tasks or in general to act outside the boundaries of their legal competence. Enterprises were given the right to report ministerial infractions to state arbitration and receive financial compensation.[19] These guarantees of enterprise independence were given more sweeping and categorical expression in the Law on Enterprises.

But this is not enough to overcome the overwhelming impression of continuing *opeka* by the ministries. In particular it appears that now that the ministries have been forced to accept less than 100 per cent *goszakazy* they put pressure on enterprises to sign ostensibly 'voluntary' contracts, by threatening the regularity of their supplies, the imposition of punitive prices and *normativy*, and the removal of recalcitrant managers. The Vladimir Tractor Factory has been freed from *goszakaz* altogether, but is unable to refuse the contracts which the ministry imposes on it, despite the fact that they guarantee that it will make a loss, because the factory depends entirely on the ministry for funds and resources.[20] A recent survey of enterprise managers found that 93.9 per cent believed that ministries did not observe the law that they could not set enterprises *normativy* and indicators above limits set by the Council of Ministers, nearly 75 per cent that higher organs continued to give directives outside their competence, and 53 per cent that rules on planning were not being observed.[21] The State Arbitration has been very reluctant to adjudicate *goszakaz* disputes, while enterprise directors suggest that they would not last long in their jobs if they went to arbitration.[22] It has been suggested that under the new system the ministry has maintained its right to impose output indicators in enterprises, but can now evade responsibility for providing inputs, leaving enterprises in a worse situation that they were in before.[23] The author of this report implies that the supply system has degenerated to a mix between barter and blackmail. One supplier of essential inputs to his enterprise (the giant Uralmashzavod) demanded as part payment metal pipes, scrap metal, kitchen fittings, rest home vouchers and a telephone in the flat of the doctor of the director's wife!

Reports of this type – and there is an increasing number of them – suggest that the introduction of the *goszakaz* system is indeed beginning to have some effect, although whether in the form expected is open to doubt. Although enterprises can be pressured by ministries to sign 'voluntary' contracts which in effect maintain ministry control over the non-*goszakaz* portion of enterprises' capacity, it appears that they are often unable (and in the case of contracts signed across branch boundaries perhaps increasingly losing the desire) to enforce the fulfilment of the contracts. Enterprises are prepared to break contracts of the delivery of non-*goszakaz* production if they cannot get the price or non-monetary payments that they expect. This has produced chaos in the Soviet economy, particularly for enterprises which rely on inputs from contract deliveries for the fulfilment of the *goszakaz* responsibilities.[24] While some see this chaos as a necessary condition for the development of a more rational market allocation of resources,[24] Gorbachev made it clear in his first presidential decree after receiving special powers that he did not.[26] The maintenance of plan discipline – in modern parlance, contract or delivery discipline – was always the ministries' primary function. Its apparent collapse is clearly a major indicator of the *de facto* decline in ministries' power.

An area in which there is some difference of opinion over whether the ministries have lost power or not is in the allocation of funding, particularly investment resources. Some commentators suggest that ministry access to enterprise funds has been or will be greatly reduced.[27] But at the same time the press is full of complaints from enterprises that they are still required to pay high percentages of their profits into central ministry budgets.[28] This touches on a key aspect of economic reform, since the reformers have stressed the desirability of 'new-type' ministries relying on such economic levers as taxation and credit regimes. Deductions into ministry budgets are effectively a form of taxation, and the reformers want such deductions to be set at reasonable levels and to be equal for all enterprises. There must be considerable doubt as to their reasonableness and no effort has been made to make them equal. They are still set on the basis of *normativy* for each individual enterprise, and smack over-poweringly of the subsidization of poorly performing enterprises through the punitive taxation of successful enterprises.[29] This has always been seen as having a negative effect on incentives. As for credit, it is increasingly granted and rates set by branch banks operated by the ministries. They clearly use their control of credit to put pressure on enterprises. One example involves a ministry's bank refusing an enterprise credit because the workforce insisted on putting forward for election as director someone the ministry did not approve of. The enterprise was driven to near bankruptcy by the financial policies of the ministry.[30]

In summary, the picture with regard to the powers and functions of ministries as expressed both in legislation and practice is a patchy one. Legislation talks boldly of enterprise independence, but leaves considerable room for the operation of the existing industrial ministries. In practice, the ministries continue to behave in their traditional way when they get the opportunity. That opportunity still comes their way regularly enough, although not as regularly as in the past. Their reduced control over non-*goszakaz* production, with its knock-on effect on the *goszakazy* themselves, is particularly noteworthy.

Structural and staff changes

The authorities consider that the reduction in the ministries' functions and powers has been sufficient to make possible a significant reduction in their administrative capacities, in terms of both staff and structures. Given that the staff cuts actually came before the legal changes in functions, it is indeed likely that they were designed to force the ministries to reduce their interference in enterprise activities (simple budgetary reasons should also not be ruled out). There was a period around the middle of 1989 when the Soviet media were very impressed by the data which revealed an army of 18 million bureaucrats which soaked up around 44 billion rubles a year and swamped the country in paper.[31] Very few of these bureaucrats in fact worked in the central apparatuses of the ministries, and so do not concern us here. In fact, something like 15 million of them, costing 38 billion rubles per annum, worked in enterprises. It appears that the staff of state administrative agencies before the cuts began stood at about 1.5 million, with only about 120,000 of these working in Moscow ministries. The general target for the original cuts was a halving of both figures.[32] While most ministries seemed to cut staff by between 30 and 40 per cent, it was claimed that the administrative apparatus as a whole shed about 600,000 jobs, including 60,000 in the central ministries.[33]

The cuts were clearly substantial, and certainly enough to have caused great alarm among ministerial officials. Reports referred to people spreading rumours and lies about their colleagues in order to direct the axe away from themselves and a general decline in the 'moral-psychological atmosphere' in collectives. In one case, an ambulance had to be called to the commission for redundancies to deal with the overwrought bureaucrats, while the main Moscow casualty hospital was said to have received three or four suicidal ministry workers a day![34] There were complaints from enterprise managers that in this difficult period ministerial officials under review were even more reluctant than usual to take risks and responsibility for decisions.[35]

In considering the significance of these cuts, some attention has to be paid to where redundant personnel went. One press report states that very few people found it necessary to turn to labour exchanges to find new work.[36] Usually people were offered and accepted jobs within the ministry, whether in one of its enterprises (in Moscow),[37] research institutes or some vaguely defined administrative unit. Very few went to work 'directly in production' (presumably engineering positions), with the overwhelming majority continuing in administrative work. A significant number were simply appointed to posts in the apparatus which had been vacant at the time the cuts were introduced.[38]

This last approach is perhaps only the most straightforward method of arranging the cuts in such a way that they mean nothing. One should also be very suspicious of the large number of redundant officials moving into ministries' research institutes and design bureaus. Such organizations have long been used as a way of overcoming limits placed on administrative staff numbers,[39] and recent references can be found to new institutes being established specifically to provide a home for displaced bureaucrats.[40] The 'researchers' presumably spend their time drawing up 'methodological documents', i.e. operating procedures, which in their old jobs would simply have been described as directives to enterprises. One article refers to ministerial staff commissioning research projects for themselves before their transfer to research institutes.[41] One should be even more suspicious of staff being transferred to production and science-production associations (POs and NPOs) or kontserny. As we will see later it seems that these are the latest repositories of the functions of former middle-link bodies such as glavki, VPOs, GPOs, etc, and that more often than not a transfer to one of these bodies will mean no change in function or even workplace, although the 'transferred' worker will be formally taken off the ministry's payroll.

The staff cuts campaign has been accompanied by a series of ministerial amalgamations. Over the last few years six agricultural ministries have been amalgamated into Gosagroprom (since itself abolished); two timber and paper ministries were combined; the Ministry for Livestock Machine Building was amalgamated into the Ministry of Agricultural Machine Building, which in turn was itself fused with the Ministry of Automobile Industry; the Ministries of Heavy Machine Building and Power Machine Building were combined into one; and the Ministry of Light and Food Industry Machine Building was abolished. These changes left fifty-five ministries in existence, and were said to have produced significant staff cuts, although not more than ministries were subjected to anyway.[42] Then in July 1989 in one blow the new Supreme Soviet passed a law reducing the number of ministries to thirty-seven at both all-union and union-republican levels.[43] These new amalgamations, in the case at least of the merging of the Ministries of Ferrous and Non-ferrous Metallurgy into the Ministry of Metallurgy, led to a further 50 per cent staff cut. It also enabled the reduction of the number of subdivisions in the ministry from fifty-two to twenty-seven, suggesting that the amalgamations led to structural consolidation.[44]

The other attack on the capacity of ministries to operate in the old 'command-administrative' way has been on their 'middle link'. This is the administrative link between the central ministry apparatus and the ministry's enterprises. Traditionally this link was provided by the glavnye upravleniia or glavki of the central ministry apparatus. These were units of the ministries which passed on in operational form the policies and directives of the ministry leadership. Given the strict vertically hierarchical nature of Soviet administration only the *glavki* had the right to give operational orders to their enterprises, something which the 'staff' (or 'functional', to use Soviet terminology) units of the apparatus certainly did not have.[45]

There is not the time here to provide even a brief history of the middle link since the first attack on the *glavki* in the late 1960s.[46] Suffice it to say that from the late 1960s the *glavki* were replaced by supposedly new bodies, the *vsesoiuznye promyshlennye ob"edineniia* (VPOs).[47] While differing in no way from the *glavki*, they survived until Gorbachev came to power, when again the middle link was subjected to savage attack. In very rapid succession the VPOs were abolished and replaced in some cases by *glavnye proizvodstvennye upravleniia*. For a while much hope was placed on new *gosudarstvennye proizvodstvennye ob"edineniia* (GPOs), whose Statute was passed into law in September 1987.[48] The GPOs, like all their predecessors, were billed as being qualitatively new organizations, appropriate for a decentralized economy in that they would have relatively small apparatuses directly dependent for their material maintenance on the enterprises they served and often physically located in those enterprises. However, few would have been greatly surprised when evidence began to appear that the vast majority of GPOs were simply VPOs operating under a (slightly) different name. After being criticized and having their Statute cancelled in a Council of Ministers decree in April 1988,[49] they gradually faded out of sight.

With the demise of the GPOs it seemed for a while that the ministries would finally be forced to come to terms with a genuine 'two-link' system. The final outcome is still unclear, but a number of strategies on the part of the ministries are becoming evident.

'Glavkization' of the NPOs

Without a radical change in the entire central planning and management system one would expect the 'middle link' to keep appearing, no matter what administrative reorganizations were undertaken. Some commentators dismiss the danger of the 'glavkization' of the POs and NPOs, because they have direct production responsibilities which insulate them from the dangers of 'bureaucratism'.[50] However, there are some very suspicious POs and NPOs appearing on the scene. Back in 1986, with the abolition of the VPOs in the Ministry of Construction and Road Machine Building the head of the old VPO 'Soiuzliftmash' went to head the NPO 'Liftmash', 'with nearly the same tasks and powers'.[51] In 1988 the PO 'Mosavtotrans' was described as a former *glavk*.[52] A 1989 article in *Ekonomicheskaia gazeta* described in some detail the creation of 'middle link' NPOs. The Ministry of Petrochemical Industry had transformed its VPO 'Soiuzasbotekhnika' in the NPO 'Asbotekhnika', while the Ministry of Construction and Road Machine Building's VPO 'Soiuzinstrument' had become the NPO 'Instrument'. The Ministry of Machine Tool Industry had replaced its *glavk* Glavdrevstankoprom with the NPO 'Drevmash', which contains the eight POs, sixteen factories, two design bureaus and one institute that had previously been under the *glavk*. The same ministry had substituted the NPO 'Stankoliniia' for the *glavk* Glavstankoliniia, including in it according to *Ekonomicheskaia gazeta* eight POs and one factory and *no* research for design organizations. (Another source states that the new NPO contains sixteen factories and eight design bureaus under the famous Machine Tool Association im. Ordzhonikidze, the director of which is also the general director of the NPO.[53]) The author of the *Ekonomicheskaia gazeta* article found these transformations dangerously irrational, and incontrovertible evidence that the ministries were again engaged in a blatantly formalistic 'changing nameplates'. He doubted that the *khozraschet* principles on which the NPOs and POs would be forced to operate would be enough to overcome their clearly 'command-administrative' origins.[54]

'Glavkization' of functional units

Just as some suspicious NPOs and POs have appeared, developments in the so-called 'functional' units of some ministries also arouse suspicion. The traditional system has been that the line middle-link organizations have been directly subordinate to deputy ministers, and all operational directives have to go down that hierarchy. The 'functional' units in the central apparatus have had no powers to give direct orders. The logic of the current reorganizations is that the ministries will no longer be responsible in any major way for giving direct operational orders. The 'strategic' tasks for which the ministry is now to be responsible are best left to the 'functional' administrations. Thus, some Soviet commentators see the reorganization as involving a strengthening of the functional administrations of the central apparatus.[55] Some even hint that there might be a movement towards the so-called *funktsional'ka* (functionalism) of the First Five-Year Plan, when functional units of the state administration were given direct administrative powers over enterprises. That approach has ever since been viewed negatively, as weakening the direct lines of management.[56] Movement in this direction, in which a line organization receives obligatory directives from a number of different functional units, seems unlikely to go far. What does seem possible is the 'glavkization' of the central functional apparatus, i.e. quasi-line organizations set up within a nominally functional unit. To some extent this development is designed simply to soak up displaced staff, with the central apparatus in some ministries managing to increase their overall staff levels at a time of savage staff cuts.[57] However, it is likely designed to help fill the bureaucratic vacuum left by the dissolution of the middle link.[58] One approach has been to greatly expand the importance within the central apparatus of the Chief Economics Administration. This is a relatively new unit, designed to answer criticisms in recent decades that Soviet administration has been short on economics expertise. Ministries can now take advantage of this demand for greater attention to economics to set up the Chief Economics Administration as a major operation management body (almost certainly staffed by the traditional engineers rather than economists).[59] Another approach has been to set up a number of specialized Technical Administrations. Thus, the Ministry of Petrochemical Industry set up seven new Chief Technical Administrations for its sub-branches.[60] One source reveals that one can now find Chief Economics Administrations with eighteen to twenty departments, Chief Scientific-Technical Administrations with fifteen to twenty, and Chief Production Administrations with twenty to twenty-five. Each of these departments can have up to ten deputy heads running their own sectors. Up to 45 per cent of the staff of these departments and sectors are directly involved in the operational affairs of enterprises.[61] One commentator sums up the situation in the Ministry of Petrochemical industry by declaring that despite the fact that the ministry is officially on the two-link system, what with the developments under way in the POs and NPOs and the central apparatus, the middle link is still very much there.[62]

Otdely and kontserny

The fluid nature of ministerial structures at the moment is demonstrated by the fact that a new structural unit of the Ministry of Metallurgy created in September 1989 as a Chief Technical Administration with the improbable name 'Nikel'med'kobalt' (and elsewhere in the same article openly described as a *glavk*),[63] no longer features in the ministry's structure. Indeed the structure of that ministry is now a combination of *otdely* (departments) and *kontserny* (concerns). The *otdely*, of which there are twenty-six in total, cover both functional and line activities. Thus, there is a Department for Material-Technical Supplies, a (single) Scientific-Technical Department and other such functional departments, but also a Department of Ferrous Alloy Industry, a Department of Heavy Nonferrous Metals, etc. The directory of the ministry (in the foyer of its building in October 1990) then listed a series of *khozraschet* organizations. They are presumably intended to be more independent of the ministry than the *otdely* and more dependent and therefore responsive to the enterprises that finance their continued existence. First, there are eight *kontserny*, with such names as 'Metallurgprom', 'Spetsstal'', etc.[64] All but two are situated in the ministry's central headquarters (the other two are situated elsewhere in Moscow). These are clearly the old *glavki* under a different name. There is, then, a whole series of various types of organization in the *khozraschet* category, including two NPOs and three POs situated in the central headquarters!

The Ministry of Metallurgy is clearly keeping its organisational options open, but it seems probable that it is placing its main hope on the *kontserny* as the continuation of the middle-link tradition. While not all *kontserny* are the pure inventions of the ministries – some, such as the 'Noril'sknikel'' *kontsern* have had to fight hard for their existence[65] – most would seem to be pretty cynical exercises in maintaining the middle link. One senses that the struggle with the middle link is virtually hopeless. With the branch-based central planning and management system still in place there is a demand for middle-link bureaucratic control which will always be met by some sort of middle link administrative apparatus.

Alternatives to the ministries

A strategy of the opponents of the ministries has been the establishment of alternative structures. On occasions these seem designed potentially to replace the ministries; at other times they are presented as a means of gingering up the present ministries and their staff by setting up alternative management structures for disgruntled enterprises.

The first move towards an alternative was the establishment of the so-called 'inter-branch state associations' (*mezhotraslevye gosudarstvennye ob"edineniia*) or MGOs. The original three still get the most attention in the press. They are Moscow's 'Kvantemp' and Leningrad's 'Energomash' and 'Tekhnokhim'. The MGOs combine a number of enterprises and R&D organizations, including some of the biggest enterprises of the major industrial ministries, in independent administrative structures free from ministerial subordination.[66] The MGOs took over or established a number of 'firms' with service type responsibilities, 'Kvantemp' has five such firms, looking after supplies, construction, foreign trade, training and credit. The last is described as a commercial bank.[67] 'Energomash' also has its own bank, set up after its enterprises' withdrawals from their ministries led to such serious credit problems for some that they were unable to pay their wages bills. The 'Energomashbank' has a paid up capital of 20 million rubles, and supposedly provides credit, factoring and share underwriting facilities.[68] The MGO's 'firms' are *khozraschet* organizations, i.e. they are expected to be financially self-supporting. They get a share of the profits of the activities they service, but are held materially responsible in a way which is not described in any detail for any failures to deliver contracted services.[69]

The MGOs were set up on a 'democratic' and 'anti-bureaucratic' basis, meaning that they were voluntary associations of financially and legally independent organizations and that the central apparatus was kept to an absolute minimum. They are run by a central board made up of the directors of the component units. The board's decision originally had to be unanimous. There are also more specialized central councils, in which the various chief engineers, chief designers, standardization managers, etc. meet.[70] The small central administrative apparatuses (in the case of 'Kvantemp', twenty-two staff; eleven for 'Tekhnokhim'),[71] which one imagines are based in the central office of the base organization, are funded directly by the component units.

The removal of the MGOs from ministerial supervision does not at all mean that they are free of the strictures of the Soviet central planning system. They still receive *goszakazy* from the central planning authorities, i.e. the obligatory state orders which have 'replaced' the old planning targets. They are also subject to the full range of *limity*, *normativy* and budget deductions that normal Soviet enterprises are subject to. It has to be said that those involved in the MGOs do not sound too concerned about these central controls.[72] More difficult it seems is the matter of supplies. 'Energomash' has been resisting pressure to set up its own supply organization, since it wants to operate on a wholesale basis with the regional supply organization Lenglavsnab. This sounds like a dangerous approach, since the general wholesale supply system is as yet in a rather unpromising infancy. So far Gossnab refuses to allow the MGO to go onto wholesale trade, and it might have to give up and follow the route of 'Kvantemp'.[73] 'Kvantemp', as already mentioned, has its own supply 'firm'. Presumably, given that 'Kvantemp' has a *goszakaz*, it has some access to centrally allocated supplies. However, it appears that it is also expected to go out on its own looking for supplies. Its director refers to its requirements for silicon, a very scarce and centrally controlled resource, to produce solar power stations. Its supply firm found a potential supplier, an enterprise of the Ministry of Non-ferrous Metallurgy. However, as was to be expected, its entire output was accounted for, for years ahead. But when the MGO offered a share in the profits to be made on the solar power stations, the enterprise, now on *khozraschet* and therefore interested in finding independent sources of funding, put in some additional investments on its own account and increased production sufficiently above the *goszakaz* level to meet the MGO's order.[74]

This cameo sums up the thinking behind Gorbachev's current policy for industrial reform. The *goszakazy* guarantee the meeting of the nation's most important requirements. But then through *khozraschet* enterprises will, on the one hand, have enough financial pressure put on them through the threat of bankruptcy, and on the other, enough opportunity to increase profits and the returns to their workers, to encourage significant amounts of above-*goszakaz* production. To determine whether the strategy will work, either for the MGOs or for the economy as a whole, requires analysis which goes beyond the bounds of this paper. However increasingly there are aspects of the MGOs' behaviour that sound ominous in terms of enterprise independence. Firstly, many of the 'democratic' procedures have proved unworkable, particularly the need for unanimity in decision making, and more familiar Soviet hierarchical patterns have been introduced.[75] The MGOs use their own banks and insurance funds to blackmail constituent units and to engage in that classic ministerial procedure of shifting the burden of loss-making enterprises onto profitable ones.[76] The deductions that 'Tekhnokhim' makes from enterprise profits go into a central fund for investment and fundamental research, and also for subsidizing lagging enterprises.[77] 'Kvantemp' has an 'insurance fund' which it uses to redistribute profits from successful enterprises to loss-makers. It also has a 'joint-stock commercial bank' which buys technical innovations from the MGO's institutes and then sells them on to its enterprises. Enterprises which are unwilling to put the innovations into production have their interest rates increased.[78] As one commentator has put it, the new bodies were supposed to be 'complexes of independent enterprises'; instead they are 'independent economic complexes'.[79] While they might have independence from ministries, that does not mean that producer units have autonomy. Even their independence from the ministries is open to question. The head of 'Tekhnokhim' has declared that while initially they were 'drunk with their freedom from the ministry', they now realize that some links have to be retained, particularly in the area of supplies.[80]

While the MGOs were the original versions of the new type of structures, they are always bracketed in discussions and legislation with various other potential bodies known variously as *kontserny*, *kontsortiumy* and *assotsiatsii*. As we have already seen, the ministries have quickly jumped in and started setting up *kontserny* of their own, which appear to be known more than yet another variation on the *glavk* theme. In another variation the new *kontserny* are in fact old 'abolished' ministries under a new name. Thus, it is somewhat suspicious that N.M. Ol'shanskii, the minister of the former Ministry of Mineral Fertilizers, is now the freely elected chairman of the 'state association' (*assotsiatsiia*) Agrokhim (Agricultural Chemicals), operating under the auspices of the Ministry of Chemical Industry.[81] It is openly recognized that the new *kontsern* Gazprom (Gas industry) is nothing more than the former Ministry of Gas

Industry, set up two days after it was announced that the Ministry of Gas Industry was to be merged with the Ministry of Oil Industry.[82] Depending on one's point of view this step was either a cynical exercise by gas industry officials to frustrate the merger or their justifiable demonstration of dissatisfaction over lack of consultation.[83]

A recent table showing the structure of the Soviet industrial sector listed four MGOs as apparent equivalents to ministries in the machine-tool sector, 'Chasprom', 'Kriogeneika', 'Mashpriborservis', and 'Prompribor'. I must admit to having no information on these new organizations, but three of them sound very much like parts of the old Ministry of Instrument Making. Presumably they split off when the ministry was merged into the Ministry of Electrotechnical Industry, along the lines of the *kontsern* 'Gazprom' (which, curiously, is not listed). Other new structures listed are the *assotsiatsiia* Agrokhim and the MGOs Tekhnokhim and Strommash.[84]

An optimistic view of these new alternative structures would seem them as an essential element in the destruction of the traditional ministries, providing a more disaggregated industrial structure and even a degree of competition,[85] and making a first step towards creating Western-style industrial corporations. The pessimists would say that they are simply another form of bureaucratic control over producers (and consumers), designed to operate in an unchanged command economy and therefore inevitably displaying the same behavioural traits as the ministries. For the pessimists, whether they are truly independent of the ministries or not is irrelevant. It is certainly far too early to declare that the optimists are right.

Centre–periphery relations

Like so many Sovietologists, particularly those dealing with the central organs of administration, I have been guilty in the past of neglecting the federal and multinational nature of the Soviet Union. I am now being made to pay for my sins, and some account, albeit brief and inexpert, of the effect on the central ministries of the breakdown in relations between the centre and the periphery is essential. Reference to the periphery is of course somewhat misleading, since one of the main anti-centre forces is the RSFSR.

The central industrial ministries have never been popular in the regions, because of their habit of neglecting infrastructural development in those areas where they build their factories, the enormous disproportion between enterprise taxes going into ministry funds compared to regional funds, and in the Baltic States in particular the overwhelmingly Russian workforce of the union enterprises. The central ministries stand to lose a great deal if the republics and regions succeed in obtaining economic independence. As yet that independence is far from won, but the issues are becoming increasingly stark.

The regions are not specifically demanding the dissolution of the central ministries. But they do demand the right to exercise sovereignty over all enterprises on their territory. The demand is not for the right to enjoy the same 'command-administrative' powers that the ministries have exercised in the past – that does not fit in with the market ideology of most of the regions. However, they do demand the right to set the conditions under which the enterprises operate, in terms of provision of infrastructure, vetos over particular forms of environmentally hazardous and socially undesirable activity and, perhaps most importantly, the right to levy taxes. Thus, the Latvian Parliament has recently been considering a package of taxation and finance laws. These foresee that Latvia will determine the share of the profits of union enterprises to be paid into central budgets, while setting a tax rate of 57.5 per cent for payments into the republican budget. Central legislation sets the rate at 22 per cent.[86] Enterprises are finding themselves increasingly subjected to such demands from regional authorities at all levels. The threat to ministry control of their enterprises and their funds through an increase in regional autonomy is considerable.

The republics are also interesting because they might appear to be offering a model of administrative restructuring that the centre could follow. A number of republics, most noticeably the RSFSR, have abolished all their branch ministries. The RSFSR has set up a single Ministry of Industry, and a range of independent self-financing *kontserny*.[87] This would appear to be close to the radical model set out at the beginning of this paper. As usual, however, scepticism seems to be required. Little is known of the activities of the Ministry of Industry, and the published comments of the minister are not particularly enlightening.[88] There is evidence to suggest that the new *kontserny* are nothing more than the old ministries operating under a different name.[89] The market as yet no more exists in the RSFSR than in does in the USSR, and in those circumstances it is not surprising that new structures have trouble finding their way and old structures continue to behave as they always have.

Conclusion

A brief conclusion would be that on balance, while the ministries have undergone some traumatic changes in structure and functions over the last five years, with their capacity to operate in the traditional 'command-administrative' way at least threatened, they have nevertheless managed essentially to maintain that capacity. That is enough on its own to raise doubts about the depth of economic reform as so far implemented.

It would be nice to leave it at that. However, as much as we might dislike and fear it, no paper on the contemporary Soviet Union can avoid concluding without some speculation on the future. Have the 'command-administrative' instincts of the ministries and a conservative economic policy with them won out, or is the radical scenario still a viable one?

It would take a brave person to predict which way economic reform will go, either in the sense of what the official policy will be or in the sense of how successfully any policy decided on might be implemented. It appears likely that the rhetoric of radical reform will continue to dominate, meaning that the ministries will continue to feel themselves under pressure or find it tactically expedient to continue to subject themselves to reorganizations, even up to and including their own abolition. Such abolition is likely to take the form of a change of name plates, such as has already been seen in a couple of cases.[90] There is likely to be a continuing heavy emphasis on putting the middle link onto *khozraschet*, i.e. getting the enterprises to pay directly for the upkeep of 'their' bureaucrats. One senior ministry official put it to me in terms of enterprises, if they choose to, sending their 'representatives' in the coordination of activities, strategic planning, etc. None of that represents a real break from the past or anything like a move to the radical model set out at the beginning of this paper.

Clearly part of the explanation for the lack of genuine movement towards that model is that the ministries themselves do not want it to happen. But a more important explanation is that the context in which the ministries operate does not allow such movement. The market does not exist in the USSR, and it is therefore pointless talking about independent enterprises and the disappearance of the traditional ministries. The lack of the market is to be explained far more by the lack of political will and consensus, the lack of psychological acceptance at all levels of society, and the enormity of the problems involved in introducing the market into a chronically deficit economy than by ministerial opposition. The fate of the reform, and therefore of the ministries themselves, does not depend on the ministries alone.

Notes

1 For some recent accounts, see A.C. Gorlin, 'The power of the Soviet industrial ministries in the 1980s', *Soviet Studies*, 37, no. 3, July 1985, pp. 353–70; D.A. Dyker, 'The power of the industrial ministries', in D. Lane (ed.), *Elites and Political Power in the USSR*, Elgar, Aldershot, 1988, chapter 8.
2 For a more detailed account of the general approaches to reform of the ministries, see S. Fortescue, 'Soviet bureaucracy and civil society', in C. Kukathas and D.W. Lovell (eds.), *State and Civil Society in Gorbachev's USSR*, Longman, London, forthcoming.
3 *Pravitel'stvennyi vestnik* no. 21, 1989, pp. 4–5.

4 For examples of this approach, see *Ekonomicheskaia gazeta* no. 26, 1989, and no. 36, 1990, p. 6.

5 For an expression of this approach, albeit masked by 'progressive' language, see the speech by the Minister of Metallurgy at the October 1990 Central Committee plenum. *Pravda*, 11 october 1990, p. 6.

6 Most of the statues for individual ministries that flowed from the General Statute have lòst legal force for the simple reason that most of the ministries to which they applied no longer exist. The ministries replacing them do not have individual statutes.

7 For the text of the 1967 Statute, see *Sobranie postanovlenii* no. 17, 1967, Article 116.

8 *Sobranie postanovlenii*, no. 38, 1987, Article 122, para. 1.

9 For the texts, see *Izvestiia*, 1 July 1987, 11 August 1989, and 12 June 1990.

10 *Izvestiia*, 30 March 1990, pp. 1 and 3.

11 *Izvestiia*, 11 August 1990, p. 2.

12 For the text of the Presidential decree establishing the Fund, see *Pravda*, 10 August 1990, p. 1.

13 *Ekonomika i zhizn'*, no. 9, 1990, pp. 12, and 21, no. 14, 1990, p. 21.

14 For the text of the Council of Ministers decree, see *Ekonomika i zhizn'*, no. 45, 1990, p. 19.

15 In measuring the increase in the ministries' powers of appointment we have to remember that the *nomenklatura* system of the regional party organs has broken down.

16 *Izvestiia*, 29 June 1990, p. 2.

17 *Pravda*, 10 September 1990, p. 2, *Izvestiia*, 21 June 1990, p. 2; the Minister of Metallurgy at the October CC plenum. *Pravda*, 11 October 1990, p. 6.

18 *Delovye liudi*, June 1990, p. 21; *Izvestiia*, 25 June 1990, p. 2.

19 There have indeed been cases of enterprises referring ministerial infractions to the courts and arbitration. For example, *Izvestiia*, 23 March 1988, p. 3; 5 April 1988, p. 2.

20 *Moscow News*, no. 13, 1989, p. 13. For other cases, see *Izvestiia*, 22 October 1989, p. 2; R.F. Kallistratova, 'Perestroika and the future of arbitration', *Sovetskoe gosudarstvo i pravo*, no. 5, 1989, p. 39.

21 Kallistratova, *Sovetskoe gosudarstvo i pravo*, no. 5, 1989, pp. 36–43. One half of those surveyed saw no need for ministries.

22 *Sovetskoe gosudarstvo i pravo*, no. 5, 1989, p. 39.

23 *Izvestiia*, 19 march 1990, p. 2.

24 *Ekonomika i zhizn'*, no. 4, 1990, p. 12.

25 *Izvestiia*, 25 June 1990, p. 2.

26 This was a decree demanding the fulfilment of existing contractual obligations. *Izvestiia*, 28 September 1990, p. 1.

27 *Izvestiia*, 28 June 1990, p. 2.

28 *Izvestiia*, 25 June 1990, p. 2.

29 A. Åslund, *Gorbachev's Struggle for Economic Reform. The Soviet Reform Process*, Ithaca, Cornell University Press, 1989, p. 135.

30 *Izvestiia*, 5 November 1989, p. 3. Some commentators have claimed that ministries deliberately but enterprises into impossible financial situations in order to increase their hold over them. *Voprosy ekonomiki*, no. 12, 1988, p. 44.

For more on branch banks pressurising enterprises, see *Ekonomicheskaia gazeta*, no. 37, 1989, pp. 14–15.

31 *Pravda*, 9 April 1989, p. 2; *Izvestiia*, 15 October 1989, p. 2.
32 *Sotsialisticheskaia industriia*, 10 November 1987, pp. 2–3; *Ekonomicheskaia gazeta*, no. 5, 1989, p. 6; A.G. Khudokormov, *Ekonomicheskie korni biurokratizma* Ekonomika, 1988, Moscow, p. 81.
33 *Izvestiia*, 8 June 1989, p. 2; *Ekonomicheskaia gazeta*, no. 35, 1988, pp. 6–7.
34 *Sotsialisticheskaia industriia*, 10 November 1987, pp. 2–3, and 26 December 1987, p. 2; *Ogonek*, no. 30, 1990, p. 24.
35 *Pravda*, 11 February 1988, p. 3; *Moscow News*, 17 January 1988, p. 3.
36 *Moskovskaia pravda*, 24 July 1988, p. 2.
37 It was said that enterprise managers were reluctant to admit to having any vacancies, because ministries would then force them to accept redundant ministerial officials. *Moscow News*, 14 February 1988, pp. 8–9.
38 *Moskovskaia pravda*, 24 July 1988, p. 2, and 14 February 1988, pp. 8–9.
39 *Izvestiia*, 25 August 1986, p. 2, and 23 July 1986, p. 2.
40 *Moscow News*, 13 August 1989, p. 5; *Izvestiia*, 15 October 1989, p. 2.
41 *Moscow News*, 17 January 1988, p. 3.
42 There are, in fact, very conflicting figures. See *Pravda*, 30 July 1987, p. 1, and 21 September 1987, p. 2; *Sotsialisticheskaia industriia*, 10 November 1987, pp. 2–3; *Moscow news*, 14 February 1988, pp. 8–9.
43 *Isvestiia*, 6 July 1989, p. 1. Ten of these are 'service' ministries (finance, justice, foreign affairs, etc); six are in the defence industry; four in construction; five in transport, power and communities; and twelve in industry and resources, including four in the engineering sector. For a somewhat different, and more official, breakdown, see *Pravitel'stvennyi vestnik*, no. 18, 1989, p. 2.
44 *Pravitel'stvennyi vestnik*, no. 22, 1989, p. 1; *Izvestiia*, 14 September 1989, p. 2.
45 For a brief discussion of the powers of 'functional' departments, see S. Fortescue, *Science Policy Making in the USSR*, London, Routledge , 1990, p. 66.
46 The middle link receives more detailed attention in the original version of this paper presented at the Third World Congress.
47 See L. Holmes, *The Policy Process in Communist States. Politics and Industrial Administration*, London, Sage, 1981; W.J. Conyngham, *The Modernization of Soviet Industrial Management. Socio-Economic Development and the Search for Viability*, Cambridge, Cambridge University Press, 1982, esp. chapter 6.
48 *Sobranie postanovlenii*, no. 47, 1987, Article 156.
49 *Sobranie postanovlenii*, no. 17, 1988, Article 46.
50 *Izvestiia*, 1 January 1987, p. 2.
51 *Pravda*, 18 August 1986, p. 1.
52 *Pravda*, 22 October 1988, p. 3.
53 *Sotsialisticheskaia industriia*, 28 June 1988, p. 1.
54 *Ekonomicheskaia gazeta*, no. 6, 1989, p. 8.
55 *Pravda*, 21 September 1987, p. 2; *Izvesiia TsK KPSS*, no. 1, 1989, p. 70.
56 V.B. Aver'ianov, 'Content of the activity of the apparatus of state management and its organizational structures', *Sovetskoe gosudarstvo i pravo*, no. 6, 1988, p. 67.
57 *Pravda*, 9 April 1989, p. 2.

58 *Pravda*, 8 December 1987, p. 2; *Sotsialisticheskaia industriia*, 12 August 1987, p. 1; *Izvestiia*, 1 July 1989, p. 2.
59 *Pravda*, 9 April 1989, p. 2.
60 *Ibid.*
61 *Ekonomicheskaia gazeta*, no. 6, 1989, p. 8.
62 *Pravda*, 9 April 1989, p. 2.
63 *Izvestiia*, 14 September 1989, p. 2.
64 *Kontsern* is a very fashionable word at the moment, along with other Anglicisms such as *konsortsium* and *assotsiatsiia*. They are apparently by their very 'Westernness' highly market-oriented connotations. The ministries have rapidly taken advantage of these 'progressive' connotations and appropriated the words for themselves.
65 *Izvestiia*, 14 September 1989, p. 2; *Pravitel'stvennyi vestnik*, no. 24, 1989, p. 2.
66 More details on the MGOs can be found in the original version of this paper.
67 *Moskovskaia pravda*, 12 January 1989, p. 2.
68 *Izvestiia*, 6 June 1989, p. 2.
69 *Izvestiia*, 22 October 1989, p. 2.
70 *Izvestiia*, 6 June 1989, p. 2.
71 Although for the first signs of expanding apparatuses, at least in terms of requirements for new office space, see *Delovye liudi*, June 1990, p. 21.
72 See the comment that 'Energomash' would be 'unable to operate outside the old system even if it wanted to'. *Izvestiia*, 6 June 1989, p. 2.
73 *Izvestiia*, 6 June 1989, p. 2.
74 *Moskovskaia pravda*, 12 January 1989, p. 2.
75 *Izvestiia*, 19 November 1989, p. 2.
76 *Sotsialisticheskaia industriia*, 27 September 1989, p. 2.
77 *Izvestiia*, 23 July 1989, p. 2.
78 *Izvestiia*, 22 October 1989, p. 2.
79 *Izvestiia*, 19 November 1989, p. 2.
80 *Izvestiia*, 22 October 1989, p. 2.
81 *Pravda*, 15 September 1989, p. 3. For details on Agrokhim, see *Pravitel'stvennyi vestnik*, no. 17, 1989, p. 8, and no. 21, 1989, p.5.
82 *Izvestiia*, 19 November 1989, p. 2.
83 *Sotsialisticheskaia industriia*, 27 September 1989, p. 2. For details on similar transformations of other ministries, see *Pravitel'stvennyi Vestnik*, no. 24, 1989, p. 23, and no. 25, 1990, p. 9; *Inzhenernaia gazeta*, 31 August 1990, p. 2.
84 *Ekonomika i zhizn'* no. 40, 1990, p. 12.
85 See the element of competition in the bus-making *kontsern* Avtrokon. *Pravda*, 20 September 1990, pp. 1–2.
86 *Kommersant*, no. 42, 1990, p. 4.
87 For an outline of a similar approach in Latvia, see *Ekonomika i zhizn'* no. 1, 1990, p. 14.
88 *Izvestiia*, 28 July 1990, p. 2; *Kommersant*, no. 27, 1990, p. 4.
89 *Pravda*, 9 October 1990, p. 3.
90 Such an approach is clearly seen in the speech of the Minister of Metallurgy at the October 1990 CC plenum. *Pravda*, 11 October 1990, p. 6.

Part III

Effects of perestroika on Soviet life

8   Employment and the reallocation of labour in the USSR

Sheila Marnie

Introduction

The USSR is in the process of deciding how to make and manage its transition to a market-type economy. With regard to employment and the labour market, this transition will mean the end of a system of guaranteed employment, as unprofitable enterprises are forced to close down, and others are no longer able to 'hoard' superfluous workers. For the first time, the Soviet Union is trying to come to terms with unemployment and define the forms and amount which already exist in the country. The legislation related to the economic reform is expected to include a new Employment Act, which will set out the type of provision to be made for anticipated large increases in unemployment.

How prepared is the Soviet Union to manage such changes in employment practices? How is reallocation to be achieved? Do incentives and mechanisms exist to facilitate job changes? Are new policies being designed to ensure a minimum social consensus for the economic changes envisaged and to protect certain sections of the population? Other East European countries are faced with similar problems, but the lessons for the Soviet Union from this quarter are limited, since, the scale and regional diversity of the Soviet labour market make it a special and more complex case.

The three main questions addressed in this paper are as follows:

1. Has perestroika so far led to any significant increase in unemployment? Calls for the large-scale reallocation of labour, involving 19 million or more employees, have led to predictions of increases in frictional unemployment. Recent Soviet discussion of unemployment is examined which already existed in the pre-perestroika period or to a new phenomenon, that is, to examine the extent to which current unemployment has been inherited, rather than created, by perestroika. The novelty so far may be the open discussion of unemployment, rather than any significant increases.

2. Has perestroika been successful in changing patterns of labour utilization and bringing about the reallocation of redundant labour from the main industrial branches of the economy to the service sector and consumer goods industries? One of the themes of perestroika has been the need to eliminate wasteful use of resources, including labour. since the late 1980s it has frequently been stated that as the industrial branches of the economy undergo restructuring, redundant workers will be reallocated to the service sector and consumer goods industries, in order both to improve labour utilization and to improve the supply of goods and services to the population. Recent employment data are examined to establish whether redeployment patterns have in fact followed such policy statements, and whether labour utilization has become less 'wasteful'.

3. How prepared is the Soviet Union for any future rise in unemployment? It is important to look at the type of labour market which has existed until now in the Soviet Union, at past attempts to rationalize and reallocate labour, and at the existing government employment institutions and regulations relating to redundancies, in order to establish what sort of experience the USSR can drawn on when tackling the new problems involved in restructuring. An attempt will be made to identify those sections of the population most likely to be affected by any future increases in unemployment, and to look at the type of provision being made for them.

The discussion of these questions is organized as follows: it begins with an account of past employment policy and the previous approach to redundancies; it goes on to consider recent Soviet discussion of unemployment and recent redeployment policies and patterns; it then summarizes reports on the draft employment act which is currently being prepared; and finally, it draws some conclusions with regard to the above questions.

The Soviet labour market and the previous approach to redundancies

Allocation of labour

Since the 1950s the labour market in the Soviet Union has been subject to much less central control than other aspects of the economy. Workers on the whole find jobs independently, and factories/organizations advertize their own vacancies and are responsible for their own staff recruitment. In the mid-1980s, around 85 per cent of all hires took place 'at the factory gate', that is, without any form of organized state allocation.[1] Workers are also free to quit and change jobs, and turnover rates show a high degree of mobility.[2]

In theory, there has been a commitment to full employment, which is guaranteed through the practice of 'planning from resources', of creating a sufficient overall number of workplaces to employ the working age population. Balances have been drawn up in order to plan the matching of manpower and workplaces. In practice, however, the balances have been drawn up only at the aggregate level, and regional 'balances' have not been achieved. There are currently estimated to be 2.8 million job vacancies (first shift) in the national economy,[3] and there are reports of labour shortages in most areas of the country. (Approximately 139 million are employed in the national economy, 120 million of them in the state sector; see appendix 1.) These shortages have been coupled more recently with reports of excess manpower and lack of employment opportunities for young people in the Central Asian Republics.[4]

The fact that labour force participation rates could not be expected to increase,[5] and that the number of new entrants to the labour market has been lower than in the previous decade, made it unlikely that the 'balance' could be achieved by drawing on labour 'reserves' within the population. However, in the absence of any changes in the economic system, this seemed to be the dominant preoccupation of planners in the 1980s. In the words of one Soviet commentator: 'the sense of employment policy has in essence amounted to meeting the demand of the economy for manpower, looking for new sources of manpower.'[6] This meant, for example, that pensioners were given incentives to continue working, that only very limited possibilities of part-time and home-based work were offered, and that further expansion of full-time study was discouraged. Any healthy adult was obliged to work for all of his/her adult life; the choice not to work did not exist.[7]

In this context the term used for 'unemployed' (*nezaniatye*) meant those *not employed* in the state economy, who were looked upon as potential 'reserves' which should in some way be 'drawn in' to the state sector.[8] The question of whether the *nezaniatye* were actively seeking employment in the state sector was not usually raised.[9]

Thus the dominant concern of the last twenty years has been that of finding additional manpower at all costs, which does not suggest that the USSR has much expertise to draw on now, when faced with the task of devising suitable labour market policies for the proposed structural changes.

The previous approach to redundancies

Although the number of redundancy type dismissals has until now been minimal (1–2 per cent in the 1970s; 4 per cent per year *planned* for the twelfth five year plan, 1986–90[10]), there has always been the idea that they were inevitable if the economy were to be restructured, and that they should and could be carried out in a 'planned manner'. Even those specialists who criticized the planners one-sided view of the worker as a 'labour resource', a resource to be planned like any other input, rather than something more human, seemed to believe that the way to protect the social rights of workers was to *plan* the elimination of uninteresting low-skill jobs and the redeployment of released workers, thus avoiding unemployment.[11] There has long been a contradiction between the usual calls for less planning as a way to improve the working of the economy, and the calls of most Soviet labour specialists for more planning of labour allocation, in order to combat hoarding and to avoid unnecessarily long spells of open frictional unemployment.[12] The calls for more planning have stemmed largely from a reluctance to admit to any form of unemployment because of the important legitimation role played by full employment in Soviet politics; but also to a firmly embedded traditional Soviet principle that unplanned individual mobility is wasteful and should be discouraged.[13]

Redundancy dismissals and planning

For over twenty years Soviet specialists have pointed to the hoarding of workers in Soviet enterprises, and stressed the need to find some mechanism to ensure the 'releasing' of superfluous workers and their redeployment in more productive jobs. The number of superfluous workers was commonly said to represent 15–20 per cent of an enterprise's workforce.[14] In order to do this either an effective incentive had to be given to managers to 'release' workers, or planners had to gain more information on actual enterprise manpower requirements in order either to set releasing targets or limit the enterprise's allocated wage fund. An enterprise's labour demand was calculated on the basis of its output target: the amount of labour required for the fulfilment of the output target was based on the amount required in the previous plan period with some allowance for planned productivity increases. Throughout the 1970s and 80s experiments based on the example of 'Shchekino' were used to try and offer enterprises incentives to release workers.[15] Schemes such as 'attestation' of workplaces were used to try and collect information on enterprise manpower requirements.[16] Most recently, the 1986 wage reform was an attempt to give enterprises an incentive to rationalize by increasing the centrally-set wage tariffs for all categories of workers, but asking enterprises to finance the increase out of their own funds.[17] The 1987 Enterprise Law also offered enterprises two types of self-accounting models, the second of which offered the enterprises the chance to benefit from reducing their workforce.[18]

Releasing entered the planning vocabulary, and targets for releasing manual labour were included in the enterprises' plans. Various adjectives were used to describe what are apparently different forms of releasing, namely 'relative freeing', 'conditional freeing' and 'absolute freeing'. These were, however, terms used above all in the technical planning literature, and did not necessarily correspond to actual workers being made redundant. The planning system was geared towards the production of increasing volumes of output, and the concept of labour releasing has until now been part of output planning, not employment policy. In this context the concept of labour releasing has referred to productivity growth measured in higher volumes of output per unit of labour or labour time. Current reports of x-numbers of released workers still do not correspond to a number of dismissed workers, but to a productivity increase, relative to a previous productivity level, calculated in terms of labour, with productivity gains being the result of increasing output, rather than decreasing labour expenditure.[19] Worker requirements were estimated as the equivalent of a work-time fund, which includes overtime, worktime for repair, etc. Thus, time rather than numbers of workers is reduced (although actual employment levels may be reduced by non-replacement of retired workers) and the planning of potential unemployment has had little to do with actual people and their welfare.[20]

Redundancy dismissals and the law

According to the Soviet Constitution, citizens have the right and duty to work. The state has the responsibility of providing workplaces. However, responsibility for finding alternative employment for released workers has until now rested with the enterprise. This has been consistently quoted by Soviet specialists as a major disincentive for enterprises to release their surplus manpower.[21] They have usually advocated that the state assume responsibility for redeployment through the network of labour offices (see below) under the State Committee for Labour and Social Questions.

There has always been legislation which foresaw the possibility of redundancy-type dismissals. The Labour Code has allowed managers to dismiss workers in connection with 'liquidation of the enterprise, institution, organization, reduction in the number and composition of staff'.[22] Before a manager can dismiss a worker due to reduction in numbers employed, the worker has to be offered an alternative job within the same enterprise, or management has to prove that no alternative exists. In the case of liquidation, the 'higher standing body', i.e. the ministry in the case of industrial enterprises, and the job placement bodies have to solve the problems of job placement of the released workers.[23] Should the worker not accept the alternative job, or if there is no alternative to be offered, the dismissal procedure (*uvol'nenie*) is used. (Workers refusing the alternative may also quit, without waiting to be dismissed. They have then come under the voluntary quit category *tekuchest'*, which covers voluntary quits and disciplinary dismissals.)[24] The written agreement of the enterprise trade union committee has been required for dismissal and the work contract has had to be terminated no later than one month after the trade union approval has been given.

A new version of the Labour Code was published in 1988.[25] The above regulations remain valid, but there is a new section specifically dedicated to 'Guaranteeing Employment for Released Workers', spelling out the rights of released workers and the procedure for releasing (Labour Code, Ch. III-A, Art. 40). The offer of alternative employment is now expressly cited as the means of guaranteeing the released worker the right to work.[26] The worker has to be given 2 months' notice, and in the case of reduction in staff numbers, has to be offered an alternative job by management within the same enterprise at the same time as notice is served. If work is not available in the same profession or specialization, or if the worker refuses transfer (*perevod*) to another job within the same enterprise, he may be placed through a Job Placement Buro (henceforth JPB) or find work independently. Management informs the Job Placement Organs of the releasing envisaged, with information on the job skills and pay level of the workers involved. A type of unemployment benefit has been introduced: the worker is given a severance payment of one month's average pay, and is guaranteed a maximum of two months' pay (including the severance payment) between jobs (three months' pay in the case of liquidation and if workers register with a JPB within two weeks of being dismissed). These payments are made by the enterprise where he/she was originally employed. The uninterrupted work service record (*stazh*: important for entitlement to pension supplements, extra vacation and other benefits) is lost if another job is not started within 3 months.

Regulations on redundancy dismissals exist in many Western European countries,[27] and Soviet specialists may have exaggerated the role of this legal disincentive to redundancy-dismissals in the past, (the economic disincentives meant in fact that the legal regulations were never actually put to the test). However, the reluctance of the state until now to assume responsibility for redeployment and unemployment benefit does seem to have run contrary to the policy statements on the need to release and redeploy millions of workers. The 1988 Labour Code gives managers more rights with regard to reallocation of the workforce within the enterprise (articles 25 and 29), and until 1988–89 policy statements, including one by Gorbachev, contained assurances that unemployment would not be tolerated in the Soviet Union. This suggests that until 1989, it was hoped to follow the East German example of encouraging enterprises to rationalize, while redeploying and retraining workers internally.

Institutions in the Soviet labour market

Job Placement Buros (JPBs) were first established in 1969 in the RSFSR.[28] They have been under the jurisdiction of either the Republic State Labour Committee or the local labour 'organs' attached to the local government. They were first set up to help after the 1965 Economic Reform when enterprises were expected to release workers, who would need help in redeployment. Such large-scale releasing never occurred. Since then the JPBs have grown in number, and at the end of 1989 there were reported to be 812 job placement centres and over 2,000 buros (and *filiali* – branch offices).[29]

There has always been some ambiguity surrounding their exact status and functions: they could be designed to help workers with their independent job search, or they could be seen as agents through which the state could try and increase its control over both worker mobility (discourage voluntary 'unplanned' quits) and enterprise demand.[30] Such ambiguity is still inevitable as long as employment policy remains caught between the 'looking for reserves' mentality, and proposals for change which depend on other market-type changes.

Both the 1988 Labour Code and a 1988 Resolution[31] suggested that they should be expanded and take over the main responsibility for redeployment of released workers. These buros, however, have, always been understaffed and poorly financed. (Until now most of their financing has come from fees charged to enterprises for use of their services.[32]) The wage of a JPB employee is reported to be lower than the national average, and it is difficult to find qualified staff to work in them.[33] Financially they have been dependent on the local enterprises and local government authorities. They are still enterprises and local government authorities. They are still not computerized. On the whole they are looked on with suspicion by workers, and only those who have great difficulty in finding work independently register with them. (Women and elderly who would like part time or home-based work; former prisoners; school leavers with poor school records, etc.) Enterprises are likewise uninterested in taking on the type of workers which tend to be sent to them by the buros.[34] (They have never been obliged to employ a worker sent by the JPB, nor has the worker been obliged to accept the job.) Since 1988, enterprises have been required to register all vacancies with the JPBs, but one article suggests that they only register those which are difficult to fill.[35]

It is usually suggested that state employment offices should also organize and coordinate retraining programmes for released workers. At present most retraining is organized by the enterprises. Job security and legal disincentives to release workers may have acted as an incentive to enterprises to retrain their own workforce, especially since the legal regulations on redeployment within the enterprise have been much laxer. However, another aspect of inefficient utilization of labour in the USSR has been the fact that obsolete machinery is not scrapped. Workers have been kept working at low-productivity machinery, which in turn requires more workers for repair work.[36] There is a shortage of skilled workers to operate more sophisticated machinery and one of the causes for machinery breaking down is manning by underqualified workers.[37] In 1988, 6.3 million workers (about 5 per cent of those employed in the state sector) were given training or retraining at their place of work, but the number had actually decreased from 7.9 million in 1980.[38]

Thus, if this skeleton institutional framework is to provide the foundation for a network of state employment agencies, there is no sign that it is prepared for such a task. Since it is the unskilled workers who are likely to be released first, state retraining centres and schemes would seem necessary. Apart from good intentions expressed in the 1988 resolution on 'guaranteeing rational employment', there is no sign of state organization in this field.

Recent discussion of unemployment and redeployment

Existing forms of unemployment

Since 1988 there have been some attempts to come to terms with and define the existing forms of unemployment. There has been mention of seasonal unemployment in agriculture and summer tourist resorts;[39] of school leavers having difficulty finding jobs;[40] and particularly of a growing unemployment problem in the Central Asian republics. In 1989 a figure of 13 million, was given for the *nezaniatye* working-age population (those not in state employment);[41] in August 1990, 8 million were reported to be *nezaniatye*, in that they were unemployed due to the seasonal character of their work, were inbetween jobs, were invalids (Group III), housewives, or refused to engage in 'socially useful labour.'[42] Figures of 4–6 million were given as estimates of unemployed (*bezrabotitsa*), those who are not in state employment but who could be, with half of these living in Central Asia and Kazakhstan. More recently we have been given a figure of 2 million,[43] which is an estimate of the State Committee for Labour and Social Questions (Goskomtrud). This estimate is the first to allow for an element of voluntary unemployment: it refers to those of working age, who are able to work, and who are actively looking for work. Most of these again are thought to be in Central Asia, but it is not clear on what basis such statistics are calculated, and Soviet specialists complain about the lack of available data.[44]

It should be stressed, however, that all these forms of unemployment have been *inherited* by perestroika. The rise in frictional unemployment which should occur due to restructuring and rationalization of the use of labour is still only a prediction. However, there have been continuous forecasts of 13–19 million workers from the 'material production sector' having to change jobs by the year 2000.[45] Here, again, the novelty is the 'having to change' aspect, since it is reported elsewhere that 25 million workers already change jobs every year, and turnover levels have always been high. The situation will only become more serious in terms of unemployment if enterprises really have to cut back their demand. Presently demand for additional labour remains high and appears to be growing: the number of vacancies (first shift) is reported to have risen from 1.5 million in 1989, to 2.8 million in 1990.[46]

There is also evidence that a large section of the population is involved in second economy activities, and that private income from such activities can represent from 15–6 per cent of total personal income.[47] Most of those involved in the second economy, however, combine these activities with state employment; private income supplements the state wage. It is possible that some of those now being categorized as unemployed will have some alternative unofficial sources of income. Should workers be shed from the state sector, it is also possible that second economy activities will provide some people with either initial cushioning, or with immediate access to legitimized private economy employment. However, current private income earnings vary greatly according to city, region, family, skill, etc., and cannot always be expected to provide ready sources of alternative employment.

Redeployment strategies

Policy statements have suggested that workers will be redeployed in the underdeveloped service sector and the consumer goods industry. In the last two years the number employed in the state industrial sector has begun to decline (in 1988 the number working in the production branches of the state sector decreased by 1.5 million, 1.2 per cent;[48] in 1989 state sector employment decreased by 1.3 million, 1 per cent; see appendix 1). This decrease is largely due to the above-mentioned wage reform; in 1989 around 1.5 million were released after the introduction of the new pay levels (about 500,000 of whom retired; this figure also probably includes vacancies which were scrapped: see Appendix 5). Employment in some areas of the state service sector, such as health and education, did increase in these years, but not to any dramatic extent. There was a decrease in employment in housing and everyday services from 1988–89 (-0.55 per cent) and in light industry (-4.23 per cent), whereas policy statements suggest increases were to be expected. Wages in both these sectors are still relatively low (Appendix 2), although the average wage in light industry increased by 11.7 per cent from 1987–8, compared with to 8.5 per cent for industry as a whole. Under the present arrangements, workers in these sectors still have less access to housing, medical services, and other perks allocated through the place of work (holiday homes, sport and leisure facilities etc.)

Since 1986 there have been two new forms of employment in the USSR: cooperatives and private individual activity. The wording of the 1988 law on cooperatives[49] suggests that they were envisaged as alternative employment in the consumer goods and service sectors for workers released from state enterprises in the period of restructuring, but also as sources of employment of 'additional' labour resources, either for those not in state employment, i.e. pensioners, housewives, etc., or those already in state employment: employees of state enterprises can take on cooperative jobs as a form of second employment (*sovmestitel'stvo*). This again reflects the ambivalence in employment policies: on the one hand the need to rationalize is stressed, and on the other, the inability to reduce labour demand means that 'reserves' are continually sought.

The numbers employed in cooperatives have risen dramatically: from 155,800 in January 1988 to 3.3 million in early 1990 (5 million including *sovmestitel'stvo*).

Given the constant high demand for labour, cooperatives may be competing with enterprises for scarce labour resources rather than offering alternative employment to release workers. Despite the fact that 1.3 million workers were released from state production enterprises in 1989, employment in material production rose by 0.1 per cent (about 86,000) due to the increase in cooperatives.[50] Cooperatives offer high wages and attract particularly skilled workers.[51] In January 1989 two thirds of those working in cooperatives or individual work had either transferred from state enterprises and organizations or were combining the cooperative job with a state job.[52] In 1989 about 80 per cent of all cooperatives were set up alongside state enterprises. About 60 per cent of all fixed assets possessed by cooperatives are leased from state enterprises, and they buy more than 60 per cent of supplies from enterprises.[53] In the past, with releasing schemes of the Shchekino type, released workers tended to be used to man new workplaces within the same enterprise: releasing went hand in hand with enterprise expansion. This pattern seems to be continuing, with enterprises formally releasing workers, but using cooperative labour to help make better use of enterprise capacity, and to

Table 8.1. *Workforce employed by the new type of cooperatives, in individual work, at the end of each year, numerically and by per cent*

Date	Coops	Individual work
1988	0.25%	0.15%
1989	1.76%	0.18%
1989	2.9 million*	0.4 million
1990	3.3 million*	0.3 million

* Does not include *sovmestitel'stvo*, people combining state and coop jobs.

Trud v SSSR, pp. 274–276; *Ekonomika i zhizn'*, no. 6, 1990; *Argumenty i fakty*, no. 45, 1989; *Vestnik statistiki*, no. 4, 1989; *Statisticheskii press biulleten'*, nos. 10 and 5, 1989; *Ekonomika i zhizn'*, no. 18, 1990.

fulfil state orders. Such practices will not lead to more efficient utilization of labour resources, nor to the promised redeployment of labour to the service sector.

Recently, there have been regulations limiting the scale and scope of the activities of cooperatives which would seem to go against the idea of developing the consumer goods and service sectors and of easing the redeployment process. As a result of such regulations, the number of cooperatives in trade and catering has decreased. One third of cooperative workers are currently employed in construction, and only one in six in consumer goods industry, and one in eight in the service sphere[54] (see Appendix 3).

Which sections of the workforce are threatened by unemployment?

According to one Soviet sociologist,

A new fringe stratum is appearing in our society, consisting of people squeezed from production ... This stratum is made up of non-specialist white-collar workers, unskilled blue-collar workers, people approaching retirement age and young people about to enter the workforce.[55]

Such statements, however, are still predictions; for the moment the labour market remains taut. Should other changes in the economy take place, unemployment may be a problem. At the moment, any unemployment is minimal and has been inherited from the past. The groups mentioned in the Soviet articles are women and young people, and unskilled, particularly elderly unskilled workers.[56]

There is potentially a problem with the redeployment of white-collar workers in large towns, this section of the workforce being the target of separate releasing campaigns to reduce administrative staff. In Moscow in April 1988 there were 101,842 vacancies, but only 12,000 were for 'engineering and technical staff' (ITRs) and other white-collar workers; in 1989 there were about 112,000 vacancies for blue-collar workers and more than 14,000 for white-collar workers.[57] Thus, those released due to the streamlining of the state apparatus may have to look for work outside Moscow.[58] Recent reports suggest that so far they appear to have been reshuffled into other administrative jobs, and the reduction in the average annual employment figures is largely due to the recategorization of some such jobs under 'production'.[59]

The data on releasing after the wage reform show that a high percentage of those released and leaving the enterprise, actually retired about 30 per cent of those released from enterprise retired). This suggests that people of pensionable age after years of being encouraged to continue in employment after retirement age (fifty-five for women; sixty for men)[60] are now the first to be asked to leave. The Soviet population is aging, and old age pensioners currently represent 17.1 per cent of the population. By the end of 1990, pension age citizens will number 51 million.[61] The growth in the older age groups took place above all in the European parts of the country. (In the Central Asian Republics, the pension age group represents 8–10 per cent of the population.)[62] Since January 1990, workers and foremen who continue to work beyond retirement age have the right to a full pension, no matter how high their earnings[63] and in May 1990 this right was extended to all categories of employees.[64] The current situation of labour shortage in the European parts of the country should ensure that a certain proportion of pensioners benefit initially from such measures. If pensioners are among the first to be released, there may, however, be an increase in poverty among this age group. The average pension for workers and employers in 1988 was only 40 per cent of the average wage for these categories. (Average wage was 217 rubles; average pension 86.3 rubles). The minimum pension is now 70 rubles.[65] It is not always clear that whether pensioners want to, or have to continue working for financial reasons. Table 8.2 shows that about 40 per cent received a pension of below 80 rubles in 1988.

In the same year, there were 10 million old-age pensioners working in the state economy, only 400,000 of whom had part-time work.[66] Of these, 35 per cent were workers who had a right to early retirement, who may be younger and more predisposed and able to continue work. However, 13 per cent of the male working pensioners were over seventy years old, and 19 per cent of the female working pensioners were over sixty-five.[67] One fifth of the 41 million said to have an income below the minimum wage

Table 8.2. *Pensions and pensioners*

Average old-age pension (rubles per month)				
Year	1980	1985	1986	1987	1988
Amount	71.6	87.2	89.4	91.7	93.9

Size of old-age pension, July 1987 (rubles per month)				
Amount	up to 60	60–80	80–100	100–120	+ or
					= 120
% recipients	20.2	21.3	17.0	13.1	28.4

Size of family income for pensioners,* year unspecified (rubles per month)
(published 1990)

Amount	up to 50	50–75	75–100	100–150	150 +
% of	3.6	28.7	27.8	29.2	10.7
pensioner-families**					

* Old-age pensioners represent about 75 per cent of all pensioners.

** There are about 19.1 pensioner families.

Statisticheskii press biulleten', nos. 1 and 9, 1989; *Ekonomika i zhizn'* no. 18, 1990.

level are pensioners (but not just old-age pensioners).[68] There is a sharp difference in income between pensioners who work and those who live off their pension. At the end of the 1980s, a family in Moscow with pension and wage earned a total income of 280 rubles per month compared with 107 rubles per month for a family with only pension (*Ekonomika i zhizn'*, no. 18, 1990).

This section of the population seem likely to suffer if there is a wave of releasing coupled with price rises, unless the recent law (May 1990) on pensions succeeds in providing some sort of cushion for them.

The regional aspect

Reports on unemployment frequently refer to Central Asia. Here, the problem is different, in that the concern is not with finding redeployment solutions for released workers, but with creating jobs particularly for the young. Again, this is not an unemployment problem which is due to any innovations introduced under perestroika, but rather one which stems from the past inability of the planning system to coordinate population forecasts, investment plans, and productivity targets.

There have been references to mass poverty in Central Asia, with the section of the population living below an undefined poverty line being 60 per cent in Tadzhikistan; over 46 per cent in Uzbekistan; 40 per cent in Kirgizia and Turkmenistan. The average income in the region is 40–60 rubles per month and one of the causes of poverty is said to be 'mass unemployment'.[69] Such reports may be a little over-dramatic. Some of this area is rich in agricultural terms, and more information is needed on unofficial income. Another article suggests that the feudal-type social and economic relations, rather than unemployment, may account for much of the poverty in some of these Republics.[70]

It is difficult to estimate the extent of unemployment in this region. A 1987 resolution on Central Asia and the Caucasus published last year refers to over 5 million *nezaniatye*.[71] A similar resolution dated 1986 states that there is a real reserve of 3 million from the able-bodied population which could be drawn into social production,[72] of whom there are 1 million in Uzbekistan and 0.4 million in Azerbaidzhan; about 1 million, one third, are men. Women with many children are said to represent less than one fifth of the reserve and more than half of them would like to work under certain conditions.[73] This resolution gives the percentage of the working-age population which was *nezaniatye* in some of the republics in 1984, and we can get a rough estimate of the numbers involved from the 1989 census data.

If we discount the women with many children who do not wish to work (even those wishing to work, wish to do so only 'under certain circumstances'; i.e. if work is home-based or part-time), we are left with 'real reserves' of 2,700,000, or 7.7 per cent of the able-bodied population in 1989. We know that in at least two of the republics, Tadzhikistan and Turkmenia, the percentage of female *nezaniatye* is extremely high; the number of males not in state employment in these republics is roughly 38,000 and 6,500 respectively. It is not clear that cultural reasons would permit married women to work outside the domain of the home and private plot. Moreover the above resolutions should be seen in the context of the planners' obsession with finding 'reserves' which could be drawn into social production. They mention frequently that a significant proportion of these *nezaniatye* are parasites living off illegal income, which suggests that some voluntarily choose to remain outside state employment.

Young workers in Central Asia are said to have problems finding jobs. It is reported that in Uzbekistan in 1985 only 7 per cent of school leavers from rural schools were placed in industry and 6 per cent in construction.[74] In Uzbekistan in the period 1981–85, 19 per cent of the graduates of universities (*vuz*) and 39 per cent of secondary specialised institutes (*suz*) were not allocated jobs.[75] Recent statistics show that only 7.7 per cent of all Soviet school leavers found jobs in agriculture in 1974, but 42 per cent in 1987.[76] This must be due to the fact that almost all the new entrants to the labour force are now in the Central Asian republics, where the rural population is still large, and suggests that young people are working in

Table 8.3. *Non-employed in the state sector (nezaniatye) in the Central Asian and Caucasian Republics in* 1984

	Non-employed among working-age population (per cent)
Uzbekistan	22.8
Tadzhikistan	25.7
of which 94% female	
Turkmenia	18.8
of which 98% female	
Kirgizia	16.3
Azerbaidzhan	27.6
Armenia	18.0
Georgia	13.5

Vestnik statistiki, no. 5, 1990; *Izvestiia TsK KPSS*, no. 5, 1989; *Argumenty i fakty*, no. 45, 1989.

Table 8.4. *School leavers in Central Asia*

	Age 16–17 1989	Age 18–19 1989	School leavers not in employment 1985	1987	As share of 16–17 yrs in 1987 /(per cent)
Uzbekistan	823,244	757,554	4,300	8,600	1.1
Tadzhikistan	216,239	200,278	3,400	4,300	2.1
Turkmenia	144,468	145,519	1,500	2,700	1.8
Kirgizia	168,808	152,445	900	1,500	0.9
Kazakhstan	589,418	551,070	1,800	2,600	0.4
(RSFSR)	(4,052,661)	(3,903,984)	(5,500)	(7,100)	(0.1)
(USSR)	(8,691,747)	(8,238,167)	(29,900)	(36,200)	(0)

Vestnik statistiki no. 5, 1990; *Trud v SSSR*, Moscow, Goskomstat SSSR, 1988, p. 93; *Molodezh' SSSR*, Moscow, Goskomstat SSSR, 1990, p. 140.

agriculture, either from choice or necessity. Table 8.4 shows that there has been a considerable increase in the number of school leavers not entering employment immediately. Again we have no indication of the extent of choice involved.

Evidence on unemployment in Central Asia is inconclusive. Other attempts to rationalize may have served to increase involuntary unemployment in this area: investment has been cut back, which means that there may be less new work-places being created for the young generation; releasing campaigns are said to have been carried out in this area, thus contradicting other calls to increase the numbers employed in the state economy.[77] However, more knowledge on the extent of involuntary unemployment is required before referring to mass unemployment.

New employment act

A new employment act ('Basic legislation of the USSR and Union Republics on employment of the population') is being prepared as part of the legislation announcing the introduction of economic reform.[78] For the first time, the legislation being considered recognizes unemployment and envisages state responsibility and provision for the unemployed. Reports suggest that the main points to be included in this legislation are as follows:

1. Citizens should have the right to choose whether to work or not. Bringing up children and looking after the elderly or invalids should be recognized as a valid form of employment, and by means of social guarantees their prestige should be raised. Citizens should have the right not to work, provided they have a legal source of income.

2. The state cannot retain a monopoly over labour resources. Workers have the right to choose to work for organizations outside state employment (cooperatives, leasing and shareholder enterprises, private farms).

3. Anyone of working age who is able to work, and actively seeks work, but cannot find employment, is to be considered unemployed (*bezrabotnyi*), and will be entitled to a benefit. The proposal for the moment is that the central government guarantees a minimum level of benefit; this would be a minimum wage (70–80 rubles per month, *Trud vs SSSR*, pp. 227–8) for those who previously worked at socialist enterprises and have lost their jobs, for those who are demobilized from the armed forces, and for those who have just finished training. The other unemployed, including first-time job seekers, would be given 50 per cent of the minimum pension (35 rubles[79]). Republics and autonomous republics can use their own funds to supplement the minimum benefit. This benefit would be paid for six months, after which, if the worker has not found employment, he will be offered a wage to do social work. If, after six months, the worker goes on a retraining course, he will be paid the minimum wage for the duration of the course.

4. The state should take on full responsibility for employment services. The state and not the enterprise should be responsible for job placement of released workers. The existing job placement buros and centres should

be reorganized, and funded by the state, not by enterprises. The state network of employment services should be responsible for the job placement, career advice, training and retraining.

5. The centre should still draw up programmes to help with employment problems of women, young people, people near retirement age, invalids, certain territorial units.

6. There is also a proposal to set up an employment fund to help finance the benefits and employment services, contributions to which would come from a special enterprise tax, and possibly from a voluntary social insurance.

Point (1) acknowledges for the first time that employment and unemployment may be voluntary; point (2) that employment does not mean state employment. Point (3) gives the embryo of a state unemployment benefit scheme, although the proposed payments seem very low, especially for new entrants. Point (4) recognizes state responsibility for helping in the redeployment of unemployed workers, but there is still no clear picture of how the proposed state system will differ from the current placement service.

The significance of this legislation may be primarily symbolic, in that unemployment is recognized as a problem for which state provision should be made. It should herald the end of the previous criminalization of unemployment, whereby the non-employed were classified (and sometimes arrested) as 'parasites'. In practical terms, little support is offered to the long-term unemployed, in that the type of benefit proposed falls short of the schemes currently being implemented in other East European countries.[80] Unless the individual republics have substantial funds with which to supplement the state benefit, the severance payments made by the enterprise (2–3 months of previous average wage) will remain the main form of financial support available to the unemployed.

Conclusion

There has been some speculation that economic restructuring would lead to large-scale labour reallocation, and consequently to a significant increase in unemployment in the USSR. So far there is no evidence of either phenomenon. What there has been is an increase in the *discussion* of unemployment, as well as attempts to define the existing types of unemployment. There has long been evidence of frictional and seasonal unemployment in the Soviet Union (although the amount of such unemployment has never been alarming, it was never admitted to in the days when any mention of unemployment was taboo), and for some time there have been reports of unemployment in the Central Asian Republics.

Here, it is difficult to distinguish between voluntary and involuntary unemployment because the only data published so far refer to all those not employed in the state sector, whether seeking state employment or not. The main point about such cases of unemployment, however, is that they are not new, although it is possible that attempts at rationalization have made matters worse.

Perestroika promised to encourage the more rational use of resources, including labour, and to promote the reallocation of redundant workers from the main industrial branches of the economy to the service sphere and consumer goods industries. While there has been some decrease in annual average employment in material production since 1988, much of this is due to the wage reform, and does not represent any permanent change in the pattern of labour utilization. Cooperatives were supposed to provide an alternative source of employment for workers released from state enterprises, and to help develop the service sphere and consumer goods production. I have argued, however, that cooperatives have become an *additional* rather than an alternative source of employment, with demand in the state sector remaining high. Moreover, the majority of cooperative workers are employed outside the spheres of service and consumer goods production.

Past employment policies and the previous approach to redundancies have left the Soviet Union with very little experience on which to draw when tackling current labour market problems. Employment policy has been dominated by the need to find additional labour resources for the state sector, and enterprises have been encouraged to redeploy redundant workers internally, in order to avoid the question of open unemployment. In practical terms the past experience of redundancy-type dismissals is almost non-existent. Skeleton legislative and institutional frameworks do exist, but institutions in particular require a vast amount of human and financial investment. Soviet attitudes to the problems of the unemployed point to a lack of intellectual preparation for labour market reform. Some refuse to consider the problems, insisting that unemployment is incompatible with socialism, and must not be tolerated; that investment policy can be planned to avoid it.[81] Others insist that unemployment will not be a problem, because of the underdeveloped service sector and the need to expand the production of consumer goods.[82] Some do recognize, however, that it may be a problem automatically transforming lathe turners and fitters into hairdressers and cooks.[83]

There is evidence that about 30 per cent of all those made redundant due to the wage reform, and who had to leave the enterprise, actually retired. This suggests, firstly, that redundancies do not necessarily lead to increased mobility and reallocation and, secondly, that pensioners will be one of the first sections of the population to suffer from involuntary unemployment.

The draft Employment Act currently under discussion represents the first serious attempt at tackling changing patterns of employment and unemployment. So far, however, there has been more fiction than fact surrounding labour market reform in the Soviet Union; as in other areas of the economy, real changes are still being awaited.

Notes

I am most grateful to Anders Åslund, Silvana Malle and John Micklewright for comments on earlier versions of this paper.

1 The main form of organized placement is the allocation of graduates to their first jobs, which they are officially supposed to keep for three years. See S. Malle, 'Planned and unplanned mobility in the Soviet Union under the threat of labour shortage', Soviet Studies, 39, no. 3, July 1987, pp. 357–87. See also A. Kotliar, 'Sistema trudoustroistva v SSSR', Ekonomicheskaia nauka, no. 3, 1984.

2 The turnover rate for industry in 1987 was 12 per cent. Trud v SSSR, Moscow 1988, p. 258. It is reported that 25 million workers change jobs every year. See A. Nikitin, 'Kak pomoch' bezrabotnomu', Pravda, 6 April 1990.

3 See interview with V.I. Shcherbakov in Ekonomika i zhizn', no. 24, 1990, pp. 4–5. Estimates of vacancies vary; if those in the second and third shift are included the number is much greater.

4 I.E. Zaslavskii, 'Obespechenie zaniatostí v usloviiakh perestroiki', Rabochii klass i sovremmennyi mir, no. 5, 1988.

5 The labour force participation rate was 82 per cent in 1987. Trud v SSSR, Moscow, Goskomstat SSSR, p. 9.

6 L. Chizhova, 'Regulirovanie zaniatosti naseleniia', Planovoe khoziaistvo, no. 8, 1988.

7 For discussion of this, see 'Pogolovnaia zaniatost' i rynok truda', interview with Prof. S. Otsu and Prof. V. Kostakov, conducted by M. Berger in Izvestiia, 11 January 1989, p. 7.

8 This usually refers mainly to people working on private agricultural plots or bringing up children at home. In 1988 there were 13.3 million nezaniatye, of whom about 8 million came under the above categories (see Appendix 1). According to Trud v SSSR, p. 4, between 1961 and 1970 15 million workers were 'drawn' from this 'reserve' to cover state labour demand.

9 See the resolution in Izvestiia TsK KPSS, no. 5, 1989, pp. 27–32, 'O privlechenii k obshchestvenno poleznomu trudu nezaniatoi chasti trudosposobnogo naseleniia v soiuznykh i avtonomnykh respublikakh Srednei Azii, Zakavkaz'ia i Severnogo Kavkaza', Postanovlenie Sekretariata TsK KPSS, 31 March 1986. This gives figures for the nezaniatye population in Central Asia and the North Caucasus in 1984, which have been since been reported in the West as figures for the 'unemployed' in these regions. See, for example, 'Reality of unemployment now recognised', Social and Labour Bulletin, no. 3–4, 1989, p. 301.

10 A study of displacement in the Bashkir region is often quoted. This gives an annual rate of 1 per cent for 1968. A. Aitov, *Tekhnicheskii progress i dvizhenie rabochikh kadrov*, Moscow, 1972, p. 21. Similar estimates are made in A.J. Pietsch and H. Vogel, 'Displacement by technological progress in the USSR', in J. Adam (ed.), *Employment Policies in the Soviet Union and Eastern Europe*, London, Macmillan 1982, pp. 147–50; and D. Granick, *Job Rights in the Soviet Union: Their Consequences*, Cambridge, Cambridge University Press, 1987, pp. 124–7. For the 1986–90 planned figures, see E. Afanas'ev and O. Medvedeva, 'Organizatsionno-pravovye voprosy pereraspredeleniia vysvobozhdaemykh rabotnikov', *Sotsialistickeskii trud*, no. 1, 1987, p. 68.

11 'Regulinavanie zaniatosti naseleniia' T. Zaslavskaia, 'Chelovecheskii faktor razvitiia ekonomiki i sotsial'naia spravedlivost'', *Kommunist*, no. 13, 1986, pp. 61–73, and 'Ekonomika skvoz' prizmu sotsiologii', *EKO*, no. 7, 1985, pp. 3–22.

12 This contradiction is discussed at length in P.A. Hauslohner, 'Managing the Soviet labour market: politics and policy-making under Brezhnev', unpublished Ph.D thesis, University of Michigan, 1984.

13 See A. Helgeson, 'Geographical mobility – its implications for employment', in D. Lane (ed.), *Labour and Employment in the USSR*, Brighton, Wheatsheaf, 1986.

14 For example, a director of one Moscow factory stated that only 80 per cent of the potential of each worker is used at his factory. V. Parfenov, in *Pravda*, 20 May 1985, p. 3. It has been claimed that 15–20 per cent of an enterprise's workforce represents hidden reserves. See I. Maslova, 'Sovershenstovanie mekhanizma pereraspredeleniia rabochei sily', *Voprosy ekonomiki*, no. 7, 1982. Kostakov, in *Izvestiia*, 11 January 1989, claims that these reserves amount to 10 million; E. Babak, 'Zashchita ot bezrabotitsy', *Ekonomika i zhizn'*, no. 15, 1990, puts the figure at 8–10 million. It is not clear, however, how this surplus is calculated.

15 See P. Rutland, 'The Shchekino method and the struggle to raise labour productivity in Soviet Industry', *Soviet Studies*, 26, no. 3, 1984, pp. 345–65. Such experiments basically aimed at giving the enterprise an incentive to release workers by allowing it to keep and redistribute among the remaining workforce a percentage of any savings in the wage fund made by releasing workers. They usually had a limited success due to the so-called 'ratchet effect', whereby the short-term rewards of releasing workers were outweighed by the long-term effect of the manpower plan in the following plan period being calculated on the basis of the reduced number of workers required to fulfil the output target in the base period.

16 See S. Malle, 'Soviet labour-saving policy in the eighties', in *The Soviet Economy: A New Course?* Nato Economic Colloquium, Brussels, April 1987, pp. 71–93.

17 J. Chapman, 'Gorbachev's wage reform', *Soviet Economy*, 4, no. 4, 1988. See also the articles in *Sotsialisticheskii trud*, no. 1, 1987.

18 See S. Oxenstierna, *From Labour Shortage to Unemployment? The Soviet Labour Market in the 1980s*, Stockholm, Almquist and Wicksell, 1990, chapter 10.

19 'Relative releasing' refers to productivity gains obtained from installed

capacity, while 'conditional releasing' refers to productivity gains as a result of the introduction of labour-saving technology, i.e. an increase in production capacity. 'Absolute freeing' takes place when the planned future employment is lower than employment in the base plan year; when the labour required for the new plan output target is lower than the labour needed for the fulfilment of the output target in the base period.

20 For an extensive discussion of this, see S. Malle, *Employment Planning in the Soviet Union. Continuity and Change*, London, Macmillan, 1990.

21 Babak, 'Zashchita ot bezrabotnitsy', is the most recent example. See also E. Manevich, 'Ratsional'nee ispol'zovanie rabochei sily', *Voprosy ekonomiki*, no. 9, 1981; also A. Kotliar, 'Sistema trudoustroistva v SSSR'.

22 Article 17 of the (1970) Fundamentals of Labour Law, *Vedomosti Verkhovnogo Soveta SSSR*, 1970, *no.* 29, Article 33 of the RSFSR Labour Code (The Labour Codes of the other republics have corresponding articles), in *Kommentarii k zakonodatel'stvu o trude*, Moscow, 1981, p. 58.

23 Article 33, RSFSR Labour Code, *Kommentarii...*, 1981, p. 68.

24 Points 42 and 43, Article 33, RSFSR Labour Code. *Kommentarii...*, 1981, p. 69.

25 *Kodeks zakonov o trude RSFSR*, Ministerstvo iustitsii RSFSR, Moscow, 1988, Article 40.

26 *Ibid.*, pp. 20–1.

27 Cf. M. Emerson, 'Regulation or deregulation of the labour market', *European Economic Review*, 32, 1988, pp. 775–817.

28 *Normativnye akty po ispol'zovaniiu trudovykh resursov*, 1972, pp. 499–508; for later statutes on the organization and operation of the JPBs, see *Biulleten'Goskomtrud SSSR*, no.8, 1979, pp. 6–9, and no. 3, 1981, pp. 3–6.

29 See J. Chapman 'The Soviet Employment Service and the Search for Efficiency', Working Paper no. 177, Report to the National Council on Soviet and East European Research, December 1984; and interview with E. Afanas'ev, *Argumenty i fakty*, no. 45, 1989.

30 Malle, 'Planned and unplanned mobility in the Soviet Union under the threat of labour shortage'.

31 Resolution of the CPSU Central Committee, the USSR Council of Ministers and the VTsSPS, 'Ob obespechenii effektivnoi zaniatosti naseleniia sovershentsvovanii sistemy trudoustroistva i usilnenii sotsial'nykh garantii dlya trudiashchikhsia', *Pravda*, 19 January 1988.

32 For more detail, see I.S. Maslova, *Ekonomicheskie voprosy pereraspredeleniia rabochei sily pri sotsializme*, Nauka, Moscow, 1976.

33 There are currently 11,000 JPB employees for the whole country. See Babak, 'Zaschchita ot bezrabotnitsy'; V. Gimpel'son and N. Rogovskii, 'Vozmozhno li u nas bezrabotitsa', *Moskovskaia pravda*, 25 April 1990.

34 A recent article describes the problems of the buros in Latvia; there is no reason to suppose that they are untypical for the rest of the country. See S. Blazhevich 'Trudoustroistvo v usloviiakh ekonomicheskoi samostoiatel'nosti respubliki', *Sotsialisticheskii trud*, no. 2, 1990, pp. 45–7.

35 *Ibid.*

36 A recent article claims that almost one-third of the metal-cutting machines and presses in Moscow are over twenty years old. 'Vozmozhna li u nas

bezrabotitsa', V. Gimbel'son and N. Rogovskii, *Moskovskaia pravda*, 24 April 1990.

37 I. Kochetkova, 'Perepodgotovka kadrov v promyshlennosti', *Sotsialisticheskii trud*, no. 3, 1990.

38 *Narodnoe khoziaistvo SSSR v 1988 g.*, Moscow, Goskomstat SSSR, 1988, p. 58.

39 Zaslavskii, 'Obespechenie zaniatosti v uslovilakh perestroiki'. The average duration is reported to be 4–6 months. Some skilled workers are also affected.

40 *ibid.*

41 See Afanas'ev in *Argumenty i fakty*, no. 45, 1989; D.J. Peterson, 'New data published in employment and unemployment in the USSR', *Report on the USSR*, Radio Liberty, 5 January 1990.

42 Report on social and economic development in *Ekonomika i zhizn'*, no. 32, 1990.

43 See Babak, 'Zashchita ot bezrabotnitsy'.

44 *Ibid*; 'Ne mogu naiti raboty', interview with A. Tille, *Komsomol'skaia pravda*, 13 September 1989.

45 Kostakov quotes the official 'Basic Guidelines for the Development of the Economy up till the year 2000', which state that the rate of growth of labour productivity should increase by 2.3–2.5 times, implying an increase of 6.0–6.5 per cent. He interprets this as meaning that the numbers employed in material production should decrease by 13–20 per cent, roughly the equivalent of 13–19 million people. Aganbegian has claimed that by the year 2000 15–20 per cent of all workers and collective farmers will be engaged in manual labour instead of 45–50 per cent as is now the case. A. Aganbegyan, excerpts from a broadcast on Soviet television, 11 December 1987, in *BBC Summary of World Broadcasts* (*SWB*), SU/0031/C/2, 21 December 1987. Others have mentioned figures of 16 million to be released by the year 2000 (interview with I. Prostikov, Deputy Chairman of the Buro for Social Development of the USSR Council of Ministers, *Pravda*, 21 January 1988, and *SWB* SU/0056/C/1, 23 January 1988; Y. Leonteva 'At the Cadre Crossroads', *Sotsialisticheskaia industriia*, 19 January 1988, and *SWB* SU/0056 C/3.); or 12–18 million from the production sphere, an average of at least 1.2 million each year (see Babak, 'Zashchita ot bezrabotnitsy'; this apparently refers to a Gosplan estimate). Kolosov, of Goskomtrud, has claimed that 50 million workers will change jobs or experience a period of unemployment in the next ten years. See report in *Sole 24 Ore*, 30 March 1990.

46 Afanas'ev, in *Argumenty i fakty*, no. 45, 1989; Shcherbakov, 1990. '*Ekonomika i zhizan'*, no. 24, Estimates and calculation of vacancies vary considerably. These figures suggest that the trend is still towards growing labour shortages, but should not be taken as the definitive figures for vacancies.

47 G. Grossman, 'Roots of Gorbachev's problems: private income and outlay in the late 1970', in Joint Economic Committee (ed.), *Gorbachev's Economic Plans*, Washington, 1987, pp. 213–29.

48 *Narodnoe khoziaistvo SSSR v 1988 g.*, p. 33.

49 Zakon SSSR 'O kooperatsii v SSSR', 26 May, 1988; *Ekonomicheskaia gazeta*, no. 24, 1988.

50 *Ekonomika i zhizn'*, no. 6, 1990.

51 The average monthly wage of cooperative workers in 1989 was reported to be 500 rubles; that of state industrial employees, 240.8 rubles. *Ekonomika i zhizn'*, no. 6, 1990, and *Narodnoe khoziaistvo SSSR v 1988 g.*, p. 377.

52 *Narodnoe khoziaistvo SSSR v 1988 g.*, p. 33.

53 Figures quoted by V. Kirichenko, chairman of the USSSR State Committee for Statistics, in *Moscow News*, no. 12, 1990, p. 10.

54 *Ekonomika i zhizn'*, no. 18, 1990.

55 F.R. Filippov, 'Sotsial'nye garantii effektivnoi zaniatosti', *Sotsiologicheskie issledovaniia*, no. 5, 1988.

56 See V. Kosmarskii, 'Vysvobodzhenie rabotnikov: nereshenye problemy', *Khoziaistvo i pravo*, no. 10, 1989.

57 Filippov, 'Sotsial'nye garantii effektivnoi zaniatosti'; *Argumenty i fakty*, no. 45, 1989.

58 In Moscow, twenty-five ministries have been eliminated as well as 2,500 middle-level administrative 'organs', and staff reduced by 70,000. In the republics, 152 ministries were eliminated, and in the autonomous republics, 192. Staff was reduced by 620,000. 'Rabochii i rynok', interview with L.I. Abalkin and V.I. Shcherbakov, *Ekonomika i zhizn'*, no. 17, 1990.

59 See *Trud v SSSR*, pp. 3–31; also 'Moskovskii bezrabotnyi – uvy, real'nost'', *Moskovskaia pravda*, 7 June 1990.

60 S. Rapawy, 'Labour force and employment in the USSR', in Joint Economic Committee, *Gorbachev's Economic Plans*, Washington, US Government Printing Office, 1987, p. 190.

61 In September 1989, the figure was reported as 43 million. See *Statisticheskii press biulleten'*, no. 9, 1989, p. 129.

62 This and following information taken from *Ekonomika i zhizn'*, no. 18, 1990, p. 14.

63 *Ekonomika i zhizn'*, no. 18, 1990, p. 15.

64 See the new pension law published in *Izvestiia*, 30 May 1990.

65 *Social and Labour Bulletin*, nos. 3–4, 1989, p. 235; see also Margot Jacobs, 'Soviet pensioners finally get a boost', *Report on the USSR*, Radio Liberty, 10 August 1990.

66 Jacobs, 'Soviet pensioners finally get a boost'; according to *Argumenty i fakty*, no. 45, 1989, the figure was 7.8 million.

67 Jacobs, 'Soviet pensioners finally get boost'.

68 The minimum wage established in 1972 is 70 rubles; *Ekonomika i zhizn'*, no. 18, 1990, p. 6. However, 75 rubles is now reportedly recognized as the poverty line, with 36 million having incomes below this level; see *Social and Labour Bulletin*, nos. 3–4, 1989, p. 235; 78 rubles is the figure given in *Moscow News*, no. 19, 1990.

69 T. Pulatov, 'Is democracy a burden on the poor?', *Moscow News*, no. 19, 1990.

70 *Moscow News*, no. 26, 1990, p. 13.

71 *Izvestiia TsK KPSS*, no. 5, 1989.

72 This is repeated in *Narodnoe khoziaistvo SSSR v 1988 g.* p. 33. A figure of 6 million *nezaniatye* is given for the country as a whole.

73 *Izvestiia TsK KPSS*, no. 5, 1989.

74 Filippov, 'Sotsial'nye garantii effektivnoi zaniatosti'.

75 *Komsomolskaia pravda*, 13 September 1989.
76 *Molodezh' SSSR*, Moscow, Goskomstat SSSR, 1990, p. 141.
77 *Izvestiia TsK KPSS*, no. 5, 1989.
78 A. Nikitin, 'Kak pomoch' bezrabotnomu', *Pravda*, 6 April 1990 and Babak, 'Zashchita ot bezrabotnitsy', The Trade Unions have also drawn up their version of the draft employment act, see *Trud*, 15 June 1990.
79 For information on minimum pension, see *Statisticheskii press biulleten'*, no. 9, 1989 and *Social and Labour Bulletin*, nos. 3–4, 1989, p. 235.
80 See J. Micklewright, 'The reform of unemployment compensation: choices for East and West', invited paper presented at European Economic Association Annual Congress, Lisbon, 1990.
81 This view is the one that has been put forward by specialists in the past, and is still held by some, such as Kotliar, head of the research institute of the RSFSR Goskomtrud. See report by Babak, 'Zashchita ot bezrabotnitsy'. See also the discussion in 'Pravo na poluchenie raboty', *Voprosy ekonomiki*, no. 2, 1989, pp. 13–83.
82 L. Kunel'skii, 'Bezrabotitsa? U nas?' *Ekonomicheskaia gazeta*, no. 36, 1989.
83 *Moskovskaia pravda*, 25 April 1990.

Appendix 1. *Labour Resources (millions)*

	1988	1989
Total labour resources (population in working age minus invalids in Groups I+II and pensioners in working age group, plus people older and younger than working age employed in the economy)	163.6	164
of which		
able-bodied in working age group	155.3	na
workers older than retirement age	7.9	na
workers below working age	0.3	na
total employed	138.5	139
of which		
in state sector	121.8	120.3
in kolkhoz	11.6	11.6
in coops (full time)	0.7	2.9
in personal subsidiary economy	4.0	4.0
individual employment	0.2	0.3
full-time students	11.7	11.9
those not in state or other forms of employment ('nezaniatye')	13.3	13
of which		
women at home with children	4.3	na
military service	4.0	na
temporary unemployed and Group III invalids	4.0	na
Foreign workers	0.1	na

Argumenty i fakty no. 45, 1989; *Ekonomika i zhizn'* no. 6, February 1990.

Appendix 2. *Average monthly wage (rubles)**

	1985	1986	1987	1988
All industry	210.6	215.7	221.9	240.8
Heavy industry	220.4	225.7	231.6	250.7
Fuel energy complex	279.4	284.5	294.7	318.5
Electric energy	210.0	216.6	226.0	251.0
Fuel industry	313.0	317.8	329.2	352.4
Metallurgy complex	257.7	264.5	271.1	296.9
Machine-Building complex	214.4	219.0	224.0	241.3
Chem. wood complex	212.1	219.2	224.2	243.2
Light industry	167.5	170.4	174.4	194.8
Textile	178.3	181.2	185.0	205.9
Knitwear	150.2	153.4	157.9	177.3
Leather, fur footwear	184.3	186.9	190.6	212.7
Food industry	188.4	194.0	206.3	219.0
Food preparation	162.4	166.3	180.7	191.2
Meat and dairy	176.5	182.8	189.6	201.9
Fish industry	342.6	353.7	373.7	400.9
Construction	236.6	244.6	257.2	288.9
Transport	220.3	228.1	239.4	260.1
Communications	159.5	164.0	175.1	196.4
Trade catering supply	149.2	152.9	155.7	165.1
Computer services	143.3	158.0	165.6	183.8
Housing and other services	146.6	149.3	154.4	168.0
Health	132.8	134.9	143.3	152.5
Education	150.0	155.7	165.6	171.4
Culture	117.3	118.1	121.6	128.2
Art	145.3	147.8	151.0	155.1
Science and Sc. services	202.4	208.2	217.4	248.4
Credit and insurance	180.9	190.9	198.6	206.4
Admin. staff	168.8	176.7	187.8	203.9

* Average wage of coop workers 1989 = 500 rubles; including those combining coop job with other form of employment; definition in *Ekonomika i zhizn'*, no. 6, 1990.

Trud v SSSR, p. 189; *Narodnoe khoziaistvo SSSR v 1988g*, pp. 377, 77–8.

Appendix 3. *Type of cooperative activity on* 31 *December* 1989

	No. of cooperatives (thousands)	No. working in them (thousands)
Total	193.4	4,851.5
Consumer goods	33.7	793.2
Public catering	5.6	53.4
Selling	1.2	14.3
Buying and selling	6.4	67.9
Public services	33.0	567.0
Storing and processing scrap metal, waste paper, etc.	3.2	92.4
Construction (apart from that under public services)	38.7	1,516.5
Design and survey (for construction)	3.1	114.5
Research design, development of programmes and information services	10.4	320.1
Agriculture	8.4	98.8
Medical services	3.3	61.2
Art design	4.5	74.1
Leisure services	2.6	53.2
Other	39.3	1,024.9

USSR State Committee for Statistics. Published in *Moscow News*, no. 12, 1990.

9   Changes in income inequality in the USSR

Henryk Flakierski

Introduction

This chapter is a part of a long-term project investigating the interrelationship between economic reforms in the Soviet Union and changes in income inequality. It aims specifically to examine how the increasing role played by the market mechanism affects the pattern of income distribution in that country. This chapter, seen as a point of departure for this long-term project, sets out to analyze what the Soviet record is in the field of wage and income distribution during the last two to three decades. Such 'stock taking' is not only valuable in itself but is also a necessary first step towards the further investigation of the complex correlation between the marketization of the Soviet economy and changes in the inequality of income.

Statistical data about income distribution in the USSR were for many years a strongly guarded secret. Only occasionally have Soviet economists been allowed to reveal the 'secret' and published in the form of a ready statement the relative dispersion of wages and incomes, usually decile ratios, without giving the frequency distribution from where it was computed. According to N.E. Rabkina and N.M. Rimashevskaia,[1] the decile ratios in the socialized sector were as follows:

1964 – 3.69
1966 – 3.26
1968 – 2.83
1972 – 3.10
1976 – 3.35
1981 – 3.00

Western economists, however, have been able, on the basis of the theoretical assumption that Soviet distribution of wages and family incomes are log-normal, to calculate the decile ratios and offer percentiles ratios without frequency distribution data.[2] Although Western economists have used a variety of different methods to estimate some decile ratios, their results are not very different from the figures pronounced by Soviet economists.[3]

Lately with the ascendance of Gorbachev and his glasnost policy, Soviet official statistics have improved. We can now find in statistical yearbooks some distribution frequencies for wages and household incomes per capita for certain years.[4] However, statistical material is still poor even by East European standards. For example, the amount of brackets in the distribution frequencies in the USSR are much smaller than those available for Poland, Hungary or Yugoslavia and, moreover, frequency distributions for wages in the Soviet Republics are given only for two years – 1981 and 1986. The same is applicable for frequency distribution of major productive sectors (industry, agriculture, construction, etc.). Given the apparent shortcomings of distributional statistics, conclusions about the relative dispersion of incomes should be treated with caution.

The dispersion of wages

From the statistical material available regarding the relative dispersion of earnings in the socialized economy in total, and that of its major sectors, shown in table A.1 (Appendix), we can draw the following conclusions:

First, based on all measures of inequality used here, the overall relative dispersion of pay in the period of 1968–1986 has increased visibly in the upper tale of distribution

$$\left(\frac{P_{99}}{P_1}, \frac{P_{98}}{P_2} \text{ and } \frac{P_{95}}{P_5}\right).$$

But for the majority of employees, the relative dispersion of wages measured by the decile ratio and coefficient of variation, has changed rather moderately.

Second, inequality of pay in the major sectors of the economy (data only for two years) does not show any visible changes. It would be tempting to infer from data of table A.1 that sectors in the material sphere, with the higher average wages (see the estimated mean, and the median in table A.1), have lower relative dispersion of pay than those with lower average wages. Hence, the Kusnetz law of an inverse relationship between the level of income and the degree of inequality would be confirmed. We can see from table A.1 that sectors like industry, construction, and transport all with average wages above the national level, have lower measures of inequality than those sectors of the economy with average wages below the national level such as agriculture. However, we should not stretch this 'regularity' too far, because we can see from table A.1 that some low-paid sectors (i.e. trade, communication) do not show such regularity, in fact in these sectors the inequality indicators are rather low, lower than in the country as a whole.

In all socialist countries up to now, the relative dispersion of wages was wider in the nonmaterial sphere than in the material one. The higher levels of inequality in the nonmaterial sphere are a reflection of the special privileges enjoyed by the upper echelons of both the administration, and the party apparatus on the one hand, and the very low pay received by the clerical personnel on the other. However, unlike in other East European countries, we do not possess for the Soviet Union data about the top earnings of the privileged upper echelons of the party and state administration; clerical employees in the administration with wages below the average in the country are lumped together with the top brass whose earnings are several times the national average. Although our data is not sufficient to compare inequalities between the material and nonmaterial spheres in the USSR, we can nevertheless judge the differences in average wages of these two sectors. As is evident from table A.1, the average wages in most sectors of the nonmaterial sphere (measured by the mean-$\bar{x}$) are much lower than those in the material sphere. Especially low are wages in education, health, and house services, as is the case in other COMECON countries as well. In the period of 1960–1980 the ratio of average wage in the material sphere to that of the non-material one has declined from 82 to 78 per cent.[5] Soviet economists explain the existence of much lower average wages in the nonmaterial than in the material sphere by pointing to the following factors:

(a) Certain sectors of the material sphere (mining construction, transport) have higher wage rates and salaries, because difficult conditions of work are much more frequent than in other sectors.
(b) Piece work is much more common in the material sphere, and this form of pay is usually higher than pay based on time.
(c) The role of premiums as a part of total earnings is higher in the material sphere.
(d) The proportion of employees with exceptionally high wages working in the remote North and Far East areas, is much higher in the material sphere.

Although the above mentioned structural factors have some influence on the differences in average pay between those two spheres, the major reason for such imbalance is rather socio-political. The stress on material production is a part of the particular growth strategy of the Soviet regime, based on the latter's ideological bias against the nonmaterial sphere as less important in creating wealth. In countries such as Yugoslavia, where this kind of bias is weaker, and the stress on services is more pronounced, average wages in the nonmaterial sphere are actually slightly higher than in the material one.[6]

Third, in the USSR the inequality of pay in industry is smaller than in the total socialized sector. The higher degree of inequality in the whole socialized sector than in industry reflects the influence of the higher degree of inequality in the nonmaterial sphere, as well as in some sectors of the material production sphere, especially agriculture.

Fourth, at a different level of comparison, we could suggest that the overall dispersion of pay in the USSR is similar to the pattern in Poland, but higher than in Yugoslavia and Hungary.[7] Evidence indicates, however, that changes in relative dispersion of pay were more strongly pronounced in the USSR than in Poland and Hungary. What is more, changes in the inequality of pay in Yugoslavia and USSR in the period of 1968–1986 are, unexpectedly, going in opposite directions.[8] In terms of the relative dispersion of wages, we observe an increase in the USSR, and a decline in Yugoslavia. The experience of these two countries in this respect suggests that the strong belief that more decentralized systems generate higher inequalities is not always accurate. In fact, highly decentralized systems of management can have smaller inequalities of pay than more centralized ones.

Interbranch differentials

As we can see from table 9.1, the inequality of pay between industrial branches, measured by the coefficient of variation has declined visibly after the 1960s, especially for manual workers; the differences in average wages between manual workers of various branches of industry has narrowed, whereas for nonmanual employees this is not the case.

As far as the level of inequality of pay between branches is concerned, (measured by the coefficient of variation (V) and the range (R)), it is higher for nonmanual than for manual workers.

All in all, the Soviet Union has much higher interbranch differentials in industry than either Yugoslavia or Poland, and, in fact, they are very high even by Western standards.[9] A similar tendency is visible as far as differences in wages between major sectors of the whole economy are concerned.

As can be seen from table 9.2, inequalities of pay (measured by the coefficient of variation and the range) are quite high, but declined gradually in the period of 1940–80. Although those indicators of dispersion have increased in the 1980s, inequality of pay has never

Table 9.1. *Interbranch pay differentials in Soviet industry, measured by the coefficient of variation and the range**

Year	The estimated mean*			Coefficient of Variation (V)			Range (R)		
	T**	M***	N.M.****	T	M	N.M.	T	M	N.M.
1950	73.7	68.4	105.0	27.2	27.2	29.8	279.0	288.0	288.6
1960	95.6	91.0	122.2	28.5	27.6	33.5	295.8	297.0	285.5
1970	141.3	134.4	172.0	22.8	21.3	27.5	235.6	233.2	263.0
1975	173.5	167.3	201.7	22.6	21.8	26.8	238.0	239.0	250.2
1980	198.4	193.2	218.0	21.7	20.1	27.6	219.0	220.0	223.4
1985	226.4	221.5	243.7	23.7	21.7	30.2	228.1	227.0	253.7
1986	231.6	226.7	249.5	23.3	21.6	28.6	231.0	225.0	250.0
1987	240.8	235.2	261.2	24.9	22.6	31.4	237.0	225.3	250.0

* Average monthly wages were recorded for 24 branches of the Soviet industry.
** Total.
*** Manual.
**** Nonmanual.
Range (R) - is the ratio of the highest to the lowest average wage between industrial branches.
Source: Trud v SSSR (Labour in the USSR), Goskomstat SSSR, Moscow, 1988.

returned to the level of the 1950s and 1960s. Despite the decline in wage differentials between sectors, the difference between leading sectors and those that trail behind in terms of average wages, is in most years the same. Those sectors, which three decades ago had average wages either above (like construction, transport, etc.) or below the national average (like agriculture, forestry, trade etc.), were in 1987 still in exactly the same ranking position.

Substantial differences in pay between branches and sectors for the same job create anomalies in the wage system. A messenger or a cleaning woman can earn more than an engineer; a highly skilled worker more than a managing director of an enterprise, if the former happens to be employed in an enterprise with very high average pay and the latter in an enterprise with very low average pay. By implication, moving from one enterprise to another can increase one's income by much more than moving up the skill ladder.

Skill differentials

Very little data exist about skill differentials in the USSR. The only data published more or less consistently are data about wages of the manual and nonmanual strata. No data about different skills of manual workers

Table 9.2. *Intersectorial pay differentials in the Soviet economy,* measured by the coefficient of variation and the range*

Year	Coefficient of variation	Range
1940	25.1	259
1945	32.1	383
1950	27.3	276
1960	26.5	242
1970	19.1	177
1975	20.6	192
1980	18.0	182
1981	18.5	186
1982	19.5	190
1983	20.0	194
1984	20.4	198
1985	20.4	202
1986	21.0	207
1987	22.2	212

*Average monthly wages were recorded for sixteen sectors of the whole Soviet economy. Seven sectors belong to the material sphere (industry, agriculture, forestry, transport, communication, construction, trade). The remaining nine sectors comprise the non-material sphere (health, education, culture, art, science, credit system, state administration, etc.).

From *Trud v SSSR* (Labour in the USSR), Goskomstat SSSR, Moscow, 1988, pp. 148–9.

is published as is the case in other East European countries. Only from time to time average wages of technical-engineering personnel and clerical personnel are published. Some available evidence on wage differences between major occupational groups in the socialized industry is summarized in table 9.3. From this we may draw the following conclusions:

1. Differences in earnings among strata have declined drastically – a tendency discernable in other East European countries. The nonmanual strata earned in 1987 on the average, not much more than manual workers, in sharp contrast with previous periods when nonmanual workers had received nearly twice as much in wages as manual workers. In the heavy industry in general, the differences have even become smaller (103.6) and in some branches of the heavy industry (machine building – electrical appliances and others) the average earnings of manual workers have become slightly higher than nonmanual workers. Such a drastic and

Table 9.3. *Average monthly pay by occupational category in state industry (manual workers = 100)*

Year	All non-manual workers	Technical-engineering personnel	Administrative and clerical personnel
1940	174.3	215.0	111.1
1945	198.1	na	na
1950	151.9	na	na
1955	145.9	na	na
1960	132.6	150.9	82.0
1965	131.8	145.9	na
1970	125.5	136.3	85.4
1975	116.2	123.8	81.6
1980	109.2	114.6	78.6
1985	105.8	110.2	77.8
1986	106.3	110.4	79.6
1987	106.7	na	na

Source: *Trud v SSSR* (Labour in the USSR), Goskomstat SSSR, Moscow, 1988, p. 189; V. Kriukov, 'Problemy Planirovania zarobotnoi platy na predpriatiakh promyshlennosti' (Problems of wage planning in the enterprise), *Socialisticheskii trud* (Socialist Labour), no. 12, 1981, p. 97; L.E. Kunelskii, *Zarabotnaia plata i stimulirovanie truda* (Wages and Work Incentives), Moscow, 1981, table 20, pp. 122–3; *Narodnoe khozvaistvo SSSR v.* 1988g, (The Economy of the USSR), Statistical Yearbook 1988.

constant decline in the status of nonmanual employees is unprecedented in any East European country, except in Poland in the period of 1980–2 when, under the pressure of the Solidarity movement, wage differentials between strata were sharply levelled off. But even in Poland this process was reversed soon after 1982.

2. Although earnings of the highly educated technical-engineering personnel are still higher than that of manual workers, the differences between those strata were substantially reduced over time. For example, in 1970 the technical-engineering personnel earnings were on average over twice as much (215 per cent) as the earnings of manual workers; in 1986 the difference between these two groups had been reduced to only 10 per cent. This tendency to reduce differences between manual workers and the technical personnel is visible in nearly all industrial branches. The biggest losers are, however, the administrative and clerical personnel. Their wages have constantly declined relative to manual wages; the white-collar average wages were in 1986, just over 75 per cent of the average manual wages in the industry.

Are the official figures in table 9.3 sufficient to justify the claims of Soviet authorities that they have overcome the manual and nonmanual dichotomy? Has egalitarianism, the great promise of a classless society, indeed been achieved? I believe that this would be the wrong conclusion. On the contrary, I wish to argue that the nonmanual/manual stratification dichotomy is still very much alive.

There are several important factors that make the official data on wage differences between manual and nonmanual wage earners inadequate for an accurate indicator of differences in well-being between these two stratas.

First, conditions of work are less favourable for manual than nonmanual employees. For example:

(a) Manual workers are more exposed to the health hazards of noise, toxic substances, high temperature, accidents, and injuries.

(b) Manual workers are subjected to tighter work discipline than nonmanual employees. Manual workers are not only subject to their superiors but are also controlled by machines and production quotas. Very often work is performed in tiring positions.

(c) Manual workers' earnings are less stable and to a larger degree depend on the supply of raw materials, the quality of tools and equipment, stoppages, and other factors over which workers have no control, especially in an environment where their participation in management is very limited or nonexistent.

Second, official distributional statistics suffer a number of important limitations, one of which is that they do not encompass all incomes from work by particular groups. Opportunities for performing extra work and therefore obtaining extra pay are not uniformly available.

Third, the housing conditions of nonmanual workers are substantially better than those of manual workers. Nonmanual families have substantially more space per person on the average than manual families. A much larger proportion of nonmanual workers' families have more modern facilities in their homes. The percentage of nonmanual households that have received new and better flats is higher than in the case of manual households. This is true both in terms of flats allocated free by state enterprises and of those allocated through different cooperative forms. These privileges are usually explained by the fact that nonmanual employees have a greater influence over and better 'connections' with the institutions making the allocation decisions. Not without importance in achieving and exercising these privileges is the 'strength and vitality' of this social stratum in pursuing its interests. Superior lobbying ability due

to better knowledge, education, and social prestige help the nonmanual
stratum get many legal and semi-legal privileges.

Although discrepancies between nonmanual and manual workers'
earnings have declined in the USSR as in other East European countries,
and they are smaller than in the Western countries,[10] differences in terms
of earnings derived from a second job, accessibility to superior housing
and working conditions are still substantial, as are differences in education
and lifestyle. Manual workers, particularly the unskilled and semiskilled
ones, are the underdogs in these societies, despite repeated rhetoric about
the privileged position of the workers. Even skilled workers are still worse
off than white collar clerical personnel, if we take into consideration
special benefits and other incomes not reported in the official statistics.

Inter-regional dispersion of wages

The Soviet Union is a country with substantial regional differences in
terms of the level of development. As a result of these differences, average
output per capita and average pay vary a great deal between republics.
Regional differences in average pay are, however, smaller than regional
differences in income per capita.

Data in table A.2 (Appendix) indicate clearly that the discrepancy in
average pay between republics, measured both by the coefficient of
variation and by range, has increased substantially over time. For
instance, in 1950 the ratio of average wages of the republic with the
highest pay (Turkmenia) to that of the lowest one (Moldavia) was 1.3:1;
in 1987, this ratio was 1.4:1 (Estonia to Azerbaidzhan). In general, such
poor republics as Tadzhikistan, Kirgizia and Uzbekistan have lost
relatively heavily in terms of average wages, with the major winners being
the Baltic republics, especially Estonia, which from 1980 firmly established
its position as the leader. In spite of the fact that differences in pay
between republics have increased substantially, those differences are still
for most years smaller than those in Yugoslavia. Only after 1982 has the
ratio of the highest to the lowest paid region been larger in Yugoslavia
than in the USSR. As for the relative ranking of different republics in the
pay scale major changes have taken place in the period under examination.

A lack of data prevents a more sophisticated measurement of pay
dispersion between republics. A noticeable exception is provided by the
data available in 1981, 1986, and although measures of dispersion for
these two years do not allow an analysis of changes in time, they at least
allow for a comparison of levels of inequality in different republics.

As we can see from table A.3 (Appendix), the poorest four republics in
terms of average wages – Azerbaidzhan, Tadzhikistan, Uzbekistan, and

Kirgizia – all have high levels of inequality of pay, higher than the more affluent republics. Especially low levels of inequality of pay exist in the Baltic republics with Estonia in a leading position in this respect. We should not, however, overlook the fact that such a clear correlation between the level of pay and the degree of dispersion of wages does not exist in all cases. For example, the republic of Moldavia with a very low level of average wages has inequality of pay lower than much wealthier republics. This kind of irregularity is as well visible in the republic of Kazakhstan. Nevertheless, for most of the republics, evidence confirms the thesis that there is an inverse relationship between the level of wages and the degree of inequality; the higher the level of wages, the lower the level of inequality and vice versa.

Per capita household income

Although wages are one of the indicators of differences in the standard of living, per capita household income reflects better the level of welfare of the population. This indicator incorporates not only wages but also the social benefits in cash and reflects the influence of the demographic structure of the household on income per capita (the ratio of active earners in the household to the total number of members in the household and the ratio of wage earners to dependents).

Before proceeding to analyze our statistical findings a few comments on the Soviet concept of household income are in order here.

Total household income, according to Goskomstat, includes the sum of all money incomes before taxation received from: state enterprises, collective farms (including individual plots of land by members of Kolkhoz), and social benefits which are taken into consideration in family budgets.

The Soviet concept of total household income has certain peculiarities which are worth mentioning here:

1. Certain items of social benefits in kind, like subsidies for kinder-gartens, resting houses, summer camps for children etc. are included in the income of the household.

2. No money income from the second economy, (legal or illegal) was included up to now in the Soviet category of household income. Such private activities as construction work and housing repairs, radios, televisions, car repairs, extra fees charged by doctors and nurses for special services, as well as tips of all kinds, are not included in the category of household income.

3. Special privileges derived from the state and the ability to obtain

scarce goods and services due to connections and position, are not included in the category 'household income' either. What can be included here are such privileges as attractive variation houses in the country and abroad foreign currency for travelling, and cars bought at low subsidized prices, which can be resold at market price several times larger than the subsidized official prices. Needless to say, that the beneficiaries of those privileges are the state and party elite. The omission of those privileges in the category of household income obviously underestimates the discrepancies of income between low and high income groups.

After commenting on the peculiarities of the Soviet concept of household income, we can return to our statistical analysis. From the data of table 9.4 we can draw the following conclusions:

1. In the period of 1980–8 there was an increase in relative dispersion of income per capita, most strongly pronounced when we compare the extremes of the distribution scale (P_{99}/P_1, P_{98}/P_2). For most of the distribution measured by the decile ratio (P_{90}/P_{10}) no changes can be observed. What is more, all changes in relative dispersion have taken place only between 1980–5, after that period no changes are observed in any measure of inequality.[11]

2. The poorest one per cent of the households (P_1) received in 1988 per capita income only slightly more than one-third (36.6 per cent) of the median. This ratio, although, low by any standard of the Eastern European countries, has declined farther in comparison with the 1980 level (38.5 per cent of the median).

3. Differences at the extremes of the distributional spectrum (P_{99}/P_1) and (P_{98}/P_1) corresponding to higher and lower income groups are quite high by comparison to Poland and Hungary.[12] As in other East European countries, the larger the household the smaller the probability of belonging to the higher income brackets. Households with six persons are in the lowest per capita income brackets. There is also a negative correlation between the size and the activity ratio of the household. The activity ratios (the ratio of active earners to the size of the household) declines with the size of the household. Large households have proportionally more dependents to maintain than small households. The strong influence of demographic factors on differences in per capita household income leads to a situation in which a highly skilled worker can belong to the highest wage bracket but his household to the lowest per capita bracket, if the household has many children and, for that reason, an unfavorable earner–dependent ratio. The lowest income group (P_1) received in 1987 no

Table 9.4. *Distribution of per capita household income in the USSR (measures of dispersion)*

	1980	1985	1988
Median (M)	100.8	114.6	127.2
Mean ($\bar{x}$)	109.7	125.6	139.6
P_{99}/P_1	6.8	7.4	7.4
P_{98}/P_2	5.4	5.8	5.9
P_{95}/P_5	3.9	4.1	4.1
P_{90}/P_{10}	2.9	3.0	3.0
P_{85}/P_{15}	2.3	2.4	2.4
Q_3/Q_1	1.7	1.8	1.8
Q_3-Q_1/M	0.56	0.59	0.59
Coefficient of variation (V)	42.4	42.8	41.0

Frequency distribution for the above 3 years are given by Goskomstat, published in *Ekonomicheskaia gazeta*, no. 25, 1989, p. 12.

more per-capita income than 43 per cent of the median, whereas the highest percentile (P_{99}) received 231 per cent of the median.

The distribution frequencies on which basis the measure of dispersion were calculated in table 9.4 show that although the proportion of Soviet citizens receiving less than 75 rubles per capita has declined, still about 36 million inhabitants (or around 13 per cent) receive less than 75 rubles per month. What is more, if we take into consideration that the 1988 officially established social minimum or poverty line was fixed at the level of 78 rubles a month per person in the household, then according to Goskomstat, over 40 million Soviet citizens (or about 15 per cent of the population) lived below the poverty line. This figure probably underestimates significantly the magnitude of the problem according to some economists. Rimashevskaia has rightly emphasized that the way the official statistics calculate per capita household income underestimates the number of people below the poverty line.[13] This is so, she argues, for several reasons.

First, the official Soviet Statistics (Goskomstat), as mentioned before, include in the per capita household income not only money income but also a certain amount of social benefits in kind like subsidies for kindergartens, resting houses, sanatoria, summer camps, etc. On the basis of such per capita income concept, the social minimum is calculated. If we would eliminate the social benefit in kind from the per capita household income, then 3–5 per cent more people would find themselves below the poverty line.

Secondly, the way household budget analysis is carried out by the official statistics reduces the amount of people receiving per capita income below the poverty line. The so-called 'sectorial methods', eliminate from the sample of households covered by budget analysis[14] those households which are not linked with one of the official sectors of the national economy. Pensioners' households are the prime victims of such elimination, followed by households of students, those temporarily out of work, and those who live on the streets. All those groups are the poorest of the poor, and need social support the most. by eliminating those most vulnerable groups (in Soviet society) from budget analysis, the number of people living below the poverty line is reduced.

According to Rimashevskaia, if these and other shortcomings of budget analysis would be removed, then not 15 per cent but 20–25 per cent of the total population of the USSR lives under the poverty line.[15]

But, let us examine more closely who are those poor households living below the poverty line in the USSR. According to Goskomstat, nearly half of them are families with a lot of children. Particularly in the Central Asian republics and Azerbaidzhan, about one-third are young families and 20 per cent are pensioners. Some economists see the structure of the group below the poverty line slightly from a different angle. A lot of children in a family is only one cause of poverty. The other factor is the low level of wages and pensions. Nearly 40–50 per cent of all families below the poverty line are families with low wages. In most cases, the active members of those families are employed in the nonmaterial sphere where average wages are very low. Therefore, to raise the per capita household income above the poverty line, it is necessary to raise substantially the minimum wage. Considering that the average national earner–dependent ratio in the household is 1:5 (each active member of the household must maintain 0.5 dependents), and the poverty line is 78 rubles, the minimum wage should be no less than 117 rubles per month 78 × 1.5 = 117). But the reality is completely different. For the last couple of years, the official minimum wage was frozen at 70 rubles a month. Needless to say, the social minimum of 78 rubles a month is related to the national average income per capita and it constitutes approximately just over 50 per cent of the national average per capita income. In a country the size of the Soviet Union where the way of life and the standard of living are so diverse, some poor republics have average per capita incomes below the official poverty line (e.g., Uzbekistan – 71.4 rubles, Tadzhikistan – 58.9 rubles). Hence, over 50 per cent of people in these republics have incomes

Table 9.5. *Real income per one person in the household in Soviet republics (as a percentage of the USSR)*

	1975	1980	1985	1987
Russian Federation	109	110	110	109
Ukraine	92	91	96	96
Belorussia	96	98	102	104
Uzbekistan	66	67	64	61
Kazakhstan	92	93	91	92
Georgia	83	88	99	104
Azerbaidzhan	63	64	68	70
Lithuania	114	110	108	111
Moldavia	79	81	82	84
Latvia	123	123	121	124
Kirgizia	73	70	70	70
Tadzhikistan	61	58	55	54
Armenia	76	80	82	86
Turkmenistan	77	73	71	72
Estonia	128	131	128	131
Coefficient of variation	24.2	24.6	24.2	25.1
Range	210.0	226.0	232.7	242.6

Socialnoe razvitie i uroven' zhizni naselenia SSSR (Social Development and the Standard of Living of the Soviet Population), Goskomstat, Moscow, 1989, p. 99.

per capita below the poverty line. To lift all families below the poverty line to the social minimum level would require, according to some economists, over 10 billion rubles without even taking into consideration the inflation process, which has already eroded the established social minimum. In view of the economic situation in the Soviet Union, with a huge money overhang, this is obviously unlikely to happen. The official social minimum will remain just an indicator which helps to establish how many families live below the poverty line, but without practical consequences.

Inter-regional dispersion of per capita household income

The Soviet Union is a country with vast regional differences in terms of level of development and demographic structures. As a result, per capita household income varies a great deal between republics. What is more, the differences have a tendency to increase with time, becoming, obviously, one of the major factors of tension between nationalities in the USSR.

As can be seen from table 9.5, dispersion of per capita household income among republics (measured by the coefficient of variation and the range) has constantly increased in the period of 1975–87. Estonia, the leader in all years under investigation, had nearly 2.5 times more per capita household income in 1987 than the poorest republic of Tadzhikistan. The relative ranking of various republics in terms of per capita household income has changed slightly; Estonia and Latvia are undisputed leaders, with Tadzhikistan, Uzbekistan, Turkmenistan lagging further and further behind the national average. The only republics who have changed their relative position are Georgia, Armenia and Moldavia. The largest one, the Russian Federation had exactly the same position in 1987 as in 1975 and is ranked immediately after the leading Baltic republics.

What are the causes of those huge differences in per capita income between republics, and is there a possibility of reducing them in the near future? The conventional wisdom is that the demographic structure of the population explains to a large degree the differences in per capita household income, and with it the differences in the standard of life. It is a statistical fact that in those republics where the ratio of dependents, especially children, to the active part of the household is high, there is a low per capita household income and vice versa.[16] Needless to say, the demographic structure of households and the size and ratio of earners to dependents, to some degree, depend on such factors as culture, tradition and form of religion. However, there are economic factors which influence the demographic shape of the household. It is a fact that the gainfully occupied rate is much lower in the underdeveloped republics than in the more developed ones. For example, in 1984 only 10 per cent of the able-bodied people were not employed in the USSR as a whole, whereas in Azerbaidzhan this figure was 27.6 per cent, in Tadzhikistan 25 per cent, and in Uzbekistan 22.8 per cent. It is worthwhile to stress that among those able-bodied people in the Asian republics who are not gainfully employed, only 20 per cent are mothers of big families.[17] The situation is indeed peculiar; women cannot find work because men work in many so-called women's professions (retail trade, services, etc.). Many factories employ workers from other republics instead of their own idle labour force. We are dealing here with hidden and not so hidden unemployment. An increase in the proportion of the gainfully occupied population would increase the earner-dependent ratio in those republics, as a result, income per one person in the family would increase. The changes that this will happen, are, however, very small. In most of those republics, as is the case in the Soviet Union as a whole, output is stagnating or falling, hence we can expect an *increase* in unemployment both hidden and open.

Reducing the differences in per capita household income between republics would require a reduction in the differences of average wages between republics. As we have seen in our previous analysis (see table A.2

in Appendix), in reality differences in wages between the 'poor' and the 'rich' republics have actually increased; wages have grown faster in the 'affluent' republics than in the less 'affluent.' The major reason for such development is linked with the differences in the industrial structure of the economy of the various republics. The highly paid, preferential industries, requiring highly skilled labour are not located in the Asian republics. As a result of such one-sided process of industrialization, a much larger percentage of the population is employed in the lower paid industries of the productive sphere, or in the lower paid nonmaterial sphere.

To reduce those differences in the standard of living would require large sums of investment funds to be reallocated in favour of the less developed republics in order to them to create a more efficient industrial structure. Given a stagnant economy in the USSR with investment declining both absolutely and relatively to the national output and considering the nationalistic fever sweeping most republics, such redistribution of funds on a big scale is very unlikely. In the foreseeable future, we can expect that all these forms, will rather work to increase differences in the standard of life between republics, with all the sociopolitical consequences it entails.

Notes

1 'Raspredelitelnie otnosheniia i sotsial'noe razvitie' (Distributional Relations and Social Development), *EKO*, no. 5, 1978, p. 20; E. Fedorovskaia and E. Alexandrova, 'Mekhanizm formirovania, i vozvyshenia potrebnostei' (The mechanism of forming and increasing needs, *Voprosy Ekonomiki*, no. 7, 1984, pp. 15–25.

2 See J. Chapman, 'Soviet wages under socialism', in A. Abouchar (ed.), *The Socialist Price Mechanism*, Durham N.C., Duke University Press, 1977, pp. 246–81. Chapman's estimates are based on fitting a long-normal distribution with parameters derived from the equation in Rabkina and Rimashevskaia, *Osnovy differentsiatsi zarabotnoi platy i dokhodov nasileniia*, Moscow, 1972; P. Wiles, *Distribution of Income: East and West*, Amsterdam, North Holland, 1974; A. McAuley, *Economic Welfare in the Soviet Union*, London, Allen and Unwin, 1979, chapter 9.

3 See A. Bergson, 'Income inequality under Soviet socialism', *Journal of Economic Literature*, 22, September 1984, pp. 1052–99.

4 *Sotsial'noe razvitie i uroven' zhizni naseleniia SSSR* (Social Development and the Standard of Living in the USSR), Goskomstat SSSR, Moscow, 1989; *Trud v SSSR* (Labour in the USSR), Goskomstat SSSR, Moscow, 1988.

5 See L.E. Kunelskii, *Zarabotnaia plata i stimulirovanie truda* (Wages and Work Incentives), Moscow, 1981, table 20, p. 200.

6 See H. Flakierski, *The Economic System and Income Distribution in Yugoslavia*, Armonk, N.Y., M.E. Sharpe, 1989, table 1, pp. 24–9.

7 See H. Flakierski, *Economic Reform and Income Distribution – A Case Study of Hungary and Poland*, Armonk, N.Y., M.E. Sharpe, 1986, tables 1 and 6; *The Economic System and Income Distribution in Yugoslavia*, Armonk, N.Y., M.E. Sharpe, 1989, table 1.

8 Flakierski, *Economic Reform and Income Distribution*, chapter 2.

9 *Ibid.*, Table 4 and note 10, 11 on page 94.

10 Intersystem comparisons of discrepancies in manual and nonmanual earnings are difficult to make precisely because of differences in the definitions of manual and nonmanual employees. However, the differences in earnings of these groups in the two systems are too substantial to be a result of different statistical classifications alone. The decline in discrepancy of earnings between manual and nonmanual employees is a tendency observed as well in the Western world after World War II. The relative decline in earnings of professional and clerical workers is well illustrated in the Western literature. See A.B. Atkinson, *The Economics of Inequality*, Oxford, Clarendon Press, 1975, table 5.1, p. 76. However, this process has gone much farther in the East European countries than in the capitalist ones, and the relative position of nonmanual earnings reached such a low level. This ratio is usually around 2:1 in most Western countries. See A.B. Atkinson, *Economics of Inequality*, R.J. Nicholson, 'The distribution of personal income', in Atkinson (ed.), *Wealth, Income and Inequality*, Harmondsworth, Penguin, 1973. As far as the prewar period in Poland and Hungary is concerned, the ratio of nonmanual to manual earnings was much higher than after the war. M. Kalecki's estimates indicate a ratio of 2.2:1 for the prewar year of 1937 for Poland (see 'Porównanie dochodu robotników i pracowników umysłowych z okresem przedwojennym' – Comparisons of blue- and white-collar workers' income with the prewar period), *Kultura i społeczenstwo*, no. 1, 1964, table 2, pp. 35–40. In prewar Hungary we observe a tendency like that in Poland. (See Z. Ferge, *A Society in the Making*, Harmondsworth, Penguin 1972, table 5/4 p. 172.

11 Distributional frequencies for all the republics were published the first time by Goskomstat only for 1988, hence no changes in time in relative dispersion of per capita household income can be analyzed. However, the percentiles calculated on the basis of the data for 1988 are suggestive as far as differences in inequality between republics are concerned. In republics with average low incomes per capita relative dispersion of per-capita household income is very high; Kirgizia, Azerbaidzhan, Turkmenia are the leaders in this respect. The more prosperous republics in terms of average per capita household income such as the Baltic republics have a much lower degree of inequality of distribution. For example the decile ratio in Lithuania and latvia is 2.4, whereas this measure of inequality for the national economy as a whole is 3.0 in 1988. The same picture emerged by using all other measures of inequality.

12 See Flakierski, *Economic Reform and Income Distribution*.

13 See N. Rimashevskaia, 'Prozhitochnyi minimum' (Social Minimum), an interview with Rimashevskaia, in *Argumenty i Fakty* (Arguments and Facts), no. 14, 7–13 April 1990.

14 In all East European countries budget analysis refers to household and not to families. A multihousehold is defined as a group of two or more living in the same dwelling (or room) and combining part of all their earnings and other

income in order to meet the needs of the household. A single household refers to any person who maintains himself alone. Although most households are family households, composed of wife, husband, and their children, there are households composed of family *sensu stricto* plus members of the so-called extended family (cousins, grandparents, etc., or people not related to the family at all). There are also households where the people do not comprise a family or an extended family but just a group of people living together under the same roof and joining their incomes to maintain themselves.

15 According to the Economic Commission of the United Nations, families who have less than two thirds of the national average per capita income are considered poor. The following 'guideline' would put the incomes of 28 per cent of the Soviet families below the poverty line. The average per capita household income in the Soviet Union was in 1989 around 150 rubles a month.

16 In 1979 according to the population census in the russian Federation, Ukraine, Baltic republics, the dependent-earner, ratio was 0.5, in the same time in Azerbaidzhan, Kirgizia this ratio was 1.0 and reached 1.3 in Tadzhikistan. The extreme differences in this ratio is nearly three-fold.

17 See, *Pravitel'stvennyi vestnik*, no. 21, 1989.

Appendix

Table 1. Distribution of wages and salaries in the socialized sectors of the USSR (measures of dispersion)

	All the economy					Industry		Agriculture		Transport		Communications		Construction		Trade		Housing services		Health		Education		Science		State administration	
	1968	1972	1976	1981	1986	1981	1986	1981	1986	1981	1986	1981	1986	1981	1986	1981	1986	1981	1986	1981	1986	1981	1986	1981	1986	1981	1986
Median (M)	101.9	115.2	130.8	149.0	160.8	175.0	192.8	125.1	140.4	174.5	186.8	134.3	146.8	178.8	191.3	124.8	133.2	125.5	134.1	119.8	125.6	125.7	138.4	165.7	180.6	140.0	149.6
Mean (X̄)	109.0	125.0	142.8	163.0	177.2	188.0	206.6	135.6	152.6	188.8	201.5	141.1	155.7	192.0	205.7	132.7	142.4	135.4	144.9	129.3	136.0	139.4	156.0	179.0	194.3	151.8	162.8
$P_{95}:P_1$	5.5	6.6	7.0	7.2	7.8	5.8	5.6	6.5	6.7	6.3	6.1	4.3	5.0	5.8	5.9	5.1	5.5	6.1	6.4	6.2	5.1	8.3	9.8	6.1	5.9	6.3	6.8
$P_{95}:P_2$	4.5	5.3	5.6	5.7	6.1	4.7	4.6	5.2	5.4	5.1	5.0	3.6	4.1	4.7	4.8	4.2	4.5	5.0	5.0	5.0	5.1	6.5	7.5	5.0	4.8	5.1	5.5
$P_{90}:P_5$	3.3	3.8	4.0	4.0	4.3	3.5	3.4	3.8	3.8	3.7	3.6	2.8	3.1	3.4	3.5	3.2	3.3	3.6	3.6	3.6	3.7	4.5	5.0	3.6	3.5	3.7	3.9
$P_{95}:P_5$	2.6	2.8	2.9	3.0	3.1	2.6	2.6	2.8	2.9	2.8	2.7	2.2	2.4	2.6	2.7	2.4	2.6	2.7	2.7	2.7	2.8	3.2	3.5	2.7	2.6	2.8	2.9
$P_{90}:P_{10}$	2.1	2.3	2.4	2.4	2.5	2.2	2.2	2.3	2.3	2.3	2.2	1.9	2.0	2.2	2.2	2.1	2.1	2.2	2.3	2.3	2.3	2.6	2.8	2.2	2.2	2.3	2.3
$P_{85}:P_{15}$	1.6	1.7	1.8	1.8	1.8	1.7	1.7	1.7	1.7	1.7	1.7	1.5	1.6	1.7	1.7	1.6	1.6	1.7	1.7	1.7	1.7	1.8	1.9	1.7	1.7	1.7	1.7
Q_3-Q_1/M	0.5	0.55	0.57	0.6	0.6	0.52	0.50	0.55	0.56	0.54	0.53	0.43	0.47	0.51	0.52	0.48	0.52	0.53	0.54	0.53	0.54	0.62	0.67	0.53	0.52	0.54	0.5
Coefficient of variable	43.6	45.3	43.9	42.3	42.6	36.3	34.8	42.8	43.0	38.5	37.2	35.5	37.4	36.0	35.1	38.8	39.8	40.9	41.0	42.4	42.2	47.4	48.7	38.1	37.0	41.0	40.6

P_5, P_{25}, etc., refer to the 5th, 25th, etc., percentiles of earnings ordering wage and salary earners from low incomes to high incomes; e.g. P_5 refers to the bottom 5% of earners and P_{95} refers to the top 5%.

Q_1 is the lower quartile.

Q_3 is the upper quartile.

The coefficient of variation (%), computed by dividing the standard deviation by the mean.

Socialnoe Razvitie i uroven žizni naselenia SSSR (Social Development and the population's standard of living in the USSR). Goskomstat SSSR, Moscow, 1989, pp. 78–9.

Appendix
Table 2. *Average monthly wages in Soviet republics (as a percentage of the national average)*

	1940	1950	1960	1965	1970	1975	1980	1981	1982	1983	1984	1985	1986	1987
Russian Federation	102.4	102.3	103.1	102.6	103.4	105.1	105.2	105.4	105.6	105.7	105.8	105.9	106.2	106.5
Ukraine	97.3	97.7	97.1	97.3	94.4	91.6	91.8	91.5	92.0	91.9	91.8	91.5	91.5	91.2
White Russia	86.4	83.6	78.4	83.5	87.2	86.1	88.8	88.8	88.7	89.0	90.5	91.4	92.3	93.6
Uzbekistan	89.7	92.8	87.0	92.4	94.1	93.7	92.1	92.1	89.9	89.7	87.4	86.4	84.8	82.3
Kazakhstan	90.0	96.6	101.1	101.6	101.4	101.2	98.9	98.8	98.0	98.8	98.1	98.1	98.5	98.2
Georgia	100.6	99.1	92.8	89.9	87.0	81.6	86.0	86.1	86.2	86.6	87.4	88.2	87.2	87.3
Azerbaidzhan	106.9	102.8	95.9	93.6	89.8	85.8	87.9	88.5	87.4	86.1	86.4	85.5	82.7	81.3
Lithuania	91.8	84.1	89.8	92.8	98.0	97.6	98.3	98.3	98.4	98.6	99.5	99.9	99.5	100.6
Moldavia	80.7	79.1	83.6	84.9	84.3	80.2	81.9	81.4	82.3	83.4	84.0	83.0	82.7	82.2
Latvia	94.9	97.0	97.4	98.4	103.0	100.4	101.5	101.4	101.7	101.7	103.0	103.1	103.0	103.0
Kirgizia	91.2	90.0	92.9	92.2	92.3	92.0	87.6	87.1	85.8	85.7	85.5	85.5	85.1	84.5
Tadzhikistan	110.3	97.5	97.1	99.5	96.4	93.4	86.1	85.7	84.3	83.4	83.2	83.0	82.8	81.8
Armenia	103.6	92.8	94.2	96.0	100.8	95.1	96.6	96.4	95.7	95.3	95.7	94.8	94.3	94.1
Turkmenistan	106.3	103.3	105.3	105.9	106.6	111.5	104.3	103.7	102.4	101.6	101.1	100.5	98.7	97.8
Estonia	97.3	99.4	101.6	103.5	110.9	109.6	111.7	111.8	110.8	111.1	112.7	113.2	113.0	112.9
Coefficient of variation (v)	8.7	7.9	7.9	6.6	8.0	9.9	9.1	9.1	9.2	9.2	9.5	9.8	10.1	10.7
Range	136.7	130.6	134.3	127.0	131.6	139.0	136.4	137.3	134.6	133.2	135.5	136.4	136.6	138.9

Appendix
Table 3(a). *Distribution of wages and salaries in the Soviet republics (measures of dispersion)*

	All the Economy		Russian Federation		Ukraine		Belorussia		Uzbekistan		Kazakhstan		Georgia		Azerbaidzhan	
	1981	1986	1981	1986	1981	1986	1981	1986	1981	1986	1981	1986	1981	1986	1981	1986
Median (M)	149.0	160.8	155.5	168.9	139.7	151.5	137.4	152.8	132.2	138.4	142.0	154.2	129.6	139.6	127.0	133.1
Mean (X)	163.0	177.2	170.0	185.7	151.9	165.0	148.9	165.8	145.3	152.1	156.3	170.2	142.2	155.0	140.2	147.6
$P_{99}:P_1$	7.2	7.8	7.2	7.6	6.7	6.9	6.4	6.6	7.6	7.6	7.7	7.9	7.4	8.4	7.9	8.3
$P_{98}:P_2$	5.7	6.1	5.7	6.0	5.4	5.5	5.2	5.3	6.0	6.0	6.1	6.2	5.9	6.5	6.2	6.5
$P_{95}:P_5$	4.0	4.3	4.0	4.2	3.8	3.9	3.7	3.8	4.2	4.2	4.2	4.3	4.1	4.5	4.3	4.5
$P_{90}:P_{10}$	3.0	3.1	3.0	3.0	2.8	2.9	2.8	2.8	3.0	3.0	3.1	3.1	3.1	3.2	3.1	3.2
$P_{85}:P_{15}$	2.4	2.5	2.4	2.5	2.3	2.4	2.3	2.3	2.5	2.5	2.5	2.5	2.4	2.6	2.5	2.6
$Q_3:Q_1$	1.8	1.8	1.8	1.8	1.7	1.7	1.7	1.7	1.8	1.8	1.8	1.8	1.8	1.9	1.8	1.8
$Q_3:Q_1/M$	0.6	0.6	0.58	0.59	0.56	0.56	0.55	0.55	0.59	0.59	0.6	0.6	0.59	0.63	0.61	0.62
V	42.3	42.6	41.8	41.3	41.7	41.3	39.7	39.3	44.8	44.5	44.6	43.8	45.5	47.5	47.0	48.0

For source, see table A.2, p. 000.

Appendix
Table 3(b). Distribution of wages and salaries in the Soviet republics (measures of dispersion)

	Lithuania		Moldavia		Latvia		Kirgizia		Tadzhikistan		Armenia		Turkmenistan		Estonia	
	1981	1986	1981	1986	1981	1986	1981	1986	1981	1986	1981	1986	1981	1986	1981	1986
Median (M)	147.7	161.7	128.4	138.8	150.8	164.5	131.3	141.0	131.5	136.8	140.1	153.1	153.0	159.8	163.3	177.1
Mean (X)	161.2	176.9	139.0	151.1	164.4	180.6	143.4	154.4	144.4	151.2	155.6	169.8	168.6	176.3	178.7	194.5
$P_{99}:P_1$	7.0	7.2	6.4	6.8	6.9	7.5	7.0	7.3	7.5	8.0	8.4	8.3	7.7	7.9	7.2	7.5
$P_{98}:P_2$	5.6	5.7	5.1	5.4	5.5	5.9	5.6	5.7	5.9	6.3	6.6	6.5	6.1	6.2	5.7	5.9
$P_{95}:P_5$	4.0	4.0	3.7	3.9	3.9	4.2	4.0	4.1	4.2	4.4	4.5	4.5	4.2	4.3	4.1	4.2
$P_{90}:P_{10}$	2.9	3.0	2.8	2.9	2.9	3.0	2.9	3.0	3.0	3.2	3.2	3.2	3.1	3.1	3.0	3.0
$P_{85}:P_{15}$	2.4	2.4	2.3	2.4	2.4	2.5	2.4	2.4	2.5	2.5	2.6	2.6	2.5	2.5	2.4	2.5
$Q_3:Q_2$	1.8	1.8	1.7	1.7	1.8	1.8	1.8	1.8	1.8	1.8	1.9	1.8	1.8	1.8	1.8	1.8
$Q_3:Q_1/M$	0.57	0.58	0.54	0.56	0.57	0.59	0.57	0.58	0.59	0.61	0.63	0.62	0.6	0.6	0.58	0.59
V	40.6	40.1	41.1	41.5	40.6	40.8	43.4	43.8	43.8	44.6	46.5	45.3	43.3	43.0	40.2	39.7

10 Estonia's economic development 1940–1990 in comparison with Finland's

Jan Åke Dellenbrant

As a result of the annexations of Estonia by the Soviet Union in 1940 and 1944, a fundamentally new political and economic order was introduced. As in other parts of the Soviet Union the political system was dominated by the Communist Party and the system of Soviets. The economy was based on the Stalinist central planning system and the agriculture was collectivized. Gradually, Estonia also became an integral part of the all-union Soviet economy. During most of Estonia's independence period, the political and economic structures had to a large extent resembled that of the West European countries. The new social transformation was performed with extremely harsh methods, and the benefits of the reorganization were questioned by many Estonians from the outset. On the other hand, it was pointed out by the Soviet authorities that Estonia's economic development would prosper as a result of the integration into the Soviet economy. Also, the new system was said to be more advantageous for the working class which constituted a majority of the population.

During the Gorbachev era, questions were more openly raised about the benefits of the social transformation inaugurated by the communists. In many cases, this development was considered detrimental to the social and economic performances of Estonia. In order to shed light on this problem, a comparative analysis will be carried out in this chapter, where the development of Estonia will be compared with other countries and the Soviet republics, and especially with its Northern neighbour, Finland.

Historically, the two countries Estonia and Finland have shown some important similarities. The cultural and linguistic connections are obvious. During the major part of the interwar period, both countries were dominated by agrarian and social democratic parties. Finland was looked upon by many Estonians as a model for social and economic development. By the end of the 1930s the two countries had achieved comparable standards of living.

As a result of the incorporation of Estonia by the Soviet Union, the two countries departed on largely different roads of development. In Estonia the traditional Stalinist economic system was introduced, while Finland

194

followed a capitalist development strategy, albeit with strong governmental regulations.

A comparative approach

In this study, a comparison between the developments of Estonia and Finland will be made in the fields of economic and social performances. In particular, the situation shortly before the Soviet attack on the Baltic countries in 1940 and the situation preceding the Estonian declaration of independence in 1990 will be compared. Arend Lijphart has pointed out that in order to make meaningful comparisons between different political systems it is necessary that the units of analysis are in certain critical aspects similar.[1] In a number of aspects, including economic development and living standards, Estonia and Finland had reached comparable levels before the Second World War.

A number of scientific studies comparing the economic and social development in capitalist and socialist countries have been undertaken.[2] Many of these studies have compared the USSR with other countries on a macro level. There are fewer studies published that compare smaller units, as the republics of the USSR with units of analysis outside the socialist (or formerly socialist) countries. In this respect, the present study is an exception from the rule. Partly, the relative lack of studies of this kind could be explained by difficulties in data collection. The statistical data originating from socialist countries have been computed differently. Access to regional data has been limited. Also, the quality of the statistics from these countries could be questioned in many respects. But by comparing the situation for the case of Estonia in 1940 and 1990 many of these difficulties could be overcome. The statistics of the independent Estonia were collected in a similar way as in most Western Countries. Also, the statistical information from the glasnost period in Estonia is more reliable and available for more variables.

The case for a comparative approach is strengthened by the works of Adam Przeworski. In his analyses of transitions from authoritarian to more democratic rule in West European countries at the beginning of this century and in contemporary Latin American and East European countries, Przeworski has found a number of similarities in the processes.[3]

Scope and method

The comparison carried out in this paper could be regarded as an analysis of the result of the modernization processes in the two countries. More precisely, the outcomes of a capitalist and a socialist development strategy will be analyzed in a long-term perspective.

In early formulations of the modernization theory, it was pointed out that there was generally a high degree of covariation between modernization indicators. Where advanced cultural, technological, and economic life are introduced on a broad scale, similar processes of social mobilization could be discerned. Eventually, this development would also affect the political system.[4]

It seems, however, that the early proponents of modernization theories underestimated the size of these factors. The modernization process has proceeded at a much faster pace than originally anticipated. This becomes evident from the exponential growth of international trade during the last decades.[5] This rapid change, however, does not diminish the usefulness of a modernization approach. On the contrary, there are even more reasons to observe modernization and its consequences.

In this chapter, the pace of modernization will first be studied for the two units of analysis. The reasons for different outcomes will be analyzed. After that some consequences of the development will be discussed. In particular, the prospects for further successful reforms in Estonia will be discussed. Of course, no *general* evaluation of the economic and social performance of capitalism and socialism can be made within the framework of this chapter. The comparison is based on the two units of analysis – one with an essentially capitalistic development strategy but including strong government regulations, the other with a socialist strategy of the particular type that was introduced by Stalin in the Soviet Union as early as in the 1920s.

In this chapter, the pace of modernization will first be studied for the two units of analysis. The reasons for different outcomes will be analyzed. After that some consequences of the development will be discussed. In particular, the prospects for further successful reforms in Estonia will be discussed. Of course, no *general* evaluation of the economic and social performance of capitalism and socialism can be made within the framework of this chapter. The comparison is based on the two units of analysis – one with an essentially capitalistic development strategy but including strong government regulations, the other with a socialist strategy of the particular type that was introduced by Stalin in the Soviet Union as early as in the 1920s.

The present investigation is based on a number of indicators measuring economic and social performance. The general level of industrial development will be analyzed for the two countries. Moreover, indicators measuring the standards of living will be of great use. The latter type of indicators may be used for an evaluation of the results of economic development. The standard of living is also dependent of political decisions concerning the distribution of wealth. Among indicators measuring living standards the purchase power of industrial workers will be used as well as data concerning health care. The same indicators cannot be used for the analysis of the situation in 1940 and the situation on the eve of the 1990s. This is due to the fact that data collection methods have changed over time. But it will be possible, nevertheless, to compare the status of the two countries in the field of living standards.

The comparison carried out in this chapter is to a large extent based on the methodology elaborated by this author in the book *Soviet Regional Policy*.[6] Here, the fifteen Soviet republics were compared in terms of political and socio-economic development. Among the indicators used were per capita national income, capital investments, number of hospital beds, housing space. Also used were indicators measuring political recruitment. In that study, it was possible to show that the Baltic republics enjoyed the highest living standards in the Soviet Union. It could also be established that the gap between the highest economically developed republics and the least developed did not change significantly over time during the period investigated, that is, 1956–1973. There was also a high degree of covariation between the political and economic indicators for all republics but the three Baltic states. Here, the levels of political recruitment were far lower than expected. Some of these results could be distorted, however, by differences in the role of the second economy in the regions of the USSR.[7]

Two other studies have been important sources of inspiration for this paper. In a book on the regional economy of the Soviet Union, I.S. Koropeckyj and Gertrude E. Schroeder gathered papers on general development problems as well as the economic development in individual regions of the Soviet Union. In Schroeder's chapter on living standards it becomes clear – by the use of a number of different indices from Soviet statistics – that the Baltic republics have enjoyed a higher standard of living than most other areas of the USSR. Schroeder concludes that

systemic ills are least manifest, in general, in the relatively high-income Baltic republics and most evident in least affluent Transcaucasia and Central Asia, where 'second economy' activities also seem most prevalent.[8]

In another important study, by Alastair McAuley, an analysis is made of money and personal incomes of Soviet citizens as well as other welfare indicators. One of the results of this major scientific investigation is that the degree of economic inequality – as measured by total income per capita – was greater than expected in the Soviet Union.[9] Both Schroeder's and McAuley's investigations are, however, confined to intra-Soviet comparisons. In this chapter, the comparison will be made also with a country outside the Soviet Union.

This cross-country comparison is, of course, not devoid of problems. Quite often, different collection methods in the two countries under focus make it impossible to compare data. Another, more sophisticated, problem is that certain types of data are emphasized during different periods of economic development. For example, in Soviet statistics there is a predominance of statistics that measure the level of industrialization, for example, the production of steel, heavy machinery, and raw materials. In the so-called post-industrial society, where service and commerce play a more important role, the industrialization indicators deserve less attention.[10] In the present study, statistics that have been collected in a similar way have been selected as far as possible. Furthermore, pure industrialization indicators have been avoided completely.

Quite naturally, statistical comparisons will never give a complete picture of socioeconomic development and living standards. But it seems impossible to make meaningful comparisons without some quantification of the material. The statistical material will also have to be supported by other sources, including interviews with scholars.

The main primary material for this study originates from Finnish and Estonian statistical publications. In some cases, also Soviet statistics have been used. Furthermore, different scientific analyses of Finnish and Estonian social and economic development have been used. Both Western and Soviet literature has been consulted, although the main usage of the Soviet literature has been concentrated on the Gorbachev period. As mentioned, interviews with scholars have been carried out. Of special importance have been consultations at the Institute of Economics of the Estonian Academy of Sciences.

Economic and social performances in the interwar period

In his analysis of the economic structure of independent Estonia, Uno Kaur has divided the interwar years into four distinct periods:

(1) Establishment of economic foundations 1918–24;
(2) Expansion and prosperity 1925–29;
(3) Crisis and depression 1930–33;
(4) Economic recovery and expansion 1934–50.[11]

Even before the economic expansion of the 1930s, independent Estonia had achieved a comparatively high level of economic development. This is evident from calculations on per capita incomes concerning some West European countries (table 10.1).

Table 10.1 indicates that Estonia did not differ substantially from the Scandinavian countries. It even ranked before Finland. However, the data

Table 10.1. *Average annual per capita incomes in international units (for the period* 1925–34)

Country	Per capita income
Estonia	241
Denmark	286
Germany	276
Finland	131
Lithuania	83
Sweden	283
England	478
USA	552
USSR	119

Following Colin Clark, an international unit is computed as the average quantum of goods and services which could be bought with one dollar in the USA during the period of analysis (1925–34).

Kaur, note, 11, p. 204.

must clearly be considered uncertain as they include observations from both the economic expansion period of the 1920s and the following depression. The data must overestimate the position of Estonia. But apart from these problems, there is clear indication that the economic situation in Estonia during this period compared in a relatively favorable way with Scandinavia.

When comparing Estonia and Finland, one should bear in mind that the population of the latter country was almost four times higher than that of the former. In 1940 Estonia had 1,054,000 inhabitants while Finland had 3,887,000.[12] This, of course, gave Finland a larger potential for future economic growth. But other indicators – for example, the level of urbanization and the structure of employment – show that at the end of the 1930s Estonia's level of development was comparatively high.

The level of urbanization could be used as an indirect index of industrialization. Industrial activities tend to be concentrated in space. Thus, the growth of cities is usually associated with the growth of industrial activities. In 1940 the level of urbanization in Estonia was even somewhat higher than Finland's (table 10.2).

In 1940, both Estonia and Finland were predominantly rural societies. The urban share of the population was higher, though, in Estonia. At this time, small-scale agriculture and, especially, forestry played an important role in Finland's economy, factors which contribute to the understanding of the relatively low share of urban population. The differences between

Table 10.2. *Urban/rural population as a proportion of the total population* (1940)

Country	(%) Urban	(%) Rural
Estonia	34	66
Finland	23	77

Narodnoe knoziaistvo SSSR 1922–1972 gg–, Moscow, Statistika, 1972, p. 681.
Annuaire statistique de Finlande, Helsinki, Bureau central de statistique, 1943, p. 9.

Table 10.3. *The structure of employment measured in per cent of total employed population* (1934/40)

Country	Industry and construction	Agriculture and forestry	Other
Estonia	16	68	16
Finland	16	60	24

Estonian data from Kaur, as in note 11, p. 100. These data refer to 1934. Finnish data from 'Population by industry', *Statistical Surveys* (Helsinki), no. 63, 1979, p. 338. These data originate from 1940.

the two countries in terms of urbanization should not be overestimated, however. Even if some differences did exist, the urbanization index could be interpreted as being on comparable levels in Estonia and Finland.

Another indicator measuring industrialization and the modernization of society is the structure of employment. Data from the 1930s and 1940 indicate that no significant differences between Estonia and Finland existed in terms of employment levels in industry and construction *versus* agriculture and forestry (table 10.3).

Although data originate from different years, there is no doubt that the employment structures in Estonia and Finland were similar at the end of the 1930s. Both countries were dominated by agriculture and forestry-related activities, although the industrial work force was growing. The figures for 'Others' in table 10.3 indicate that the tertiary sector still was relatively small in the two countries but still larger in Finland.[13]

At the end of the 1930s Estonia still maintained a level of prosperity comparable to the Nordic countries. This is evident from calculations by Sirje Sinilind concerning wage/price relations in Estonia and Finland. According to official statistics a Finnish worker could buy slightly more food for his hourly wage than his Estonian counterpart (table 10.4).

Table 10.4. *Amount of food that could be bought by a blue-collar worker in 1938 with his hourly income.*

Item	Estonia	Finland
Pork	400 g	420 g
Beef (roast)	410 g	660 g
Small herring	1750 g	1620 g
Rye bread	1770 g	1650 g
Wheat bread	960 g	580 g
Milk	3.0 l	3.6 l
Potatoes	8.4 kg	8.9 kg
Sugar	780 g	950 g

Sirje Sinilind (pseudonym for Juhan Talve), *Estonia in the Prison of Nations*, Stockholm, Estonian Information Centre, 1984, p. 25.

Using the data in table 10.4 it could be argued that the standard of living of Estonian workers was at least 90 per cent of the standard of Finnish workers. These data are restricted to the working-class population, but nevertheless they give an approximate picture of the situation at large.

The conclusion that the Estonian living standard amounted to about 90 per cent of Finland's is supported by several investigations, among others those carried out by contemporary scolars.[14] But it should be stressed that these kinds of international comparisons were still relatively uncommon in the 1930s, as the statistical data were not highly refined. Following calculations by V. Lindberg the per capita national income of Estonia was 367 Estonian kroon in 1927–28 and the corresponding per capita national income of Finland was 397 kroon. In 1936 the Estonian national income per capita was about 400 kroon. During the last years of the 1930s, the gap between Estonia and Finland remained the same or decreased slightly. On the other hand, Finland's predominantly agrarian orientation would tend to somewhat underestimate the Finnish income.[15]

A comparison of economies and living standards in the 1980s

During the 1980s a considerable interest in assessing the Estonian socioeconomic development arose as a result of the reemergence of large nationally-oriented movements, such as the popular front. Several concepts for economic self-determination were presented. In one version of these from 1988 it was stated that Estonia's economic development had been slowed considerably through its inclusion into the administrative planning system.[16]

At the end of the 1930s the economic social and demographic developments of Estonia and Finland were on about equal levels, but at present Estonia has lagged behind considerably. For every year we have moved farther from the top positions of the list of developed states in terms of subject objective indicators as average life expectancy of the population, infant mortality, national income, standard of living etc... The fact remains that the quality of our lives has continuously deteriorated during the last decades.[17]

A number of indicators show clearly the low economic standard of Estonia according to the programme. The authors point at life expectancy and infant mortality as important indicators. The comparison is made with countries outside the USSR and not with other Soviet republics. If the latter comparison is carried out it is clear that Estonia enjoys the highest standard of living – together with Latvia and Lithuania – of all Soviet republics.[18] As pointed out by Alastair McAuley the per capita personal incomes in the Baltic republics exceeded the USSR average by 15 per cent or more in 1970.[19] An elaborate programme for economic self-determination for Estonia was presented in 1989, the so-called IME-Programme. Also here, comparisons were made with the Nordic countries.[20]

The Estonians clearly wish to compare themselves with the West European countries and not with the USSR at large. It is also stressed in the IME-Programme that the sole solution to Estonia's economic problems is to introduce indigenous reforms. The economic development of the USSR as a whole had reached a *cul-de-sac*, according to the IME-Programme.

From 1940 to the end of the 1980s, the level of urbanization changed dramatically in both countries under review. In 1989–1990 both Estonia and Finland have a majority of urban dwellers. But as in 1940 the urbanization level in Finland in 1990 was somewhat lower than in Estonia (table 10.5).

In both 1940 and 1990, the levels of urbanization in Estonia were higher than in Finland. This could partly be explained through the larger territory of Finland. Also the total number of urban dwellers in Finland was greater than in Estonia due to differences in population size. The total population in Estonia was 1,573,300 in 1989; the corresponding figure for Finland in 1990 was 4,972,798.[21]

The employment structure in the two countries in the 1930s was remarkably equal (table 10.3). The comparatively large urban population of Estonia would, no doubt, have the potential of being part of a rapid industrialization process. This industrialization indeed took place at a more rapid pace even than in Finland. But by the end of the 1980s Finland had already reached the post-industrial society where the industrial work force tended to decrease (table 10.6).

Table 10.5. *Urban/rural population as a proportion of the total population* (1989/1990)

Country	(%) Urban	(%) Rural
Estonia	72	28
Finland	61	38

Narodnoe khoziaistvo Estonskoi SSR v 1988 g, Tallinn, Olion, 1989, p. 10. (Estonian data are for 1989). *Statistical Yearbook of Finland*, Helsinki, Central Statistical Office, 1989, p. 40. *Förhandsuppgifter om befolkningsförändringar kommunvis*, April 1990, Helsingfors, Statistikcentralen, 1990. p. 3.

Table 10.6. *The structure of employment measured in per cent of total employed population* (1988)

Country	Industry and construction	Agriculture and forestry	Other
Estonia	43	12	45
Finland	30	10	60

Narodnoe khoziaistvo Estonskoi SSR v 1988 g, p. 213. *Statistical Yearbook of Finland*, 1989, p. 328.

By 1990 almost two thirds of the Finnish population was employed outside the industrial and agricultural sectors. Instead, a growing number of employed persons was engaged in trade, communications, and different types of services. This shift of employment towards communications and services has been also observed in other countries entering the so called post-industrial society. From table 10.6 it becomes clear that this process has been slower in Estonia. In fact, the service sector – as in the Soviet Union as a whole – in Estonia has been underdeveloped.

In the preceding section a comparison of wage/price relations in Estonia and Finland was made, using calculations by Sinilind. This author also made the same comparison for the 1980s. It turns out that in 1983 the Estonian worker could buy somewhat more food with his hourly income than he could do in 1938, while the Finnish worker could buy about three times more (table 10.7).

In table 10.7 it is clearly seen that the near equality in purchasing power between Finnish and Estonian workers has vanished. While the situation for the Estonian worker is only characterized by minor change since 1938 the Finnish worker could buy far more. An approximate estimate would be that the living standard for the Estonians is about 40 per cent of the

204   Jan Åke Dellenbrant

Table 10.7. *Amount of food that could be bought by a blue-collar worker in 1983 with his hourly income*

Item	Estonia	Finland
Pork	455 g	1370 g
Beef (roast)	250 g	630 g
Small herring	1235 g	4990 g
Rye bread	6250 g	3750 g
White bread	4545 g	2860 g
Milk	3.9 litres	10 litres
Butter	294 g	900 g
Sugar	1289 g	3160 g
Eggs	8.3 pieces	15.3 pieces
Sausage	400 g	1540 g
Wheat flour	2380 g	4860 g
Coffee	50 g	860 g
Cheese	340 g	860 g

Sinilind, *Estonia in the Prison of Nations*, p. 26

Finns. Certainly, the living standard has increased also for the Estonians over time. But in making this wage/price comparison one should not forget the severe shortages of food that are prevalent in Estonia – as well as in other parts of the Soviet Union. Only one item, bread, is relatively cheaper in Estonia.

The differences between Estonia and Finland are also apparent using other indicators on people's welfare. In the IME-Programme, infant mortality was specifically mentioned. According to the official statistics of Estonia, the Soviet Union, and Finland infant mortality, that is, infant deaths before the age of one year, is significantly higher in Estonia. In 1989 the mortality rate in Estonia was 14.6 per 1,000 live births, while in Finland the corresponding rate was 6.1 in 1987. Although Estonia's mortality rate was lower than in many other Soviet republics – Turkmenia represented the highest with 54.2 – it was more than twice that of the Nordic countries. Moreover, it seems that the infant mortality rate in Estonia and other Soviet republics is no longer decreasing after the middle of 1970s. Most probably, this tendency is related to increased levels of air and water pollution as well as a general decline in the health care system.[22]

The decline of social conditions in the Soviet Union is recognized also by official Soviet authorities. In the annual report for 1989 of *Goskomstat* (The USSR State Committee for Statistics) it was pointed out that the development of living standards had stagnated. Housing construction even declined. The health care system remained on an insufficiently low level.[23]

Some of the tendencies noticed in Estonia were also found in Finland. But in general the socioeconomic development of Finland was characterized by rapid growth. The statement that the living standard of Estonia was approximately 40 per cent of Finland's seems on the whole plausible.

Decreasing or increasing divergence?

In 1984 a book was published whose main thesis runs contrary to that of the present paper. In his work *Dva berega – dva obraza zhizni* (Two shores – two ways of life) Vladimir Petrov stated that as late as in 1980 the living standards of Estonia and Finland were on an equal level. According to Petrov the levels of consumption of the inhabitants in Estonia and Finland were comparable:

At present the level of daily consumption of the population in the Estonian SSR not only equals but for a number of products also exceeds the corresponding level of many developed capitalist countries. And when comparing prices on some categories of food ours is cheaper than in England.[24]

According to Petrov, the situation in Estonia was even more favourable than in Finland due to the social security system of the former country. It seems correct to dismiss Petrov's analyses as sheer Soviet propaganda. Clearly, he overstates the positive sides of the Estonian development. But some data presented by Petrov could also be used as an indication of the possibility that the divergence between Estonia and Finland occurred relatively late: Petrov's data refer mostly to the period 1970–80. During the economic discussions of the 1960s in the USSR it became clear that the existing planning system had exhausted most of its possibilities and that far-reaching reforms had to be carried out. But due to bureaucratic resistance and other problems the actual reforms were not implemented.[25] The failure of these reforms must be taken into account when determining the point of time when Estonia's and Finland's paths of development diverge.

Also Estonian sources indicate that the divergence point occurred during the 1960s. The authors of the IME-Programme refer to the deterioration of the last decades. The works of the Estonian economist Kalev Kukk show that from 1968 and onwards the differences in per capita national income between Finland begin to differ substantially. While in 1968 the GNP development gap was small the differences in 1988 were substantial. According to calculations favourable to Estonia Finland's per capita national income was three times higher in Finland than in Estonia. Following Kukk's analysis there is even a possibility that Estonia's per capita national income had stagnated in the 1968–88 period.[26]

These data give an indication that the increasing divergence could have occurred some time in the 1960s. At this time it was clear to many observers that the central planning system had to be substantially altered or even replaced by a system oriented towards profitability and market thinking. But neither in Estonia nor in the USSR at large it was possible to overcome the obstacles to economic reform.

Conclusions

Available data show clearly that the levels of socio-economic development in Estonia and Finland were close to equal around 1940. In 1990, Estonia's standard of living could be assessed to be about 40 per cent of Finland's.

The foundation for Finland's prosperous development was a capitalist strategy. Situated between the East and the West Finland could profit from relatively favourable trade relations with the USSR.

Estonia's relative poverty could more specifically be explained by the inability of the planning system. Within this system it was impossible to create a consumer-oriented society and also to solve the severe environmental problems. Estonia started to lag substantially behind Finland from the 1960's and onwards. A real market-oriented economy now appears to be the sole solution.

In November 1989 a USSR Law on Economic Sovereignty of the Baltic Republics was passed.[27] Although hitherto this law played more of a formal role it gives possibilities for further change. More important at this stage are the republic level laws in Estonia passed in 1989 and 1990. The new Enterprise Law, the decisions on joint-stock companies and on an Estonian currency, as well as other measures taken lay the legal foundations for the transition to a market economy.

This paper will end with a paradox: During the last decades the Soviet leaders in Moscow have devoted considerable interest in promoting good relations with Finland, utilizing this country as a bridge in East–West relations. Estonia, on the other hand, has constantly been caught in the centralist planning which in practice has meant that many Estonian products had to be delivered to other parts of the USSR, especially to the Russian republic. The differences between good neighbourly relations and semi-colonial exploitation also contribute to the understanding of the outcomes of economic and social policy in Estonia and Finland.

Notes

1 Arend Lijphard, 'The comparable cases strategy in comparative research', *Comparative Political Studies*, no. 8, 1975, pp. 158–77.
2 See, for example, Igor Birman, *Ekonomika nedostach*, New York, Chalidze

Publications, 1983; Paul Marer, *Dollar GNPs of the USSR and Eastern Europe*, Baltimore, Johns Hopkins University Press, 1985; Gertrude E. Schroeder and Imogene Edwards, 'Consumption in the USSR: an international comparison', paper prepared for the US Congress, Joint Economic Committee, Washington, GPO, 1981; Irving B. Kravis, Alan Heston, and Robert Summers, *World Product and Income: International Comparisons of Real Gross Product*, Baltimore, Johns Hopkins University Press, 1982; and Anders Åslund, 'How small is the Soviet national income?', in Henry S. Rowen and Charles Wolf, Jr. (eds.), *The Impoverished Superpower: Perestroika and the Military Burden*, San Francisco, ICS Press, 1990. For a thorough analysis of these attempts at comparison, see the article by Åslund.

3 Adam Przeworski, 'Democracy as contingent outcome of conflicts', in Jon Elster and Rune Slagstad, *Constitutionalism and Democracy*, Cambridge, Cambridge University Press, 1988.

4 Karl Deutsch, 'Social mobilization and political development', *American Political Science Review*, 55, no. 3, 1961, pp. 493–514. For broader discussions of the modernization process, see Daniel Lerner, *The Passing of Traditional Society*, New York, Free Press of Glencoe, 1958 and Seymour Martin Lipset, *Political Man*, Garden City, Doubleday & Co. 1969.

5 Lucian W. Pye, 'Political science and the crisis of authoritarianism', *American Political Science Review*, 84, no. 1, 1990, pp. 3–19.

6 Jan Åke Dellenbrant, *Soviet Regional Policy: A Quantiative Inquiry into the Social and Political Development of the Soviet Republics*, Atlantic Highlands, Humanities Press, 1980.

7 Several works by Gregory Grossman give thorough insights in the second economy, e.g.'The "second economy" of the USSR', *Problems of Communism*, 26, no. 5 Sept–Oct 1977, and 'The "Shadow economy" in the socialist sector of the USSR', in *The CMEA Five-Year Plans (1981–1985) in a New Perspective: Planned and Non-Planned Economies*, NATO, Economics and Information Directorates, 1982.

8 Gertrude E. Schroeder, 'Regional living standards', in I.S. Koropeckyj and Gertrude E. Schroeder (eds.), *Economics of Soviet Regions*, New York, Praeger Special Studies, 1981, p. 149.

9 Alastair McAuley, *Economic Welfare in the Soviet Union: Poverty, Living Standards, and Inequality*, Madison, University of Wisconsin Press, 1979.

10 Cf. Peter O. Aven, 'Quantitative indicators for international comparisons: the IIASA approach', Ms, IIASA, 1990, pp. 3–4.

11 Uno Kaur, 'Wirtschaftsstruktur und Wirtschaftspolitik des Freistaates Estland 1918–40', *Commentationes Balticae*, 8–9, no. 3, Baltisches Forschungsinstitut, Bonn, 1962, p. 87.

12 *Norodnoe khoziaistvo SSSR 1922–1972 gg*, Moscow, Statistika, 1972, p. 681. *Annuaire statistique de Finlande*, Helsinki, Bureau central de statistique, 1943, p. 9.

13 Soviet data from 1940 – which were collected with different methods – give a more unfavourable picture for Estonia. According to *Trudovye resursy Pribaltiskikh Sovetskikh Respublik*, Riga, Zinatne, 1967, p. 34, the following employment structure existed in 1940: industry 11 per cent; agriculture and forestry, 71 per cent; other branches, 6 per cent.

14 Jaan Laas, 'Gody truda i nadezhd', *Vechernyi Tallin*, 16 October 1989.
15 Laas, 'Gody truda i nadezhd'.
16 Kontseptsia khoziaistvennogo rashcheta Estonskoi SSR (tezisy)', *Sovetskaia Estoniia*, 30 September 1988.
17 *Ibid.*
18 Dellenbrant, *Soviet Regional Policy.*
19 McAuley, *Economic Welfare*, p. 111.
20 *Kontseptsia IME*, Tallin, Problemnyi soviet IME, 1989.
21 *Narodnoe khoziaistvo Estonskoi SSR v 1988 g*, p. 10. *Förhandsuppgifter om befolkningsförändringar kommunvis*, April 1990, p. 3.
22 *Sem'ia*, no. 7, 1990. *Yearbook of Nordic Statistics*, Stockholm, Nordic Council of Ministers and Nordic Statistical Secretariat, 1990. *Sostoianie zdravo-ochraneniia i zdrovia naseleniia Estonskoi SSR sa 1988 god*, Tallin, Minzdrav ESSR, 1989. The ecological problems are discussed in Romauld J. Misiunas and Rein Taagepera, *The Baltic States: Years of Dependence 1940–1980*, Berkeley, University of California Press, 1983, pp. 227ff.
23 *Izvestiia*, 28 January 1990.
24 Vladimir Petrov, *Dva berega – dva obraza zhizni*, Tallin, Eesti raamat, 1984, p. 93.
25 Jan Åke Dellenbrant, *Reformists and Traditionalists: A Study of Soviet Discussions about Economic Reform, 1960–65*, Stockholm, Rabén & Sjögren, 1972.
26 Kalev Kukk, 'Nepoluchennye dokhody Estonii', mimeo, Tallin, Institut ekonomiki AN ESSR, 1990.
27 'Zakon Soiuza Sotsialisticheskikh Respublik Ob ekonomicheskoi samo-stoiatelnosti Litovskoi SSR, Latvyskoi SSR i Estonskoi SSR', *Izvestiia*, 2 December 1989.

Index

209

SELECTED PAPERS FROM THE FOURTH WORLD
CONGRESS FOR SOVIET AND EAST EUROPEAN STUDIES,
HARROGATE, JULY 1990

Edited for the International Committee for Soviet and
East European Studies by Stephen White, University of Glasgow

Titles published by Cambridge

Market socialism or the restoration of capitalism?
edited by ANDERS ÅSLUND

Women and society in Russia and the Soviet Union
edited by LINDA EDMONDSON

The Soviet Union in the international political system
edited by ROGER E. KANET, DEBORAH NUTTER MINER and
    TAMARA J. RESLER

The Soviet Union and Eastern Europe in the global economy
edited by MARIE LAVIGNE

The Soviet environment: problems, policies and politics
edited by JOHN MASSEY STEWART

New directions in Soviet history
edited by STEPHEN WHITE

Printed in the United States
By Bookmasters